"Most of the media interest in America's ██████████████████████ ry
operations. But some of the most important ████████████████████ ly
behind the scenes by civilians striving to ██████████████████████ ld
withstand Taliban assaults. Jonathan Addleton was one of those civilians on the
front lines. His journals provide an intimate, important and illuminating window
into the challenges of nation building, the cost of war and the experience of civilians
in the midst of military conflict."

> —**Max Boot**, Jeanne J. Kirkpatrick Senior Fellow in National
> Security Studies, Council on Foreign Relations, author of
> *Invisible Armies* and *The Savage Wars of Peace*

"A profound work of intense humanity . . . no civilian has written an account like
this of their experience in the Afghan war . . . a significant contribution to the
growing literature of America's involvement in Afghanistan . . . very compelling."

> —**Carter Malkasian**, former senior advisor, ISAF commander
> in Afghanistan and author of *War Comes to Garmser*

"Jonathan Addleton writes with precision and gentle, understated emotion about
Afghanistan's endless torment. His memoir is an important, eloquent extension of
the brave service he performed for the State Department and his country."

> —**Thomas Mallon**, critic, essayist, novelist, and author of *Finale*,
> *Henry and Clara*, and *A Book of One's Own*

"Throughout his distinguished career, Ambassador Jonathan Addleton has been
an exemplar of what American public service is all about—and of the promise of
American leadership. Addleton's stirring account is as close as any reader can get to
diplomacy's frontline in the twenty-first century."

> —**Ambassador Bill Burns**, former deputy secretary of state, and
> president, Carnegie Endowment for International Peace

"As the senior embassy representative in southern Afghanistan, Jonathan
Addleton experienced a unique side of the conflict, involving travel to remote
places and personal contact with Afghans of many different views. His deeply
personal reflections capture the human drama of the war and provide an account
of experiences in the field not available elsewhere."

> —**Ambassador James B. Cunningham**, former U.S. ambassador
> to Afghanistan; senior fellow, Atlantic Council

ALSO BY JONATHAN S. ADDLETON

Undermining the Center: The Gulf Migration and Pakistan
(Oxford University Press, 1992)

Some Far and Distant Place
(University of Georgia Press, 1997)

Mongolia and the United States: A Diplomatic History
(Hong Kong University Press, 2013)

THE DUST OF KANDAHAR

A Diplomat among Warriors
in Afghanistan

Jonathan S. Addleton

NAVAL INSTITUTE PRESS
ANNAPOLIS, MARYLAND

This book was brought to publication with the generous assistance of Marguerite and Gerry Lenfest.

Naval Institute Press
291 Wood Road
Annapolis, MD 21402

Library of Congress Cataloging-in-Publication Data
Names: Addleton, Jonathan S. (Jonathan Stuart), 1957– author.
Title: The dust of Kandahar : a diplomat among warriors in
   Afghanistan / Jonathan S. Addleton.
Other titles: Diplomat among warriors in southern Afghanistan
Description: Annapolis, Maryland : Naval Institute Press, [2016] | Includes
   bibliographical references and index.
Identifiers: LCCN 2016030991| ISBN 9781682470794 (alk. paper) | ISBN
   9781682470800 (epub)
Subjects: LCSH: Addleton, Jonathan S.—Diaries. | Afghan War, 2001—Personal
   narratives, American. | Diplomats—United States—Biography. |
   USAID/Afghanistan. | United States. Army. Infantry Division, 3rd. | Afghan
   War, 2001—Campaigns—Afghanistan—Kandahar. | Kandahar
   (Afghanistan)—Politics and government.
Classification: LCC DS371.413 .A38 2016 | DDC 958.104/72092 [B]—dc23 LC
record available at https://lccn.loc.gov/2016030991

∞ Print editions meet the requirements of ANSI/NISO z39.48-1992
(Permanence of Paper).
Printed in the United States of America.

24 23 22 21 20 19 18 17 16   9 8 7 6 5 4 3 2 1
First printing

All photos are part of the author's collection.

CONTENTS

Introduction   1

Chapter 1.   August   9

Chapter 2.   September   14

Chapter 3.   October   35

Chapter 4.   November   52

Chapter 5.   December   70

Chapter 6.   January   84

Chapter 7.   February   102

Chapter 8.   March   123

Chapter 9.   April   135

Chapter 10.   May   161

Chapter 11.   June   173

Chapter 12.   July   189

Chapter 13.   August   213

Afterword   233

Acknowledgments   239

List of Acronyms and Abbreviations   241

Glossary   243

Index   245

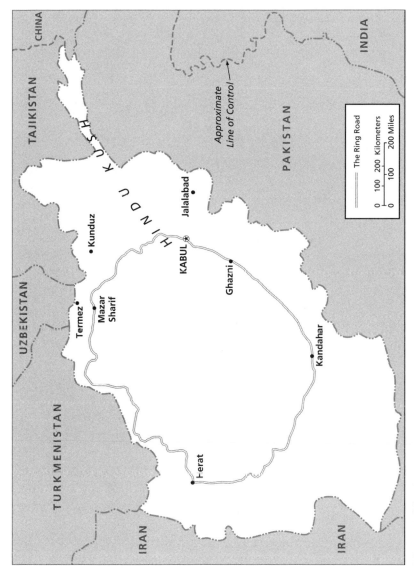

Map 1. Afghanistan

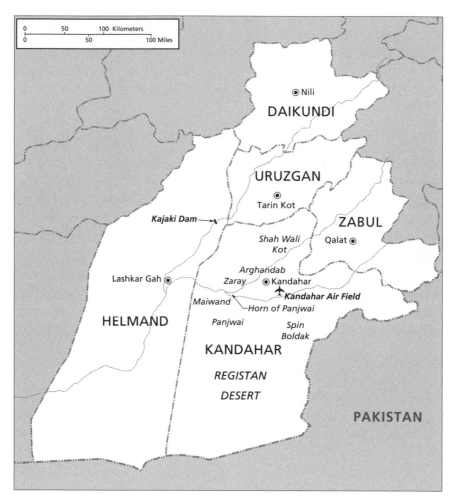

Map 2. Southern Afghanistan

THE DUST OF
KANDAHAR

—✦—

INTRODUCTION

At the age of fifty-five I went to war. I did not wear a uniform or carry a gun, but I worked alongside those who did. Sometimes I travelled outside the wire, on occasion walking through potential kill zones in some of the most violent parts of Afghanistan. On one cruel day in early April, in what should have been the start of spring, I was part of a small group attacked by a suicide bomber in Zabul; a fellow diplomat, my Afghan American translator, and three of the American soldiers who were accompanying us were killed.

Our work focused on Kandahar and the districts that surrounded it. It included Maiwand, Zaray, and the Horn of Panjwai, straddling grape orchards and pomegranate fields, as well as the main highway west to Herat. It was a place where dozens of American and Canadian soldiers as well as hundreds of Taliban lost their lives. Other provinces in this region included Uruzgan, where the Australians spilled their blood and treasure, and Zabul, guarded in places by Romanian troops who controlled Highway One north to Kabul.

Spin Boldak to the southeast bordered Pakistan. A central point in the heroin smuggling network, it was a busy, vibrant, and violent town that also marked the main trade route to Quetta, and then to Karachi on the Arabian Sea. Most of the long border between Afghanistan and Pakistan was open and easily crossed, punctuated at almost every point by small valleys, narrow ravines, and high mountains. It was through these mountains that the insurgency organized multiple rat lines, bringing in explosives, young recruits, and supplies from Pakistan.

We often rode in Black Hawk helicopters. The female waist gunner on one flight from Kandahar to Spin Boldak was young and small, almost as young and small as my daughter who had just started her final year of high

1

school. From time to time we travelled by convoy, protected by the heavy metal of a dust-colored MRAP vehicle. Each time I boarded an MRAP the thought briefly crossed my mind that this vehicle might well become my tomb.

On other occasions we walked to our appointments, donning helmets and protective armor to meet Afghan officials, visit schools, and inspect irrigation works. American soldiers from the Third Infantry Division out of Fort Stewart, Georgia, provided security. Again, it was the youth of those around us that was so striking. Lieutenant Brad Cohn directed my security on several trips to Kandahar. He had only recently graduated from West Point and had actively sought combat experience in Afghanistan.

One private that I met seemed so young I was tempted to ask, "Do you have a note from your parents giving you permission to participate in this war?"

The narrative that follows details in edited diary form the year I spent during the downward slope of America's longest war, the one it fought in Afghanistan. It spans August 2012 through August 2013, providing a perspective on the civilian side of the conflict. As SCR for the U.S. Embassy in southern Afghanistan, I was charged with overseeing civilian relations in Kandahar Province as well as the adjoining provinces of Zabul, Uruzgan, and Daikundi. Together these 4 provinces had a population of more than 3 million people and covered a land area the size of Kentucky or South Korea, much of it desert. As civilians, our work involved us in several very different worlds.

One world focused on the official American presence in Kandahar and the region surrounding it, known historically in Pushto as Loya Kandahar. Nearly 140 of us represented the U.S. Embassy in that part of the country, living and working in 14 different locations. During the course of a single year, that number dwindled to fewer than 40, all assigned to one location at Kandahar Air Field. Within 2 years after that, every embassy officer serving in southern Afghanistan had departed.

Like the soldiers that surrounded us, we ate in crowded mess halls, worked behind barbed wire fences, and lived in small hooches, in some cases built inside what had once been metal shipping containers. Our numbers included political officers, agriculturalists, lawyers, and aid workers. A few were career FSOs, but most were temporary hires, recruited for a specific task over a limited period of time. Many had served in Iraq or parts of Africa. One was a former judge, another had worked as a congressional staffer, a third grew up as the son of Mennonite missionaries to Zambia. I often wondered how someone raised as a pacifist ended up surrounded by soldiers in a war like this.

Another world involved liaison with the international military forces then serving in southern Afghanistan. The soldiers were led by Major General Robert "Abe" Abrams who headed RC-South from his headquarters at Kandahar Air Field. He was assisted by three one stars: Brigadier General Chris Hughes, Brigadier General Pat White, and Brigadier General Mark Brewer from Australia. They in turn worked with the several battlefield commanders known as "battle space owners," all of them colonels.

Their mandate was to assist and train the Afghan National Army as it increasingly assumed control. The Afghans were commanded by General Hamid, a soft-spoken and highly professional career soldier. He had trained in Russia when it was part of the Soviet Union; the Soviet Union had fought its own long war in Afghanistan. At one time he had been a prisoner of the Taliban. The senior American officers respected General Hamid and his soldiers, confident that they could withstand the onslaught of the Taliban when international forces finally departed.

Working with the military brought the realities of war very close to home. Over the course of one year I attended dozens of Purple Heart pinnings, ramp ceremonies, and memorial services for soldiers killed that took place on remote and far-flung military bases scattered across southern Afghanistan. One Purple Heart pinning was for a soldier who had lost three limbs; another was for a recent West Point graduate, originally from South Korea, whose limbs also had been blown away. When paying tribute to wounded soldiers, General Abrams typically described the Kandahar health unit as "the best trauma center in the world." He also praised the stricken soldiers for their sense of duty and self-sacrifice, adding that their only assignment now was to recover, heal, and be made whole.

The ramp ceremonies were always held at Kandahar Air Field. Sometimes they took place under a hot and almost unbearable sun. More often they were scheduled for late at night or very early in the morning, when the sky seemed to stretch like a dark quilt above us, broken only by the tiny sparkling pinpricks of a thousand stars. The setting made all of us seem very small and insignificant, as if nothing that we did mattered.

Sometimes the outline of a full moon cast a brighter light on the scene below where hundreds of soldiers from many nations gathered in all their quiet solemnity to pay final respects as the flag-covered metal boxes containing last remains were carried respectfully, first on a caisson pulled by an MRAP and then shouldered by fellow soldiers to a waiting transport plane for the long journey home. Always the air crew stood at attention outside their airplane, arms lifted in a somber salute.

Almost every service included a reading from scripture, a brief summary of the soldier's life, and the sorrowful sounds of a taped version of the bagpipes playing "Amazing Grace."

The casualties came from every part of the United States. Their names reflected an even wider set of geographic origins, pointing to parents and grandparents that had come from around the world—Asia, Africa, Latin America, Europe. One detachment of soldiers in Zabul served in the Alaska National Guard, some having grown up in small communities found north of the Arctic Circle. The names stitched on their uniforms included White Feather, Boy Scout, and Pinzayak. Other soldiers were more recent immigrants from places like Uzbekistan and Nepal.

One ramp ceremony involved a young private from New York whose parents had not been happy when he joined the armed forces and were even less thrilled when he became a Navy Seal. Another was in honor of a young soldier blown up the day before by an IED. The soldiers lifting his flag-draped metal box were trailed by a black sniffer dog. Following respectfully a short distance behind his late master, the dog walked with his new handler, head cocked to one side as if waiting for the sharp crack of another explosion.

The memorial services held on distant bases were very moving, especially in the late afternoon when the dust gathered and the sun turned the hills from brown to orange and then, fleetingly, a darkened shade of gold. The chaplain would offer a few words of comfort, on occasion making the case for mercy and forgiveness. Several of the chaplains that I heard originally came from South Korea. The late soldier's commander, usually a lieutenant or a sergeant, then provided brief reflections followed by recollections from fellow soldiers—some humorous, most serious, all heartbreaking.

After the last roll call and a final playing of "Day Is Done" on a bugle that seemed to quaver with every note, we walked in silence to the front of the tent, pausing at the upturned rifle, helmet, and boots arranged as a temporary shrine, lingering briefly to touch the small metal dog tag worn only days before in battle. The boots were always brown, caked with the ubiquitous dust of Kandahar.

We also had opportunity to connect, often in surprising ways, with the people and places of Afghanistan. During the course of twelve months we met many Afghans, including tribal leaders, government officials, religious figures, and businessmen. Some clearly sympathized with the Taliban and looked forward to their return. Others dreaded it—not only because it meant the flow of foreign funds would finally stop, but also because of genuine fear for their lives.

Yet, always, it seemed that Afghans wanted to talk—anytime, anywhere, and to anybody. Once an imam who was sympathetic to the Taliban embraced me as I departed, saying, "I have no voice and no one listens to me." This is the message that he wanted the world to know: For him, justice meant the end of corruption as well as the establishment of shariah law across the country. Justice means the end of corruption as well as the establishment of shariah law across the country.

On another occasion I met with the head of the religious affairs department in Kandahar. He had served as the Taliban shadow governor in Kunduz before joining the government and had just returned from the hajj.

"Did you meet any of your old comrades from the Taliban in Mecca?" I asked.

"Oh, yes, I saw several of them."

"What did they say to you?"

"They asked why I had crossed over to the infidels."

"And what did you say to them?"

"I asked them why they had joined up with the Pakistanis."

Major contacts included Shah Wali Karzai, titular head of the Popalzai tribe and half-brother to then-president Hamid Karzai. He lived in a new housing development on the edge of Kandahar. The roast lamb and pomegranate juice that he served in his surprisingly modest home was especially delicious.

I met often with three of the four governors in Loya Kandahar—Wesa (Kandahar), Akhundzada (Uruzgan), and Naseri (Zabul). We also met with Haji Dastageeri, a soft-spoken and charismatic tribal leader with a black beard, black turban, and hairy feet who somehow managed to retain working relations with almost everyone, including the Taliban, al-Qaeda, and the Americans, even as he emerged as one of the richest men in southern Afghanistan. He owned a construction company in a place where the pent-up demand for building was insatiable.

Other contacts included judges, lawyers, mullahs, merchants, human rights activists, security officials, and the warden of Sariposa Prison. On one memorable occasion we drank tea with the so-called keeper of the cloak, a survivor in a large extended family that had suffered greatly over the preceding decades, with many members dying much too young. As his title suggests, he looked after the famous garment now locked behind three progressively smaller metal trunks in a shrine near the governor's palace in Kandahar. The threadbare cloak had reportedly once been worn by Prophet Mohammad and, more recently, had been waved before a crowd of thousands by Mullah Omar during his rise to power in the 1990s.

Our efforts at outreach followed in the footsteps of those who preceded us. Now, more than a decade later, our task was mainly to pave the way for our own pending departure. We were charged with dispelling any sense of abandonment even as we prepared to leave. As our casualties declined, the butcher's bill for the Afghans fighting this war would only increase. By early 2013 four out of every five soldiers killed on the battlefield were Afghan, not American, Australian, or Romanian.

Looking forward, it was now time for the Afghans to write their own narrative and achieve their own destiny, as they had so often done in the past. The United States and its allies would lend a helping hand where possible. But after more than thirty years of intermittent conflict it was time for the Afghans to take charge, time for the Afghans to determine if this was truly a cause worth dying for. Like the Soviets a generation earlier, the United States had finally reached its self-imposed limits in terms of what it was willing to expend in Afghanistan.

Civilian casualties also reflected this grim trend that continued long after I departed. Pervez Najib, Governor Wesa's chief of staff, was killed in March 2014, six months after I left Kandahar, blown up by a suicide bomber at the Shah Wali shrine in the Khakrez District west of Kandahar. Eight months after that the deputy governor of Kandahar Province, an acclaimed thirty-two-year-old poet named Qadim Patyal, who had been published in Peshawar and favorably reviewed by the Pushto press in Dubai, was murdered in a Kandahar classroom, leaving small children behind. He was sometimes referred to as "a politician with the soul of a poet." I often met with him. His final Facebook post was a couplet against hate: "Let's completely drain the hatred from our blood, in one Humanistan, [and] celebrate love with love."

I still don't know how I escaped a violent death following the attack in Zabul on 6 April 2013, surrounded as I was by death and violence at every turn. Five of us flew to Zabul early that morning to visit a school and meet Governor Naseri, two from Kabul and three from Kandahar. I was the oldest. Anne Smedinghoff was only twenty-five, young for an FSO who was already well into her second overseas assignment.

We talked briefly on the tarmac as we waited for our helicopter, shielding our eyes against the early morning sun, the sky a perfect blue. This was Anne's first trip to Kandahar and we were meeting for the first time. She mentioned her recent leave when she had cycled across Jordan. I also talked to my translator, Nasemi, who said he was supporting a large extended family stretching from New York to New Zealand. His own parents had only recently emigrated to the United States.

Within hours both Anne and Nasemi were dead. Two other civilian State Department employees who flew up with us that morning from Kandahar— Abbas Kamwand, an Afghan American working in the embassy Public Affairs section in Kabul, and Kelly Hunt, who headed our Public Affairs section in Kandahar—were injured, Kelly critically.

Three soldiers walking beside us were also killed that day: Staff Sergeant Christopher Ward was from Florida and led the protective detail that surrounded us. Sergeant Delfin Santos, the youngest of seventeen children, was born in the Philippines and raised in California. Corporal Wilbel Robles-Santa grew up in Puerto Rico and left a wife and two young children behind. All three soldiers were born in 1988.

I fell to the ground and rolled into a shallow ditch when I heard the first of two explosions. The engine block landed not far from where I had been standing. Expecting a Taliban attack, I prepared to die and wondered what my family would be told. Later I held Anne's and Kelly's hands as they were taken to the nearest first aid station and then again as they were taken by helicopter to FOB Apache for further treatment.

I returned to Kandahar alone in the early afternoon, picked up by the same helicopter that had dropped the five of us off earlier in the day. "Is that it?" the crew chief asked, looking first at me and then at his flight manifest with its longer list of names. "Are you the only one?"

Not a day goes by when I don't think about what happened in Zabul on that cloudless morning, recalling every moment as it unfolded, reliving endlessly what might have been. I wish a dust storm had blown up out of nowhere, causing all flights to be cancelled. I wish I could reset the tape, reconfigure the order of events, and arrange a different outcome. I wish that I had been killed instead. But I somehow did survive, surrounded by the living but still feeling very much alone.

The next day I attended the ramp ceremony for my colleagues and accompanied the remains on the long journey home. We started with five flag-draped aluminum boxes in Kandahar and added four more in Bagram, bringing the American death toll for that day to nine. The song played at the ramp ceremony at Bagram was "Abide with Me" rather than "Amazing Grace." There was another ramp ceremony when we landed at Frankfurt Airport, a chaplain entering into the belly of the military aircraft and offering a prayer.

Prior to our arrival at Dover, the control tower responded to our request for landing by announcing to all the airplanes swirling above Chesapeake Bay that dark morning: "Cleared for landing. American heroes coming home."

Three days later I returned to Afghanistan to complete the remaining twenty weeks of my allotted time, finishing the year-long task that had been set before me. Yet even now I have never quite left Afghanistan behind.

I think about it often. At odd moments memories from that year return, unprompted and seemingly for no reason at all—I remember the rush of hot air through an open Black Hawk door, the winter fires marking the kutchi encampments down below, the taste of cardamom tea in a musty government office in Kandahar, the smell of roses in the small garden outside, the dust kicked up by a Special Forces platoon returning in off-road vehicles at dusk to Tarin Kot, the gentle rustle of the wind blowing through a stand of pine trees on a lonely hill in Zabul, the brilliant night sky above Alexander's Castle in Qalat, the awful finality of a single trumpeter playing "Day Is Done" to conclude yet another memorial service for yet another young American soldier dying far away from home.

I have no ear for music, but I will never forget those few forlorn notes from that one lone trumpeter, echoing hauntingly across the Horn of Panjwai, off a brown and desolate mountaintop set above a remote and by now abandoned military outpost, somewhere in southern Afghanistan.

1

---⋄---

AUGUST

Kabul, 26 August

Overnight in Dubai followed by a noon Safi Airlines flight to Kabul. The air-bus was named "City of Kandahar." The plane was two-thirds full, a mix of foreigners and Afghans. Everyone was quiet, both while waiting to take off and throughout the flight.

The tarmac on arrival at Kabul Airport was cluttered with dozens of air-planes and helicopters, mostly of the military kind. It had rained earlier in the day and the water collecting in some places was quite deep. There was a huge traffic jam outside the airport and it took forty-five minutes to cover the short distance from the airport to the embassy.

I'm staying in an all-metal hooch, a half-size container with a small bed-room and separate bathroom. I'm tired but not too tired to enjoy listening to the birds in the trees and watching the last rays of sun against the Hindu Kush.

Kabul, 27 August

Morning meetings. Those involving security are sobering. Observation cam-eras capture almost everything. One video showed a bomb going off near the consular line, another showed the results of an RPG hitting a USAID vehicle. There was also footage from al-Jazeera showing an attack on a PRT from the Taliban point of view.

Details of the attack that killed a USAID officer in Kunar a couple of weeks ago bring the realities of this place especially close to home. It involved a suicide bomber attacking a group who routinely walked five hundred meters to a nearby government office rather than taking a more circuitous route by armored car.

News from Helmand is depressing: seventeen civilians including two women beheaded by the Taliban for holding a party that included dancing; ten Afghan policemen killed by colleagues who reportedly defected to the Taliban; and two U.S. soldiers dead because of green on blue attacks. A good day for Afghanistan is when there are no news stories about it.

Kabul, 28 August

Morning meeting with Ambassador James Cunningham. He is guardedly optimistic, suggesting Afghans will respond to the departure of ISAF in better ways than most expect.

Dinner with Deborah Kingsland, outgoing head of Kandahar PRT. Her reflections underscore the challenges ahead: problematic relations between KPRT and the regional platform at Kandahar Air Field and differing views on some issues between civilians and the military.

Spent part of evening packing, trying to find space for several new items passed out to field personnel during the past couple of days:

1. Helmet
2. Body armor
3. Cell phone
4. Satellite phone
5. Blackberry
6. Emergency locator
7. GPS
8. Flame retardant gloves
9. Ballistic dark glasses
10. Flashlight
11. Medical kit

Kandahar, 29 August

Two morning meetings—one with David Donahue from IPA, the other with Masha Hamilton, director of the Communications and Public Diplomacy Office for the U.S. Embassy. Masha is a novelist and said I should look up her Web site. Former ambassador Ryan Crocker had asked her to take the position. She is committed to being in Kabul for at least the next two years.

Afternoon flight to Kandahar on DeHaviland/Bombardier—three of fifty seats were occupied. The road from the embassy to Kabul Airport was less crowded than on Sunday, providing a few brief glimpses of Kabul street life.

It is cloudy and the trip south to Kandahar was bumpy. The landscape is mostly brown and desolate, though small villages are occasionally built into side valleys, houses hanging precariously on the ridges and cliffs of central Afghanistan.

Met on arrival by General Abrams and Third Infantry Division photographer. Outgoing SCR Andrew Haviland was also there to greet me. Drove quickly to our allotted portion of Kandahar Air Field, a dusty and desolate place permeated with foul smells from what is usually referred to as the stink pond, the obsolete sewage treatment plant that handles waste from a Kandahar Air Field population that now exceeds 30,000, most of them expatriates.

Attended evening military briefing with General Abrams and General Huggins, outgoing commander of the 82nd Airborne. This is a strange war, one that can be very violent but that also includes a strong civil affairs component. According to Andrew, there have been some positive developments—the bigger question is how long they will last.

Also briefed by two RSOs on what to expect in Kandahar. They described Kandahar Air Field as resembling a reasonably sized city, complete with its own version of a mafia as well as brothels and bars—and an undocumented population of at least two thousand, many of them third-country nationals whose contracts have expired but are not yet ready to return home.

Retired to my hooch by 11:00 p.m. My quarters are the size of a small college dormitory room and furnished with a desk, cupboard, closet, single bed, and small refrigerator. The most frustrating part as I go to bed on this first evening is that almost nothing works—no blackberry, no computer, no communications at all.

Zaray, 30 August

Accompanied General Abrams to Zaray west of Kandahar and bordering Maiwand and Panjwai. These are dangerous districts, accounting for two thirds of all violence in southern Afghanistan over the past twelve months.

At least two hundred American soldiers are reported to have died in Zaray, Maiwand, or Panjwai during the past three years. The British were badly mauled at Maiwand in 1880 during the Second Afghan War and the Soviets suffered many casualties around Zaray throughout the 1980s during the decade that they spent in Afghanistan.

We travelled by Black Hawk to FOB Pasab—a smooth ride over an interesting landscape, more varied than expected and with many grape fields. We were briefed by the military and had lunch with district governor Niaz Mohammed Sarhadi. His fellow governor from Maiwand attended, along with another fifty Afghans.

The governor was eloquent, though Andrew said he has heard it all before. According to Sarhadi, Zaray produces the "best grapes in Afghanistan." However, because of poor marketing they sell for the "price of gravel."

Sarhadi expressed appreciation for the Americans who came to Afghanistan and sacrificed their "sweet young lives" for his country. Later, making the case for education, he claimed "our minds are dark—we don't know anything and our children can't even write their names."

I spoke with both governors afterward, mentioning that in 1975 at the age of eighteen I took a bus from Peshawar to Paris via Kabul, Kandahar, and Herat. They agreed those were Afghanistan's golden years; they long to see such stability again.

More briefings throughout the afternoon followed by dinner with General Abrams. He thinks the Taliban are losing and security is better than most people realize—but poor governance may eventually bring down the Karzai government.

He also thinks the U.S. military presence will quickly wind down after U.S. elections in November. Reflecting on the U.S. Embassy in Kabul, he said Ryan Crocker's recent departure as ambassador leaves a big hole. He thinks agriculture is key to Kandahar, far more important than any other sector, including energy.

We talked briefly about personal matters. Abrams has two kids, one a high school senior. He is the youngest of six siblings; his two brothers became generals and his three sisters married Army officers. His father, General Creighton Abrams (after whom the tank is named), died in uniform. He was only thirteen when his father passed away.

Gecko, 31 August

Accompanied General Abrams and General Huggins to the Kandahar trauma center to pin Purple Hearts on two American soldiers. One stepped on an IED and lost his leg. He was unconscious and will be flown to Germany shortly. The other was more lightly injured and happy just to be alive.

After the Purple Heart pinnings I visited a nearby hospital room to see General Razziq, the Kandahar chief of police nearly killed in a bus bomb a few days ago. He is younger than I expected and badly burned, though doctors expect a full recovery. Razziq embraced General Huggins warmly and was very talkative, expressing appreciation for his "brothers" in the American Army.

Our military welcomes General Razziq, describing him as a "rock star" for his ability to provide stability and keep the peace. The embassy is more circumspect, concerned about the allegations of human rights abuse that surround him.

Accompanied General Abrams to Gecko for evening briefing, a fascinating yet unnerving experience. Once again we travelled by Black Hawk. Kandahar is very well lit despite concerns over power outages.

I fumbled repeatedly while trying to attach my shoulder straps and earphones. We travelled low to the ground, crossing a series of grape orchards before reaching our destination. Dinner included grapes and melons from southern Afghanistan.

Gecko, variously also referred to over the years as Graceland and FOB Maholic, is situated in what was once Mullah Omar's headquarters, and we met in what was once his second wife's bedroom. "Creepy," as one soldier described it. Some of those attending were also "creepy." One briefer in particular had piercing eyes and seemed to be staring straight through me throughout the evening.

2

—◇—

SEPTEMBER

Kabul, 1 September

Day trip to Kabul for meeting on green-on-blue violence. The latest example is from Uruzgan where three Australian soldiers were killed by a new Afghan recruit who sprayed their tent with an AK-47 and then escaped by motorcycle. The Afghan military reported after the fact that the killer had mentioned to his fellow soldiers that his father was a *talib*.

Travelled to Kabul in Danish C-130, a smooth and uneventful flight. Like Chinooks, the C-130 embraces the best of technology, c. 1960. The thick bundles of wires make it seem as if it was built in another age.

Disembarked on military side of Kabul Airport, guarded by members of the Mongolian military. I talked to the contingent commander named Bayar. He seemed pleased to meet someone who knew something about his country.

The conference included many generals, both Afghan and foreign. One recurring theme was that "a commander must know his soldiers." General Karimi, senior Afghan military official present, told officers to set a good example by going to the mosque more often, not just for Friday prayers. "We are a religious nation—we pay dearly when we fail to realize it."

The reality of insider threats has increased markedly—there were only two such attacks in 2007 and 2008, followed by six in 2009, eleven in 2010, twenty-one in 2011, and thirty-four so far this year. In fourteen cases the Afghan soldiers involved came from a single district in Nangahar Province, Kugyani District. Two-thirds of the attacks this year were followed by a second attack within twenty-four hours, suggesting a strong copycat effect.

Returned home on the same Danish C-130 that brought us to Kabul. This time the plane was nearly full and uncomfortable because of it. Several ISAF generals are flying down to Kandahar for tomorrow's handover ceremony. I slept briefly, spending the rest of the time reading or watching the spectacle of sleeping soldiers. I noticed one Afghan interpreter resting his head on the shoulder of the American soldier sitting next to him.

Dinner in Kandahar with Andrew Haviland, now in the final days of his Afghan assignment. He said that his younger brother had been killed in the collapse of the first tower in New York on 9/11.

Kandahar, 2 September

Attended change-of-command ceremony at Kandahar Air Field, hearing speeches from outgoing commander Huggins and incoming commander Abrams. Also met Governor Wesa from Kandahar. He is a Canadian citizen and by all accounts had a complicated relationship with my predecessor.

The color guard included soldiers from Romania and Australia, as well as the U.S. and Afghanistan. The Third Infantry Division band played the national anthems—two trumpets, a trombone, a tuba, a French horn, and drums. Mullah Rahmatullah from the Afghan army and Chaplain Walker from the Third Infantry Division delivered invocations.

General Huggins' remarks included a short Pushto poem. He thanked soldiers from Singapore, Romania, and Australia for their service. He praised his translator, Aman, saying he knew of "no greater patriot or friend." Emotional at the end, he said, "We may leave Afghanistan, but Afghanistan will never leave us."

General Abrams offered briefer comments, paying tribute to the 82nd Airborne for its sacrifice of blood and treasure. In his words, "We are committed to an Afghanistan that can stand on its own."

Afterward my Afghan American translator Kush took me on an extended tour of the boardwalk, introducing me to several other Afghan translators. Most have spent years in the U.S. All seem intrigued by my memories of an earlier and much different Afghanistan.

Attended first staff meeting chaired by General Abrams. He loathes PowerPoint and likes flat organizational structures. He prefers "we" and "ours" to "me" and "mine." He places strong emphasis on unity of effort, cultural awareness, ethics, integrity, and maintaining a strong moral compass.

Dinner at Niagara DFAC with Phil Russell. He is my new chief of staff, has ties to Tennessee, worked with former senators Bill Frist and Fred Thompson, and plans to retire in Nashville. Among other things, he mentioned his two main objectives for the coming months: strengthened ties between civilian and military personnel in the areas for which we are responsible, and the safety and well-being of those for whom we are responsible.

Also visited the nearest PX, buying three early Christmas presents for Iain, Cameron, and Catriona. Once again it is well past midnight before I finally turn out the lights and go to sleep.

Governor's Palace, 3 September

Morning trip to Kandahar PRT. We travelled in a Black Hawk, noisy but with terrific views of the landscape below.

Unloaded gear at PRT and then headed to the governor's palace in two MRAPs. Finally, I get a view of the streets of Kandahar, albeit through thick Plexiglas. Life outside looks normal, with shops, pedestrians, houses, etc. A few buildings bear bullet holes but mostly Kandahar is a city on the rebound. Every street I see is paved and there are many sidewalks and solar-powered street lights.

Entering into the governor's courtyard, I noticed the shrine where the cloak of the prophet is stored. During the early 1990s Mullah Omar briefly donned the cloak to announce his rule and proclaim the arrival of the Taliban. There is an attractive rose garden in front of the palace, Governor Wesa's pride and joy.

The governor was in good form, perhaps because he just returned from vacation in Vancouver. Relations between Wesa and Andrew might at times have been challenging, but all is forgiven on this last day. The meeting focused on education, youth development, and the governor's desire to build very expensive soccer fields.

Afterward I was told about a plot on Wesa's life a few months ago. Two Taliban entered the compound with revolvers hidden in their sandals. On entry they shot two guards, stole their AK-47s, and started firing. One American soldier was shot in the arm. The attackers were eventually killed and Wesa himself was left unharmed.

Returned to Kandahar PRT, home to ninety American soldiers and fifty civilians. The compound includes a small Afghan bazaar, a grove of pomegranate trees, and paintings of the sights of Kandahar, at least one of which dates to when the Canadians were in charge.

Evening meeting with General Abrams at Kandahar Air Field. Uruzgan is a mess. Australian Special Forces are trying to track down the killer of their three advisers. In the process they captured a facilitator and a woman riding a motorcycle with him. They also raided a nearby compound, an operation that inadvertently resulted in the death of an elderly man and his son.

President Karzai is angry, claiming the Australians are "crying for blood" and breaking all the rules of war to get it. In the meantime, the governor of

Uruzgan—whom I will meet tomorrow—denies the Australians consulted with him beforehand.

Kandahar, 4 September

Boarded C-130 for flight to Uruzgan, returning shortly after departure because one of four engines had blown out. There are few windows on a C-130 and I didn't realize what happened until we were safely back at Kandahar Air Field. The aborted flight means I miss a possible first meeting with the governor.

Attended farewell dinner for Andrew. Several expressed thanks for his contributions over the past eighteen months and I joined in. Apart from everything else, the price of serving in southern Afghanistan right now includes dust, danger, and poor living conditions.

After dinner wandered around the boardwalk, watching soldiers play soccer, basketball, and American football. I ordered ice cream and browsed in several electronic and handicraft shops. This is as close as it gets to an Afghan bazaar at Kandahar Air Field.

Kandahar, 5 September

Saw Andrew Haviland off on his plane to Kabul. He was in Afghanistan for two years, serving as SCR in Kandahar for most of it. Got serious blowback from Kandahar PRT for memo issued in my name on clearance process for cables. It is mostly my fault—I am not properly following my instincts. I should have let them comment first.

Kandahar, 6 September

More briefings—they seem endless. One was on reintegration. The numbers from the south are small, not exceeding three hundred. Yet the Australian officer involved has fascinating stories about his contacts with a Taliban commander who wants to come "in from the cold."

I have mixed feelings about what I see around me every day. General Abrams is impressive. Yet the task at hand is daunting, especially the civilian side of it. There may be bright spots at the tactical level—but strategically things are much murkier.

Received another missive from Kandahar PRT, adding to the challenge of trying to improve relations between Kandahar Air Field and KPRT. Discussed these and other issues with Phil Russell, an experienced chief of staff who brings important continuity and judgment to everything we do. As a former Marine colonel, he doubtless has a different management style. Along with everything else, he mentioned that he expects that with Andrew's departure the civilians here will again test General Order Number One prohibiting alcohol on Kandahar Air Field.

Kandahar, 7 September

Spent part of the day doing laundry and the rest of it thinking about the year ahead. Realistically, Kandahar Air Field is mostly a dismal place—rows of barbed wire, lots of traffic, the endless sound of aircraft overhead, not much of a view, and dust everywhere. It is also a surreal place, bordering on the bizarre— soldiers from several countries looked after by contractors from several other countries and hardly an Afghan to be seen anywhere.

Early in the day Phil informed me that we did indeed have a situation involving a dozen civilians who last night violated the long-standing military order prohibiting alcohol at Kandahar Air Field. He had already held a 6:00 a.m. meeting with those involved. By one account they had been celebrating a colleague's departure.

Evening briefing by military colleagues. It seems that the Taliban's summer campaign yielded few results and there may be growing dissension in their ranks. Yet the Taliban expectation is that ISAF will depart at the end of 2014— and Afghanistan will then be theirs for the taking.

Two quotes from General Abrams: "We've killed all of the dumb Taliban. It is only the smart ones who remain." And "Don't confuse activity with effectiveness. They aren't the same thing."

Kandahar, 8 September

Weekly all-hands meeting, mostly to talk about the Thursday evening drinking episode. Somehow I don't think those volunteering to serve in Kandahar can make a plausible claim their constitutional rights are being violated because they are barred from drinking beer. Once again it is after midnight when I finally return to my room—and once again I find myself going to sleep to the sound of helicopters overhead.

Kandahar, 9 September

Still trying to figure out how my daily rhythm will work. I get up at 7:00 a.m. and don't get to bed until midnight, if I am lucky.

This particular day started with the weekly Kabul conference call at 8:30 a.m. with its cast of dozens. Those of us working in the provinces participate by video. The call starts with a moment of silence for deaths on the battlefield over the past week—six names were read out today.

As for other meetings here at Kandahar Air Field, I am often intrigued by General Abrams when he holds forth. Occasionally he draws me into the conversation. I do my best but the military approach is very new to me. It is impressive on the face of it—but also has its flaws. For all the work that goes into a battle plan, notable elements of Afghan reality are missing from it. Reports suggest that the Taliban are being hit hard. But they are also very resilient. For all the fire directed toward them, they are not about to go away. When the issues are essentially theological, linear thinking has its blind spots.

Iain asked in our phone call last night if I am afraid when travelling outside the wire. I replied that I am not really afraid, rather simply stoic about it. Tonight I wrote him a more extended note, elaborating on this theme while reflecting on much else besides.

Qalat (Zabul), 10 September

Accompanied General Abrams by Black Hawk to Qalat, capital of Zabul Province. The ride was pleasant enough as we passed above a mix of mountains and deserts with a few settlements interspersed among them.

We followed Highway One north most of the way—there is plenty of traffic on the roads despite the security situation. On arrival we briefly saw Qalat Castle, a nineteenth-century structure with foundations going back to Alexander the Great.

Introductory call on Governor Naseri in his office adjacent to the PRT. En route we walked by a few pine trees and a small but lovely lawn with green grass surrounded by rose bushes. The governor did most of the talking, expounding on the importance of education. He previously worked for NGOs in Peshawar and Islamabad and has also been a college lecturer.

My eyes occasionally wandered around the room, taking in the white washed walls, red Turkmen carpets covering the floor, multicolored plastic roses in a garish vase, and blue frilly curtains with yellow tassels. I noticed a book in English sitting on his side table—*Make Today Count,* by leadership guru John Maxwell.

Naseri claims the security situation in Zabul is much better. He said school enrollment has increased from 5,000 to more than 40,000. He mentioned a recent note from the Taliban threatening to "cut off the noses and ears" of those working for the government.

Afterward met several civilians working at the Zabul PRT. Also noticed a memorial wall in the conference room with pictures of those who paid the ultimate sacrifice. One photo is of Paula Lloyd, an anthropologist who served with USAID in Zabul several years ago and was burned to death following an attack in Maiwand.

Tarin Kot (Uruzgan), 11 September

Up early for Kandahar Air Field 9/11 commemoration ceremony. I sat next to an Afghan general, the brother of Governor Sherzai in Nangahar. Soldiers from several countries attended, including Britain, Australia, and Romania.

A senior U.S. Air Force general gave remarks, the chaplain offered prayer, an airman presented a picture he had painted, another airman sang "The Star-Spangled Banner" in hushed tones, and someone else laid a wreath.

Returned to office for more meetings, then headed north to Uruzgan by Black Hawk. We again crossed a bleak landscape—mountains and deserts, mostly, with a few hardscrabble villages, and the occasional river valley.

Travelled two kilometers through Tarin Kot bazaar by MRAP to the governor's palace for long conversation with Haji Amir Mohammad Akhundzada. His family has dominated Helmand politics for at least a generation, partly because of past ties with the mujahideen—and partly, according to some allegations, possible connections to the poppy trade.

Superficially at least, Akhundzada is genuine enough when he explains his vision of development in one of the most isolated provinces in Afghanistan. He especially wants paved roads. The Australians consider him reasonably effective. A friend of the Karzai family, he may have a future in national politics.

I must have been his easiest visitor of the week. Two days ago an Australian general visited; a couple of days from now General Terry will stop by. Both soldiers are delivering the same message of concern regarding the governor's critical public comments on a recent night raid, conducted as part of a continued search for the killer, still on the run, of three Australian soldiers.

Afterward Akhundzada treated our group, both military and civilian, to lunch featuring chicken, lamb, and naan, along with sweet melons, apples, and grapes, all from Uruzgan. The view from his office toward a nearby canal with the fields and hills beyond is lovely.

Kandahar, 12 September

Dust storms cast a brownish pall over Kandahar Air Field for much of the day. The alcohol issue continues to dominate, though this seems trivial when set against unfolding events in Libya resulting in the death of Ambassador Christopher Stevens and three colleagues.

Ostensibly the violence in Benghazi was provoked by a video against the prophet posted on the Internet several months ago; concern has been expressed that a similar reaction might now emerge in Afghanistan. I am more ambivalent or at least more hopeful that Afghanistan will remain calmer on this issue than some people expect.

Kabul, 13 September

Welcomed Sergio Guzman as new SDO at Kandahar Air Field. Left later for Kabul on Beechcraft that seats seventeen passengers. We flew over rugged brown mountains and small, remote settlements before clouds moved in to cover everything.

A couple of flares lit up outside our plane as we approached Kabul, precautionary flak to divert a possible rocket attack. Driving to the embassy, it was possible to briefly glimpse local street life—traffic, shops, billboards, bodybuilding gyms, and at least two lavish wedding halls.

Kabul, 14 September

Full day of meetings, starting with breakfast with IPA head David Donahue. He anticipates a quick civilian drawdown. In southern Afghanistan that means moving from 120 people to 10 people in less than 2 years.

Spent part of morning with a senior diplomat from the Indian Embassy. We talked about Indian aid projects in Kandahar—a short road to the industrial park as well as the planned $80 million agricultural university at Tarnak Farms where Osama bin Laden once had his base.

Lunch with head of U.S. Department of Transportation Office in Kabul. She departs in two weeks, has a bleak view of the state of civil aviation in Afghanistan, and is not optimistic about what will happen when ISAF departs.

Met David Donahue again later in the day, this time in his apartment. He thinks Afghans will assume responsibility more quickly than anyone imagines—and that we should give them this chance as soon as possible.

Spent half hour at Camp Eggers, most of it thinking about my trip there eighteen months ago to meet Mongolian soldiers. Stopped briefly at Afghan market as well as PX. Walked briefly around rose garden across the street from ISAF headquarters, the calmest, greenest, and most pleasant place in all of Kabul.

Kabul, 15 September

Long meeting with several embassy colleagues on management issues. I expressed strong hope that something will finally be done about housing at Kandahar Air Field. Our people desperately need something better than the current building that leaks when it rains and is about to fall down.

Embassy Air flight to Kandahar Air Field via Tarin Kot. This time it was a half-full Dash 8. I slept part of the way, occasionally looking at the brown landscape below. The dirt tracks drawn across the mountains look precarious. I noticed a very small patch of snow atop one mountain in central Afghanistan, all that remains of the winter ice pack. The dust storms started south of Tarin Kot—the dust of Kandahar that never goes away.

Kandahar, 16 September

Meetings and e-mails for hours on end. For the second time in as many days Fiona and I connected via Skype, providing brief glimpses of Catriona in the background. Life with family in Outer Mongolia sounds perfect right now—I miss it a lot.

Spent an hour touring Camp Valdez, the base for Embassy Air. It is an amazing operation, all on a contract basis. At evening briefing learned Kandahar Air Field population has fallen to just over 25,000. More than 20,000 are Americans, divided roughly equally between soldiers and civilians.

Broke off work at 8:00 p.m. to attend ramp ceremony for four soldiers killed early this morning in a green-on-blue attack at a remote outpost in Zabul. Several hundred soldiers showed up, including senior officers from most countries at Kandahar Air Field. As the ranking civilian present, I was the last to see the flag-covered aluminum boxes lifted into the airplane.

The four dead soldiers were part of a group of six, five sleeping while a sixth stood guard. Early in the morning an Afghan policeman turned his gun on them. The two survivors are wounded, one badly. The remaining survivor attended the ceremony, a bandage on his leg, his eyes wet with tears. He looked very young.

The program started with prayer and a passage from Isaiah, read above the noise of airplanes overhead. This was followed by a taped rendition of "Amazing Grace" on the bagpipes. The chaplain paid brief tribute to each of the dead, ranging in age from nineteen to twenty-five. They came from Hawaii, Texas, Oklahoma, and North Carolina. One had been in the Army less than eighteen months, another for hardly two years.

The ramp ceremony was followed by a shorter one inside the plane—prayers and a scripture reading conducted by the pallbearers and the half dozen soldiers who accompanied them, one of them a chaplain.

This has been a terrible forty-eight hours. Another four were killed in Helmand, two British soldiers following an insider attack at a checkpoint and two U.S. Marines following an audacious attack on the major air base in the region. Three groups of Taliban arrived dressed as American soldiers and broke into the perimeter, destroying several Harriers.

Kandahar, 17 September

Trip to Panjwai cancelled. I instead spent the entire day at Kandahar Air Field. The green-on-blue attacks have a devastating impact on ISAF efforts and for security reasons our outreach is now severely curtailed. General Odierno, U.S. Army chief of staff, arrived in Kandahar in the evening. I met him briefly and then retired for the night.

Maiwand, 18 September

An awful start to the day. At least nine dead following suicide attack on civilian bus near Kabul Airport, close to three new wedding palaces and on the same road I took to catch my plane for Kandahar a few days ago. Those killed include one Russian and eight South African pilots working out of Kabul on a contract basis. The suicide bomber was an eighteen-year-old Afghan girl who drove her sedan into the bus, killing everyone.

Departed at 10:30 a.m. by Black Hawk for Hutal in Maiwand District west of Kandahar. The journey takes twenty minutes and includes tremendous views of deserts, mountains, and river valleys—as well as the occasional *kutchi* encampment.

Greeted on arrival by members of our U.S. military and civilian teams. Some 120 American soldiers live at Maiwand along with 3 civilians. The conditions are primitive and I have to admire their dedication and fortitude. The Taliban remain active, especially south toward the river.

There are 360 *karezes* in the area, and only 10 are still in operation. The rest are derelict, many having been destroyed during the Soviet era. Almost half of all those living in Maiwand are Noorzai. U.S. losses over the past 5 months include 6 dead and 70 wounded—much fewer than the 70 U.S. soldiers killed in Zaray 2 years ago.

At 1:00 p.m. district governor Saleh Mohammad Noorzai arrived along with his police chief. He must be in his mid-forties. He looks like a traditional Afghan, studied for several years in Leningrad, and spent much of his career as a policeman.

As with every other governor, he is engulfed with allegations of corruption. But he is also smart, lobbies tenaciously for his district, and was friendly enough on this occasion. As for the police chief, he looks like a tough street fighter, well acquainted with violence. I later learned he is about to depart on hajj.

We talked for ninety minutes, with Kush doing most of the translation. I sought to connect in some fashion, at one point recalling my visit to Kandahar in the 1970s and later lamely comparing the governor's experience with local *shuras* to my sister Nancy's accounts of her work on the Macon city council.

I occasionally appealed to Pushto proverbs as well as the deity: "God on the lips, murder in the heart." "It is easy to destroy but hard to build." "God will forgive us when we make mistakes, but he won't forgive us if we don't at least try." Etc., etc.

Departed Maiwand as scheduled at exactly 3:30 p.m. As we left, noticed old mud-brick British fort, still in good repair, next to the U.S. military base, a reminder that the British once briefly ruled this area—only to meet with defeat at a village north of here in April 1880. Nearly a thousand British and Indian soldiers died at Maiwand, along with several thousand Afghans.

Once upon a time the name "Maiwand" resonated across Victorian Britain. Kipling wrote a poem about it, two British soldiers received Victoria Crosses following the battle, and the fictional Dr. Watson, companion to Sherlock Holmes, was supposedly wounded at Maiwand.

Maiwand also inspired gripping Victorian era artwork, including one depicting the last of a small contingent of eleven British soldiers, just before they ran out of ammunition and mounted a final, desperate bayonet charge that ended in their deaths. Even the Afghans were impressed.

A final footnote to this story: One deceased British soldier had been the owner of a small terrier later found wandering around the Maiwand battle-field. The dog was taken to England and, to much acclaim, was given a medal, pinned on at the palace by Queen Victoria herself. Not long afterward the small dog who had survived the worst of the fighting in Maiwand was killed, struck down by a horse-drawn cart on the streets of London.

Governor's Palace, 19 September

Another day, another Black Hawk flight—this time to the Kandahar PRT to meet Governor Wesa. We mostly talked about green-on-blue attacks and broader security issues. I brought up the issue of senior Afghans who routinely seem to want to avoid security procedures at Kandahar Airport.

The security blanket that covers us is unbelievable, including machine guns on the Black Hawks and MRAPs taking us everywhere. Donning body armor and a helmet is becoming second nature. Still, I enjoy brief glimpses into a more normal world, whether involving rural landscapes from on high or fleeting views of Kandahar bazaar when we drive through town. Realistically, we are the only aliens in this landscape—Kandahar with its shops, rickshaws, and school children looks like the Pakistan I remember from the 1970s. Kandahar also has impressive houses and neighborhoods, suggesting another reality yet to be reflected in the media.

On arrival noticed again the blue-tiled shrine housing the cloak of the prophet as well as the green lawn and red roses in front of the palace—the clas-sic Afghan garden that somehow survives, despite the tribulations of the past thirty years. The conference room where we discussed security issues includes two large maps, three identical portraits of Karzai, a long wooden table—and not much else.

After the official event, Governor Wesa asked General Abrams to meet with him alone. Later the general said Wesa expressed concern about both corruption and the Taliban reintegration program.

Ate lunch at Kandahar PRT before returning to Kandahar Air Field. It has a nice dining hall; the menu today included roast beef and Cornish hen glazed in honey, another of the surprises of life in southern Afghanistan.

As we waited for helicopters, Phil Russell mentioned that KPRT was once home to several cats, brought to Afghanistan by Canadian soldiers as a form of pest control. The cats were later banned. Nonetheless, foreigners continue to befriend puppies and kittens in Afghanistan, sometimes paying as much as $3,500 to take them to North America.

Kandahar, 20 September

Morning meeting with Samaat from Uzbekistan, the regional UN representative for southern Afghanistan based in Kandahar. We talked mostly about Afghanistan, touching occasionally on matters concerning his own country as part of a much wider region that was once widely known as Soviet Central Asia.

Watched *Charlie Wilson's War* against a large concrete T-wall with a couple dozen other Kandahar Air Field civilians. Partway through the movie the mortar alarm sounded and we gathered in a nearby bomb shelter to wait out the next forty minutes.

Kandahar, 21 September

Accompanied General Abrams to Purple Heart ceremony, the result of a single incident in Panjwai—an RPG penetrated a vehicle, doing lethal damage. One soldier lost a leg and a hand. The other two soldiers will suffer no lasting physical damage. One expressed a desire to return to the battlefield, saying he still has "unfinished business" to take care of.

Also attended late afternoon ramp ceremony. Several hundred soldiers showed up. Again there was the familiar eulogy by the chaplain preceded by a reading from Psalms and followed by prayer and "Amazing Grace" on the bagpipes. This soldier was twenty-four years old and had been raised in Arkansas. He leaves a small child and expectant wife behind.

Kabul, 22 September

Left Kandahar Air Field at 1:30 a.m. on Texas National Guard C-130 bound first for Bagram and then Kabul. Finally arrived at 4:00 a.m., managing two hours sleep before driving through early morning traffic to reach ISAF.

General Allen opened the all-day meeting, highlighting the need to plan now for the close-out of PRTs across Afghanistan over the next two years. What we are experiencing in the south is happening all over the country. Yet I finished the day more pessimistic than when I started it—we face an enormous task, one that at times seems as clear as mud.

Once again walked around the pleasant rose garden across from ISAF headquarters in Kabul. This small and quiet oasis includes a green lawn, tree cover, several small pavilions, and a fountain.

The nearby hall (Milano) where we met includes a disco ball and prayer room, emblematic perhaps of two wildly divergent aspects of life in Afghanistan. Meanwhile, nineteen people have been killed in Pakistan on what was billed to the world as "Love of the Prophet Day."

Looking back, the real highlight of this long day was when I walked off the C-130 at Kabul Airport at 4:00 a.m. and saw two dozen Mongolian soldiers lined up in formation with all their gear. They had just arrived from Ulaanbaatar to start their six-month rotation in Afghanistan and were surprised to be greeted in Mongolian.

Kabul, 23 September

Attended weekly country team meeting in basement of old embassy, chaired by Ambassador Cunningham. All the names read out this week were for deaths in Kandahar. Also met Zabul PRT head Tim Bashor, picked up business cards, picked up blackberry to replace the one I managed to lose during my first weeks in Kandahar, and talked at length with an interesting colleague of Indian origin who grew up in Wyoming.

Left for airport not long after noon, passing the same spot where the South African aircrew had been killed by an eighteen-year-old female suicide bomber a few days ago.

The embassy driver was named Suleiman. He lived as a refugee in Pakistan for sixteen years, working as a taxi driver and bus conductor. We talked in Urdu, and he became quite emotional, even tearful, when he recalled the many members of his family killed over the years. Like Cambodia, this is a place where so many people must surely be counted among the walking wounded, carrying with them a deep pain that never goes away.

Returned to Kandahar Air Field, this time on Embassy Air. I still haven't tired of the views when flying over central Afghanistan. Some tiny valleys in the deepest parts of the mountains are unbelievably remote. Afghanistan as a country has been devastated by decades of war—but for those living in these isolated places life can't be much different than it was a century or even ten centuries ago.

Attended 5:00 p.m. service at Fraise Chapel, just off the boardwalk—my first church visit since arriving in Afghanistan four weeks ago. It was billed as an English service, and about fifteen people came, most of them American.

The service was led by Padre Baptiste who was raised in the Caribbean. His mother is Caucasian American and his father came from the Dominican Republic. His mother was sixteen when he was born. She is now sixty-six years old and still lives in Alabama.

Padre Baptiste's mother never married his father and never acknowledged that she had a son. She later had a second family, giving him several half siblings he has never met. His wife is from Barbados and he has two daughters. He described himself as the first and so far only Pentecostal chaplain in the British Army. Physically large and imposing, he exudes a gentle and even kind personality and I can't help but be astonished when I reflect on the places he has been and the changes he has witnessed in his lifetime.

Spin Boldak/Wolverine, 24 September

Left Kandahar Air Field at 8:30 by Black Hawk for Spin Boldak. Our route skirted the Registan Desert, a vast sea of sand that looks like the Sahara.

On arrival at Spin Boldak drove ten miles to the Pakistan border at Wesh in a convoy consisting of four Strykers. There are no windows and I didn't see much. Once at the border we were first briefed by Americans working at the site and then embarked on a walking tour that included passport control, biometric facilities, and various customs offices.

A small detachment of twelve American soldiers lives at the border, headed by a young lieutenant from Ohio who did his ROTC at Liberty University. Their quarters include a tiny lawn and the inevitable rose garden.

It felt odd standing on the sandbagged roof, looking a couple hundred yards toward Dosti Darvaza with its large Pakistani flag and red brick Frontier Corps fort in the background, not far from where the local Afghan rumor mill suggests the Taliban make IEDs and have a training camp.

Approximately 30,000 people cross the Wesh-Chaman border each day, almost all Afghans who don't require passports. Pushtun family members live on both sides of the frontier and don't think there should be a border at all.

Travelling in an envelope of security along with General Hughes, we were met by stares, occasional looks of bemusement—and a few glares reflecting deep hostility bordering on rage. One old man with a beard and broad smile was being trundled about amidst much laughter in a wheel barrow, an experience he seemed to enjoy immensely.

The U.S. Army Corps of Engineers hired a Turkish company to build a new $22 million border crossing. The chief Turkish engineer said he enjoys his work, adding that there are thirty-five Turks at the site along with two hundred Afghans, some hired from Turkmen-speaking parts of the country.

Lunch at Spin Boldak DFAC under the watchful eye of Albanian soldiers. Also met two American civilians. Their facilities are rudimentary. The command center hallways are decorated with portraits of soldiers who have died, a grim reminder of the true cost of this war.

After lunch flew to Camp Wolverine on Highway One to remember four soldiers killed in green-on-blue attack in Zabul last week: Sergeant Sapuro Brightley Nina from Micronesia, Specialist Genaro Bedoy from Texas, Specialist Joshua Nathaniel Nelson from North Carolina, and Private First Class Jon Ross Townsend from Oklahoma.

Two were younger than Iain, one younger than Cameron. All four were married and one had only recently become a father. The youngest, a devout Christian, married Brittany less than six months ago, just before he departed for Afghanistan.

The remembrance service was led by Chaplain Pak, originally from Korea. It included eulogies from friends and fellow soldiers. A lone piper played "Amazing Grace."

The saddest moment was the last roll call, a ceremony in which several names of those belonging to the same platoon are called out. Fellow soldiers respond immediately with "present," until the names of the dead are called— first once, then twice, then a third time, followed each time by an aching silence.

The chaplain's brief reflections were based on Psalm 34:18: "The Lord is close to the brokenhearted and saves those who are crushed in spirit."

Afterward joined others in a final gesture, standing at attention before portraits of the four soldiers placed below their boots, upturned rifles, and helmets as a temporary shrine.

The tradition is to briefly touch each dog tag individually and then stand at attention before moving on for a last and final time. General Hamid from the Afghan National Army attended. He said afterward he is sorry so many young American soldiers have sacrificed their lives for his country.

Returned to Black Hawks with sound of "Day Is Done" and the final gun salute still ringing in my ears. The female machine-gunner on this flight had a cute smile and was quite small—not much bigger than Catriona and probably not much older either. Travelling over the bleak landscape on the return flight to Kandahar I noticed an old mud fort disappearing into the desert.

As always, my office manager and secretary Bonnie Weaver was waiting on arrival. The day ended late—General Terry is visiting from Kabul, accompanied by Lester Holt from NBC News. The briefing was upbeat and informative. I hope the briefers are right in their relatively optimistic prognosis of this war.

Kandahar, 25 September

A mostly quiet day. Several meetings were cancelled. Had dinner at Asian DFAC, spending part of it watching cricket match between Bangladesh and Pakistan.

Arghandab, 26 September

All-day trip to Arghandab and then KPRT with Ambassador Glenn Davidson from Canada. He is from Nova Scotia and previously served as Canada's ambassador to Syria.

Flew from Kandahar Air Field in an antique CH-46 belonging to Embassy Air. The views approaching Arghandab are lovely—jagged mountains in the back, hemmed in by a large expanse of green as well as the Arghandab River shining brightly in the late morning sun. The base where we landed is picturesquely situated, set beside a small mountain looking out over fields and orchards below.

Moved out in a four-Stryker convoy, travelling perhaps fifteen miles on paved road through open countryside to a reconstructed weir funded by the Canadians, building on a USAID irrigation project dating to the 1950s.

The Canadian project cost $50 million and includes renovation of 350 miles of irrigation ditches and watercourses. Security has been good—nobody was killed in finishing this project, perhaps because the Taliban think they will one day inherit it.

We walked along the Arghandab and then crossed a small bridge, experiencing brief moments of quiet normalcy.

A few locals stared at us in bemusement. I didn't have any afghanis—if I had, I surely would have bought at least a drink from a nearby shop. Also saw wildlife—a lone crane in one direction, a crab scuttling across a slab of cement in the other.

A small Afghan fort was situated next to the Arghandab River—built of mud, it featured sandbags, barbed wire, and a couple of tattered Afghan flags.

We passed many cemeteries and a lot of colorful flags, presumably marking the graves of mujahideen killed during the Soviet period and perhaps more recently. This area was never controlled by the Soviets and later became a stronghold for the Taliban.

Our second stop was at a large new Canadian-built bridge. Again the view toward the mountains was lovely, and made even more so by nearby gardens and wetlands. This ranks among the most scenic views in all of southern Afghanistan. Overhead a couple of observation helicopters wheeled about as part of our protective detail.

Our third stop was at Governor Wesa's palace with its familiar grass lawn and rose garden, set opposite the shrine where the cloak of the prophet is kept. Governor Wesa was in good form—hosting lunch, holding forth on the usual issues, making the most of his Canadian connections.

Wesa expressed special pride in the growth of education in Kandahar, recalling his pioneering role in founding both Kandahar University and a local high school. We briefly talked about the new Afghan soccer league, the local Maiwand Heroes having just defeated a Kabul team 3–0.

Following lunch with Wesa, we boarded MRAPs for the short trip to KPRT—a route I now know very well. We then boarded our CH-46 helicopters for the journey back to Kandahar Air Field.

Joined General Abrams and Lester Holt for dinner. The Third Infantry Division will feature in an upcoming news special from New York. We spent part of the time talking about soldiers who die and ways in which the division tries to comfort those families left behind.

Tarin Kot (Uruzgan), 27 September

Morning C-130 flight to Uruzgan. General Hamid is on this trip, along with General Abrams. We separated on arrival, the generals embarking on a tour of nearby military sites while I was briefed by the PRT, a mix of Australians and Americans who work well together.

The Uruzgan DFAC is exceptionally good and offers fresh fruit as well as my favorite guava juice. The Dutch were in Uruzgan previously, leaving several mementoes behind including a small windmill. There is a memorial to ISAF soldiers killed in recent years, mostly from the Netherlands, Australia, and the United States:

> To our brothers and sisters in arms
> Thanks for all the memories
> Laughs, tears, blood and sweat
> You will always be in our thoughts
> And remain in our hearts
> All gave some
> Some gave all

Elsewhere there was this familiar British verse, seen at cemeteries across Europe marking the dead of other wars:

They shall not grow old,
As we who are left grow old;
Age shall not weary them
Nor the years condemn
At the going down of the sun
And in the morning
We will remember them.

Headed to Governor Akhundzada's office in seven-vehicle convoy of identical Australian MRAPs. The convoy was commanded by a young Australian officer. He seemed slightly jittery, perhaps because he was now responsible for a general. The bazaar in Tarin Kot seems quite normal and even flourishing.

The meeting with the governor went reasonably well. We covered a lot of territory, General Abrams focusing on reintegration while I discussed economic concerns. Last year only 14 girls graduated from high school in all of Uruzgan, a province with at least 300,000 people. As we departed, General Abrams spoke briefly with the governor, saying there has been far too much killing already and the reintegration program somehow needs to work.

Returned to Kandahar Air Field to meet one of the members of the Panjwai DST returning from vacation. He grew up as the son of Mennonite missionaries originally from Indiana, first in Zambia and later in Central America. His wife is Honduran and he has two small boys; together they manage a small farm in Honduras. I'm not sure how a Mennonite from a pacifist tradition ends up working in a war zone.

Kandahar, 28 September

The deputy SCR from Helmand dropped by for a meeting. He lifts weights, wears a heavy silver chain, and breaks most stereotypes about what FSOs should look like. We shared stories about what brought us to Afghanistan, nearly shedding tears when recalling ceremonies for soldiers who have been killed in Helmand and Kandahar.

Panjwai, 29 September

Attended monthly military award ceremony honoring two new sergeants. Also saw exhibition featuring military dogs. The dogs immediately took down two female soldiers dressed in protective gear, a frightening display of canine fighting prowess.

Departed at 3:30 p.m. with General Abrams in Black Hawks for Sperwan Ghar in Panjwai, not far from the Registan Desert. Our purpose was to attend another memorial service—this one for Sergeant Jason Swindle, killed on patrol more than a week ago.

Sergeant Swindle is survived by his wife Chelsey and son Paxton, age one. Another baby is on the way. One of five brothers from Arkansas, he leaves an identical twin behind. He joined the Army at age eighteen and died at age twenty-four, less than two weeks after arriving in Afghanistan.

The service was led by Chaplain Kim, originally from Korea. He acknowledged that everyone must surely feel grief and even anger and a desire for revenge—but, taking as his text a passage from Romans, urged those left behind to realize that neither life nor death can ever separate humanity from the love of God.

The regimental flag included battle stripes going back to Antietam, Gettysburg, and Cold Harbor. The final roll call, with its sad and lingering silence, moved me nearly to tears.

Three commanders and three fellow soldiers from Bayonet Company provided tributes. Sergeant Swindle must have ticked "Southern Baptist" on his religious preference card. One soldier seemed especially close, saying they were godparents to each other's respective children at Fort Stewart.

The memorial service ended with the familiar gun salute, a playing of taps, and a taped version of "Amazing Grace" on the bagpipes. Afterward we lined up to salute and briefly hold the dog tags in our hands. Some soldiers left gifts behind next to the boots, rifle, and helmet—military coins, military patches, even a knife.

Afterward I talked with Sergeant Major Watson and Chief of Staff Quintas. They agree these are hard ceremonies to attend—but added that those held in the field are meant to bring the platoon together to first grieve, then reflect, and finally return to their duties.

I've often thought I wanted to experience all aspects of life in my brief time on earth—and I am certainly doing so in Afghanistan. For those that experience war, it usually happens in their youth; for me, it is something I am somehow confronting as I grow old.

I never thought putting on armor plating and a helmet or buckling up in a Black Hawk would become second nature. I never imagined the histories of the United States and Afghanistan would ever become so closely intertwined, extending to even the remotest corners of this country.

Dozed off toward the end-of-evening CUA meeting at Kandahar Air Field only to be awakened by General White. "That's okay, I sometimes do that myself," he said, reassuringly. Very probably I will be exhausted throughout my time in Afghanistan.

Kandahar University, 30 September

Early-morning departure by Black Hawk to Kandahar. Met first with Ehsan Noorzai, chairman of Kandahar Provincial Council. His predecessor, Hamid Karzai's brother, was assassinated.

Noorzai was eloquent about many issues including corruption and mistakes that he said had been made by the government in Kabul. Noorzai himself studied in Germany. He is pragmatic and competent but also increasingly frustrated.

When I described the clean hands campaign against corruption in Cambodia that I had observed several years ago during an assignment there, he replied by saying the problem in Afghanistan isn't that people's hands are dirty: "They are covered with corruption from head to toe and it is impossible to ever remove it."

Also attended weekly council meeting in large room decorated with portraits of President Karzai and the former mayor of Kandahar who was killed last year. Discussion centered on efforts to remove an almond market without compensation. As bearded elders shouted, it became almost like a medieval encounter—only a king was missing to pronounce final judgment. Miriam Durrani, one of three female council members, was especially vocal.

After the meeting, walked through the impressive garden where the provincial council is located. It was a beautiful day—and I have never seen such an array of colorful flowers in Afghanistan—not just roses, but every other variety as well.

Returned to KPRT by road, looking out the MRAP window at vibrant bazaar scenes at every turn. Most people ignore our four-vehicle convoy. For Kandaharis, security has never been better.

Lunch at KPRT with Rogiya Achackzai, Kandahar's director of Women's Affairs. Two or three other women attended. Afghans have seen too many people such as myself come and go. A decade later, they are unhappy that their initial hopes have not been fulfilled. Some blame it partly on the Afghan government in Kabul while others mostly blame ISAF.

Drove to Kandahar University for final meeting of the day. Founded in 1990, it has many new buildings, a big blue mosque—and ambitious plans for the future. Chancellor Totakhil was trained in Tashkent and Moscow. He is nearly blind but wants something better for Afghanistan. Vice Chancellor Tawab speaks good English, studied in Thailand, and visited the U.S. for the first time last year.

After our office meeting we toured the new journalism department. I met several journalism students, including two women. One professor said he is seventy-two and realizes that this will be his final project.

Conversations with the journalism students went well. I mentioned my own brief and undistinguished journalism career, including one glaring blunder early on involving a failure to verify sources and talk to as many people as possible when writing a story for the local newspaper in my hometown. The students were enthusiastic yet face hugely difficult prospects, both in life and in their hoped-for journalism careers.

Returned to KPRT for informal discussion with civilian head Brian Bachman and military head Commander Starvis. We do our best despite frustration. Commander Starvis will finish his assignment in late October. He described the pace of change in Afghanistan as "glacial," meaning not much has changed in Kandahar during the past twelve months.

3

—◦✧◦—

OCTOBER

Kandahar, 1 October

Stayed at Kandahar Air Field all day. At least ten Afghans and three American soldiers have been killed following a suicide blast in Khost.

Kandahar Airport, 2 October

Morning visit to Kandahar Airport, starting with walk through new USAID-funded cool storage on Juliet Ramp. It isn't much to look at but may increase exports of grapes, pomegranates, and melons to Dubai.

Met members of Kandahar Fresh Fruit Association and Rabat Melon Cooperative in Spin Boldak, all with long beards and Taliban-like turbans. About 90 percent of their exports go to Pakistan, 8 percent to India, and 2 percent to the Middle East. The farther products are sent, the better the price.

Met airport director Ahmadullah Faizi, former Kandahar Air Field interpreter and green card holder. He says he fights battles every day to make the airport viable. He claims he also works to tackle corruption at every turn, in part by computerizing financial flows. He said the airport handles three hundred flights a month, earning $150,000—all of which he sends directly to Kabul.

We then walked around the airport rose garden, watching the occasional peacock strut about the lawn. Faizi recently built a large wire bird cage that is now home to parakeets, doves, and a colorful pair of exotic birds from Australia.

Kandahar, 3 October

Spent entire day at Kandahar Air Field, working through another excruciating management challenge. Why can't people just get along?

35

Shah Wali Karzai's Residence, 4 October

Feeling a bit better about last night. Fortunately it was more a case of one individual acting out rather than an entire unit. But I still can't understand why it should be so hard.

An eventful twenty-four hours on the war front: twenty Taliban killed across the battlefield, possibly including a couple of commanders.

In other news, an Afghan soldier assaulted a female American soldier at Pasab in Zaray. One general made this observation: "What would be the reaction if it had been an American soldier assaulting an Afghan female instead?"

Evening drive to Kandahar to meet Shah Wali Karzai, younger half-brother of President Karzai and titular head of the Popalzai. He assumed that role following the July 2011 killing of his more flamboyant brother Ahmad Wali Karzai. Rich Pacheco and Lewis Gitter accompanied, along with Kush, though Shah Wali Karzai speaks fluent English and needs no translator.

We travelled in a six-car convoy, Rich Pacheco and I riding together in an armored Toyota Land Cruiser driven by a Third Infantry Division sergeant from Puerto Rico. The route was just over twenty miles, most of it on Highway Four. It was already dark when we left Kandahar Air Field, but we saw lots of gas stations, truck stops, and traffic along the way.

We met in Shah Wali Karzai's guest house, taking off our shoes before entering. We first gathered in a side room, drinking tea and talking about Kandahar as well as his time in the U.S. following the Soviet invasion of Afghanistan.

That distant time is memorialized in a large color photograph on the wall taken when Shah Wali Karzai was an engineering student at the University of Maryland. It shows several brothers, including Hamid Karzai, with their father in their American home, decorated for the secular Christmas season—an angel on the wall, a Santa Claus on a side table.

We then walked to Shah Wali Karzai's dining room, stopping briefly to wash our hands in warm water poured by a servant bearing a curved silver jug, Afghan style.

Dinner included *kabuli pilau,* pumpkin, eggplant, chicken, and very tender mutton. We were served large glasses of fresh pomegranate juice. Shah Wali Karzai said he planted 13,000 pomegranate trees but has yet to harvest any of them.

Shah Wali Karzai still follows American sports, especially football and basketball. He is raising nine children under the age of ten—four of his own and five belonging to his murdered brother.

Death seemed very much on his mind as he rattled off names of friends and colleagues killed by the Taliban. At one point he commented dolefully,

"All of us will eventually be killed, either by the Taliban or by the American media."

Shah Wali Karzai is quite thin and much less physically imposing than his brothers. As leader of the Popalzai he hears many problems and tries to solve most of them. He said everyone fears 2014 when ISAF finally leaves. He doesn't think Afghanistan is yet fully ready for democracy. Yet he also expressed a measure of optimism about the future, noting that much has changed.

We stopped to admire Shah Wali Karzai's small lawn as we departed, surrounded by rose bushes, the smell of rose petals permeating the night air.

Returning to Kandahar Air Field by road, I occasionally looked out toward the night sky at an almost full moon. The distance between Shah Wali Karzai's house and Kandahar Air Field is about the same as from Sukkur to Shikarpur, and the journey to Kandahar Air Field somehow evoked strong memories of my childhood in Pakistan's Sindh Province so many years ago.

Kandahar, 5 October

A relatively quiet Friday. At the weekly general officers' huddle, General Abrams complained about too many uncoordinated meetings involving senior Afghans. He thinks we should take a more measured, less frenetic approach. He also thinks we shouldn't pester Afghan officials so much.

Afternoon meeting on Dahla Dam. Kabul emphasizes power projects while we think water needs more attention; this is perhaps an opportunity to address both.

Attended evening deep dive on IED networks followed by another discussion on political issues. One comment especially stands out: "The Taliban aren't really trying to fight: they just want to be perceived as fighting until after ISAF departs in December 2014."

Kandahar University, 6 October

Morning helicopter flight to Kandahar with Masha Hamilton—journalist, writer, novelist, and now in charge of public affairs at the U.S. Embassy in Kabul. She has three kids the same ages as ours, all involved in artistic pursuits. Like our adventurous son Cameron, one of them wants to visit Afghanistan.

Met vice chancellor of Kandahar University. The plan is to break ground on a new USG-supported media center later this year. But the Afghans want more, including a partnership program with an American university and a four-story rather than a one-story building.

Toured KMIC next to the governor's palace. Masha mentioned the USG grant to KMIC will be extended to February 2014, much to their relief.

Returning to our helicopters I notice pomegranate season has finally arrived and Kandahar bazaar is now full of them.

Attended evening Purple Heart ceremony for young private who lost both legs during a lapse in concentration while looking for IEDs in Zaray. He is from North Carolina and realizes he is lucky to be alive. Yesterday five American soldiers were wounded, two of them losing legs to IEDs.

Kandahar, 7 October

More meetings. After a while the subject matter discussed in one morphs into the next.

Joined generals for dinner in VIP dining room for Dr. Catherine Dale, visiting from the Congressional Research Service. She spent time with the Third Infantry Division in Iraq. More than a few women are interested in intel and I often see them walking about the command center, pistols on their hips and with a jaded look, as if they have already seen everything and by now know everything.

Attended evening Purple Heart ceremony, General Abrams once again pinning medals while several dozen officers and enlisted men looked on. He is good on these occasions, recalling the history of the medal but also interacting with his troops.

The two soldiers tonight were lucky—they were injured in IED explosions but neither lost limbs and both can expect a complete recovery. One soldier might have lost his sight except that, fortunately, he was wearing blast-proof goggles when the bomb went off.

Panjwai, 8 October

Morning flight to Panjwai. The route took us close to the red and brown sands of the Registan Desert, a vast empty quarter that extends into Pakistan and is mostly frequented by *kutchis*. The views in the other direction, toward the north, were lovely—brown hills interspersed with green irrigated areas, a view on a clear morning of the Kandahar landscape at its best.

The jagged mountain north of the Panjwai PRT is especially striking—the Americans call it Fish Mountain because of its long shape. A group from the PRT recently climbed to the top to see a small memorial to an American soldier killed a couple of years ago. The cross at the top somehow survives, at least for now.

Briefed by a cynical civilian who has probably been in southern Afghanistan for too long. We then walked to government reception hall for local *shura* hosted by district governor Haji Faisal Mohammad.

About sixty local *maliks* joined us, looking like they just came in from the hills. Most wore black turbans and black sandals and had beards that were either black or white. It looked like a gathering of Taliban. Afterward I was told at least half were either Taliban or Taliban sympathizers.

Mostly I listened to the discussion covering everything from attacks on USAID-funded workers digging an irrigation canal to complaints that a university in Kabul was recently renamed after the Tajik politician Rabbani, killed by the Taliban a few months ago.

"A new school, maybe," said one elder. "But why is the name of an old school changed to honor someone like him?"

Another *malik* complained that too many local schools had shut down. "We don't have power," he said. "And our children don't even know how to use a computer."

After lunch Governor Faisal Mohammad and Haji Agha Dastageeri (a Kandahar Provincial Council member) dropped by for a long conversation. Dastageeri took the lead on almost everything. He is soft-spoken and affects a modesty that is somewhat reminiscent of some Mongolians I have met. At one point he said, "I am a servant, not a leader."

In reality Dastageeri has a reputation in some circles for ruthlessness, having started his adult life as a mujahideen commander against the Soviets. Many years later, he seems to have also made his peace, at least for a time, with the Taliban.

More likely he is simply a canny and politically astute survivor, bending to the inevitable, depending on who is in power at what point in time, perhaps embodying the Pushtun saying, "When confronting the very powerful, either keep your distance or keep your peace."

Qalat (Zabul), 9 October

Morning helicopter flight to Qalat, capital of Zabul Province. Lewis Gitter, Brian Bachman, and Sergio Guzman are accompanying. Had lunch in PRT cafeteria served by support staff from Kenya and Macedonia. The cook is creative with oranges, cucumbers, and peppers, cutting them into funny shapes for display purposes.

Departed on MRAPs belonging to the Alaska National Guard. Some soldiers previously participated in summer exercises in Mongolia. As we left, I noticed a small collection of historic artifacts decorating the Zabul PRT—a Russian tank, an old artillery piece, and two recoilless rocket launchers.

Stopped first at Alexander's Castle, the remains of a mud-brick fort dominating Qalat. We first walked down one set of walls and then climbed to the highest point, a hill topped by a glass teahouse built by the PRT several years ago. It is now abandoned. Perhaps it will make a nice tourist attraction a few years from now.

Visited the new slaughterhouse below Alexander's Castle. It is not yet in use, the butchers having protested against the small fee each must pay to use it. A collection of kids gathered around as we departed, watching our every move and asking for pens.

Drove to *mustafiat* to visit Shamsodeen and his staff responsible for provincial budgets. He has a long beard and spent fifteen years in Pakistan where he ran a shop. But he also knows budgets, providing a glimmer of hope in an administrative setup that usually lacks even basic skills.

Tried to draw Shamsodeen out on his exploits as a mujahideen commander—but he said no one ever has good memories of war. Afterward toured his rose and marigold garden—these gardens that crop up everywhere are among the most attractive aspects of Afghanistan.

Returned to PRT for dinner. Later walked across street to Governor Naseri's residence for two-hour session that swung between optimism and pessimism about the future. Last year fewer than a dozen girls graduated from high school in all of Zabul. Yet the number of schools and students has grown tremendously.

Returned to my quarters in the dark, pausing to look up toward a brilliant night sky. By midnight, Orion's belt is close to the horizon. The PRT includes several trees, and it is nice to smell the pines and hear them gently rustle in the breeze. Zabul is at an altitude of more than three thousand feet—and much cooler than Kandahar because of it.

Qalat (Zabul), 10 October

Morning meeting with senior agriculturalist Bismullah Harifal. He said agricultural production in Zabul has increased steadily during the past ten years.

Morning meeting with Rahimullah Lodin, youngest provincial director under the Ministry of Education in Afghanistan. He recently got his BA degree in India. His father worked at the Ministry of Education before him.

Met several members of provincial council, including two women wearing burkas. The men had beards and wore black turbans. We focused on economic concerns. Again, there is this tendency among Afghans—and the Americans here, for that matter—to swing between optimism and pessimism about the future. Realistically the future will probably involve both the good and the bad.

Afterward, the two women went their separate ways while we walked to the DFAC for lunch. The Afghans piled their plates with food. The menu included Mongolian barbeque with beef and shrimp. "It is nice to try different foods," one Afghan commented. Hussein, a PRT translator from Nangahar, helpfully steered all the Afghans away from pork.

We then boarded Black Hawks for our return to Kandahar Air Field, briefly skirting a dust storm to get there. International headlines focus on an attempt by the Pakistan Taliban to kill Malala Yousafzai, a young student from Swat who had become an advocate for female education via her Internet postings. Now she has a bullet in her brain and most of Pakistan is finally outraged about it.

Kandahar, 11 October

Wrote op-ed piece for the local Pushto press, building on the fact that Malala of Swat was named by her father after Malala of Maiwand, the Afghan heroine who waved her veil like a flag at the Battle of Maiwand where she was killed in 1880. Pushtuns on both sides of the frontier will be proud of both of them. Pushtuns everywhere need heroines.

Gecko, 12 October

Dinner at Gecko, fifteen minutes north of Kandahar Air Field by helicopter. The chef is from South Africa. I had catfish with grapes and sweet melon.

Observed simulated night raid organized and undertaken entirely by Afghans. The night-vision goggles I wore cost $7,000. The Afghan soldiers were quiet and professional, creeping out of the darkness to do the jobs assigned to them. Their pick-up trucks make them look like desert rats from Montgomery's North African campaigns. The night sky and the outline of nearby mountains, barely visible through the darkness, add to the atmosphere.

On days like this I reflect back on what I saw—and I can't believe I am here at all. Perhaps I should have done my homework. I never imagined I would ever be in a war like this.

Kabul, 13 October

Accompanied General Abrams on early morning flight to Kabul on Danish C-130. Several Afghan generals travelled with us, along with a large contingent of Romanian soldiers. We are here to attend the periodic commander's conference on the winter campaign.

The conference was deadly boring, at least for amateurs like me. General Allen put a good face on things, projecting modest optimism about the next campaign. It will be the thirteenth in the long war in Afghanistan—and the last involving ISAF soldiers.

Noticed several Mongolian troops on arrival at Kabul Airport. Also met an American colonel who I last saw in Pakistan several years ago.

Met Dutch general who said he served as deputy ISAF commander in southern Afghanistan in 2006. He mentioned that ISAF killed 1,500 Taliban in three weeks of intense fighting in Panjwai. The Taliban had dug trenches. He said it was the last time they engaged in a set piece battle with ISAF.

The Dutch general closed his eyes, bowed his head, and said a brief silent prayer over lunch. I didn't realize that such open displays of faith still survived in Europe. Also met ambassadors to Afghanistan from Netherlands, Lithuania, and Sweden—plus the new NATO SCR, also from the Netherlands.

Kabul, 14 October

Attended ISAF conference all day, watching commanders review plans for the coming winter and beyond. The Afghan commanders are a mixed bunch. Several became very vocal, even passionate. Almost all of them blamed Pakistan for violence in Afghanistan, describing summer 2012 as a war that mostly involved IEDs, the materials for which they claim come largely from Pakistan.

General Allen concluded by saying, "All wars end in a political solution." He thinks the Taliban will be a factor for many years to come—but if the April 2014 elections are free and fair, the government will have the legitimacy it needs to rule.

Met General Dahl at lunch, mostly to talk about Dahla Dam. He strongly supports it, believing it is a "big mistake" to think power is more important than water in southern Afghanistan.

Attended evening gospel service at IJC—other services earlier in the day were in Czech, French, and Hungarian. About a hundred attended, mostly Americans, though I also saw uniforms from Belgium, Britain, and Singapore, as well as civilians from places like India and the Philippines.

The choir and the band, mostly African American, are very good. Looking around I felt uplifted while also contemplating mankind in all its imperfections—most specifically including that poor, miserable specimen of humanity that is me. I want to experience everything in life—including faith, if that is ever truly possible. Mostly I fail miserably.

Kabul, 15 October

Long day in Kabul involving presentations by the military, both Afghan and American. Afghanistan faces a roller-coaster during the coming months, and some Afghans are frightened about what lies ahead.

Returned to Kandahar with General Abrams on a C-130 operated by the Texas National Guard. There is something strange and even alien about the greenish glow of the cabin, the passengers hunched up with their packs, helmets, and protective gear as they try to catch brief moments of sleep.

It has been a hard weekend in southern Afghanistan—three Americans are dead, two following a suicide attack south of Kandahar. Ambassador Cunningham attended the ramp ceremony earlier this morning because one of the dead was a civilian.

Exchanged e-mails with Tina Kaidanow, Ambassador Cunningham's deputy in Kabul, on the "two Malalas" story, my draft op-ed for the local Pushto press comparing Malala, the young student in Pakistan nearly killed by the Taliban for championing female education, with Malala of Maiwand, the courageous nineteenth-century Afghan heroine who grew up near Kandahar and rallied Afghan soldiers in their time of need. Apparently Public Affairs in either Washington or Islamabad recommended that this story be killed, fearing that it might somehow feed growing conspiracy theories in Pakistan that the Americans were behind the recent attack and stand to benefit from it. I vehemently disagree, viewing it as another example of our reluctance to avoid confronting both conspiracy theorists and radical Islamist narratives directly.

Kandahar, 16 October

Latest *New York Times* editorial urges the United States to leave Afghanistan "now," noting it will take a year to remove the last of the troops. I agree that it is time to leave—but in a way that also meets our commitments, in this case including the two-year transition on which all else is based.

Qalat (Zabul), 17 October

Morning Black Hawk flight to Qalat. David Donahue accompanied along with General White, though the general mostly stayed in the background; the intent is to emphasize the civilian side of things, especially when the main event of the day was to lay the foundation stone for the Zabul Teacher Training College. The United States contribution is $1.7 million and the project is finally moving forward.

Our convoy was protected by soldiers from the Alaska National Guard. I love the last names on the uniforms—White Feather, Boy Scout, Pinzayak. Several soldiers are Alaskan natives and some come from remote corners of the state.

While at the construction site our security was supplemented by two small helicopters gamboling about in the clear blue sky overhead. Driving through town I was impressed with the commercial activity and new construction, including several buildings with glass fronts, an optimistic sign.

Governor Naseri planned the ceremony and was disappointed we could not fly the minister of education down from Kabul. Several local dignitaries spoke, including the governor, head and deputy head of the provincial council, head of the local college, and the senior line director for education.

My remarks acknowledged the workers lined up off to one side with their spades, safety goggles, and bright orange tops. Following speeches, we walked toward a large trench to lay our respective foundation stones. This was followed by soft drinks and apples set up on long tables nearby.

Afterward Governor Naseri hosted lunch—the usual *kabuli pilau,* mutton kebab, and eggplant Afghan style, all of it delicious. Dessert included very large local apples.

A press conference was held in the governor's rose garden. The one question directed toward me was about the USG commitment to Afghanistan after 2014. Will the international community remain involved? The Kandahar party then boarded Black Hawks for the trip home.

Attended a couple of meetings and then stayed up late to respond to a query from Kabul, this time suggesting an alternate approach to dealing with members of the Kandahar Ulema Council who have not been paid for many months.

The untimely fate of the "two Malalas" article continues to rankle. It seems like a small thing, but the fate of this article that would have resonated among Pushto speakers in southern Afghanistan still bothers me. I realize that Kandahar is at the end of the line—but decisions on an article like this shouldn't be made from thousands of miles away.

Tarin Kot (Uruzgan), 18 October

C-130 flight to Uruzgan. I was invited to ride in the cockpit, making for nice views as we landed at Tarin Kot.

Today's program includes a change-of-command ceremony, in this case moving from an American colonel from the Indiana National Guard to Colonel Stuart from Australia. General Allen, General Abrams, and the Australian ambassador attended, along with Governor Akhundzada and other Afghan officials.

An Australian padre dressed in black offered an invocation and benediction. The Third Infantry Division band flew up for the day to play the American, Afghan, and Australian national anthems. Most Australian soldiers in Tarin Kot wear two patches—one showing a kangaroo, the other a boomerang.

Colonel Stuart's remarks were affecting, especially when he mentioned he had visited the Tarin Kot memorial that morning to reflect on those who made the ultimate sacrifice.

Later I visited the memorial, flags from Australia, Slovakia, Singapore, Afghanistan, and the United States flying overhead. I counted more than a hundred names on the concrete wall—Australian, Dutch, and American, mostly, with a single French captain appearing on the list.

Listened to Governor Akhundzada's interview with Australian media. The Australians focus entirely on Uruzgan—for them, it defines their deployment and they are doing everything possible to make it succeed. The Australian prime minister visited a couple of days ago.

Enjoyed pizza night at outside pizza oven. Earlier, Rob Sipe showed us around, including a quick trip to the shooting range with its views toward the green valley below.

The sound of gunfire echoed off the mountains as the sun disappeared behind the clouds, as if tucking itself into bed. At one point a dozen Special Forces drove by on small three-wheel off-road vehicles covered with dust, returning home from who knows where.

Stayed up to hear the PRT country-western band—three Australians and three Americans, the vocalist a female soldier. Songs included "Sweet Home Alabama" and "Hotel California." We gazed into the night, almost all of us feeling nostalgic and thinking mostly of home.

Late-night coffee latte at Green Bean. I was served by a Nepali who had to take over when his newly arrived colleague from Kenya messed up the order.

Tarin Kot (Uruzgan), 19 October

Up early for morning flight to Nili, capital of Daikundi Province, north of Uruzgan. Waited at flight line for most of the morning. In the end the clouds never lifted and the helicopters from Camp Phoenix never arrived. Daikundi is a largely Hazara region and it is disappointing to have my hoped-for trip there once again cancelled.

Met Governor Akhundzada in his office a couple of miles from the Tarin Kot PRT. He looks tired but still briefed us on what to expect tomorrow.

The view from the new government building is lovely—corn ripening in the field; a river running through the valley; a few orchards, mostly almonds and apricots; mud-brick buildings built in traditional style, some of them newly constructed; a cemetery filled with colorful flags waving in the wind; a solitary man praying in his fields; and a long ridge of barren mountains marking the far horizon.

Akhundzada is short with chubby cheeks, a cheerful puckish expression, and a quizzical smile. He has a reputation for being mercurial and not finishing what he starts. His family embraced the mujahideen against the Soviets during the 1980s. His father was killed by the Taliban, stoking a hatred that has continued ever since.

Spent most of the evening at my computer. Had dinner in Tarin Kot DFAC with General White and Colonel Stuart—the Goan shrimp curry was delicious. Also had a haircut and looked around the several Afghan shops set up within the PRT. Unlike last night the sky is clear and dotted with tiny pinpricks of light, like a dark bed sheet quilted with stars.

Tarin Kot (Uruzgan), 20 October

Rode in large Australian convoy to government center to attend Unity of Effort conference. Governors from across southern Afghanistan—Helmand, Kandahar, Zabul, and Uruzgan—all attended, along with the deputy governor of Daikundi whose aide looked like he came from a long line of Mongolians. A dozen or so ministers and deputy ministers from Kabul also attended, along with ambassadors from Australia and the Netherlands.

I had low expectations but the conference exceeded them. One member of parliament from Uruzgan also attended, making a strong case for promoting southern Afghanistan as a whole.

General Hamid spoke, sounding low-key and sincere. If Afghans respect their army, it is because of people like him.

Sat next to minister of communications and deputy minister of water and power for lunch. The former spent many years in Sweden and the latter's family lives in London. Also met minister of health, the only female in the Afghan cabinet. She attended the Harvard School of Public Health.

Lunch was delicious—for the first time I had fried river fish. Dessert included freshly cut pomegranate. The milk tea with a slight pistachio flavor was wonderful.

The afternoon session included more speeches concluding with a final summation by Dr. Abdul Ghafar Stanikzai, director of the Uruzgan branch of the Afghan Independent Human Rights Commission. The meeting room is quite well appointed. It's "paid for with your taxes," according to General Abrams.

The Afghan cabinet ministers returned to Kabul in a Kam Air commercial flight. The rest of us—including most of the provincial governors—boarded a C-130 for the return journey to Kandahar Air Field. I sat next to Wesa. Governor Akhundzada, looking cheerful and dapper as ever, briefly boarded our plane to say his final goodbyes.

Kandahar, 21 October

Stayed up until 2:00 a.m. but slept until 9:00 a.m. Otherwise spent most of day in meetings. The next two days will be exceptionally busy, starting with a trip to Zaray tomorrow.

Zaray, 22 October

Morning Black Hawk flight to Zaray west of Kandahar. Saw lots of traffic heading toward Herat on Highway One. After internal briefings, walked to district governor Sarhadi's office next door. One wall is decorated with photographs of leading district figures, the other with large posters of four who were deceased, all killed by the Taliban, all shown as if they were floating like angels in the clouds.

Sarhadi was unsuccessful in his latest run for parliament. He spoke disparagingly about the process, describing it as rigged from start to finish. He thinks security is getting better but chooses to keep his family in Kandahar. He views current poppy policies as impossible to implement. He is frustrated at the budget process and finds it very hard to access funds.

Several local dignitaries arrived, including the local police chief. We talked briefly, mostly covering the same themes as in the conversation with the district governor. We then returned to the flight line for our short trip home.

Accompanied General Abrams and General Hughes to evening Purple Heart ceremony. Earlier Abrams had asked "those who believe in a higher power" to pray for one young soldier who had stepped on an IED in Maiwand, losing three limbs.

The soldier he was referring to is a captain and it is gut-wrenching to see him stretched out and unconscious in an ICU hospital bed. Thirty-four minutes after the explosion, he was on the operating table at Kandahar Air Field.

Abrams also pinned medals on two other soldiers—one a private, the other a sergeant. Both were on the same dismounted patrol but had been less badly injured.

Governor's Palace, 23 October

Morning meeting at Camp Valdez with General Abrams and Ambassador Cunningham, Abrams mostly offering advice on working with Wesa. Abrams thinks the governor should more aggressively pursue governance issues in his province.

Toured Third Infantry Division command center before meeting with embassy civilians at Kandahar Air Field. The ambassador is soft-spoken but got his message across: The U.S. is drawing down in Afghanistan and it is time for Afghans to take the lead.

Drove to civilian side of Kandahar Air Field to meet Director Faizi. He was dressed in suit and tie and gave a good briefing, noting many changes. He has now met three U.S. ambassadors at Kandahar Airport—Cunningham, Crocker, and Eikenberry.

Returned to Camp Valdez, stopping briefly to show Ambassador Cunningham our dismal living situation—damp, leaking, cracking, coming apart. It will take $1.5 million to replace them and that time can't come soon enough.

Helicopters to KPRT for internal briefings. We then boarded MRAP for short journey to the governor's palace. The roads and bazaars of Kandahar are busy as ever.

Governor Wesa was his usual voluble self, repeating to Ambassador Cunningham many themes I've heard before on transition, elections, corruption, etc., etc. He mentioned a recent meeting with Bill Gates in Dubai to talk about polio. He said the Maiwand Heroes finished third in the Afghan premier soccer league. Herat placed first, aided by "Afghan players especially recruited from Iran."

We then walked to the office next door to meet line directors as well as Atta Mohammad, a former Taliban leader who now heads the Kandahar Peace *shura* and completely looks the part.

This was followed by a press conference at KMIC. The toughest question was from an Afghan BBC reporter who asked Ambassador Cunningham for his views on the Durand Line. Returned to KPRT early, time enough for Green Bean coffee while waiting for our helicopters home. Said goodbye to Ambassador Cunningham at the Camp Valdez flight line—he seems to have had a good day.

Talked briefly to Ambassador Cunningham about the story of the two Malalas that will never be published—he said he was aware of my concern. Perhaps I'm becoming too obsessed with the fate of this single op-ed, but I can't understand why it was ultimately trashed.

Evening briefing—as always, I am impressed by the level of detail, analysis, and understanding that Third Infantry Division staff have about this place. It is lower-ranking soldiers that give most of the presentations. Nearly everyone seems very young.

General Abrams held forth at different times, noting a recent visit to a district governor's office in which the framed picture of General Razziq was much bigger than the one of President Karzai. When asked about it, the district governor replied, "General Razziq is a great man."

Later, General Abrams was asked about the Afghan army. In his words, "With the right *kandak* commander, it can be a thing of beauty. The Afghan soldiers—they get it."

Kandahar, 24 October

Internal *shura* on water. About fifty people attended, both civilian and military. Also talked with Shah Wali Karzai by phone, partly to wish him happy Eid al-Adha and partly to see if mullahs on the ulema council had ever gotten their salaries. He called back to say they had indeed been paid.

Kandahar, 25 October

Spent entire day at Kandahar Air Field. It ended dismally with news that two American Special Forces soldiers had been killed in Uruzgan, possibly in a green-on-blue attack.

Kandahar, 26 October

Attended afternoon ramp ceremony for the two dead American NCOs assigned to Uruzgan and killed yesterday, one twenty-two years old, the other thirty-one. Once again the ceremony included a gathering of chaplains, a reading from Psalms, and a haunting rendition of "Amazing Grace" on the bagpipes.

Staff Sergeant Kashif Memon, the oldest soldier killed, was from Houston. He left two small children and an expectant wife behind. Very likely he was Ismaili and very possibly his family originally came from Pakistan. He was killed alongside another sergeant, Clinton Ruiz.

Spent most of day at my computer, finishing the RC-South quarterly report for Ambassador Cunningham. I included several references to Malala that some will probably find annoying.

Met Under Secretary of Defense for Policy James Miller. Our last encounter was in Mongolia in May when he visited Five Hills and met with senior Mongolian officers to thank them for their service in Afghanistan.

Called Fiona and Iain before going to bed. Iain had sent an e-mail mentioning William Stafford as his favorite poet and attaching one of his more touching poems, "A Story That Could Be True." It moved me to tears, especially the part about a lost father who needed to be found.

Kandahar, Eid al-Adha, 27 October

Eid. Spent part of it making courtesy phone calls to three governors (Akhundzada, Naseri, and Wesa) and two Peace Council members (Noorzai and Dastageeri). Naseri especially holds on to every moment of such conversations, expressing extreme gratitude for our partnership as well as appreciation for the blood shed by young Americans in Afghanistan.

Naseri is dealing with fallout following the deaths of three Afghans who at their request were freed by the Lithuanians onto the streets of Qalat rather than into the hands of Afghan security. A couple days later all three were killed—possibly in an IED they themselves blew up inadvertently, possibly in some other way.

Kandahar, 28 October

Morning briefing for visiting congressional staffers, one working for Senator McCain. They seem well informed and asked good questions. But one continuing theme is that Washington is tired of this war and wants it to end.

Kandahar, 29 October

Mentioned several items at morning staff meeting including Ambassador Cunningham's off-the-record media interview in Kabul, my quarterly report, concerns expressed by Governor Sherzai in Nangahar about the incarceration at Bagram of a former "businessman" from Kandahar with apparent ties to the Taliban, and the request from our staff to not go through IJC to force the appointment of a new governor for Arghandab/Zabul—in these situations, Afghans need to take the lead.

Scheduled to meet Jehani, a poet and former VOA correspondent who lives in Arlington, Virginia. He wrote lyrics to new Afghan national anthem—unfortunately last-minute airport security concerns intruded and I missed the meeting.

Jehani is known as the poet of Kandahar and supports a greater "Pashtunistan." Kush said he once worked at a McDonald's in Virginia alongside Jehani's son. Like Kush, the son is now an interpreter for the U.S. Army in Afghanistan.

Attended several meetings. Again, much of the conversation is about the progress of governance in Kandahar, Uruzgan, and Zabul. We almost never talk about Daikundi with its largely Hazara population and female mayor; somehow, it seems to be thriving in its splendid isolation.

Evening Purple Heart ceremony—four soldiers were given the award, three badly injured and scheduled to leave for Germany tomorrow. All were involved in the same incident in Panjwai where their Stryker hit a sixty-pound IED. No limbs were lost and all of them should make a full recovery.

General Abrams said the same thing to each soldier: "You are young, you are lucky, and your most important job right now is to fully recover."

General Abrams always describes Kandahar Air Field hospital as "the best trauma center in the world." The staff, both American and Australian, are very dedicated. Reflecting the season, hospital halls and rooms are decorated in orange and black for Halloween.

Kandahar, 30 October

Met Paul McEarchern, the Australian diplomat stationed at Kandahar Air Field. His tour ends in March and his next assignment will be as DCM in Dublin. He said the Australian international presence is far too small—smaller even than New Zealand's.

Met embassy official from Kabul working on border issues. He mentioned that three of his colleagues were killed and a fourth severely wounded in a green-on-blue attack in Herat last summer. The attack lasted six seconds.

Discussions continue on the winter and summer campaigns. The military views this summer as a last chance to deal big blows to the Taliban. General Abrams is focused on Panjwai and thinks the Taliban there are reeling.

Kandahar, Halloween, 31 October

The Taliban outside Kandahar Air Field observed Halloween with a rocket attack. The timing could not have been worse—I was waiting in line for my rice and curry at the Asian DFAC when the alarm went off.

Evening video conference with Zabul—Governor Naseri may accept the ISAF investigation after all, publicly acknowledging that the three Afghans initially detained by the Lithuanians really did blow themselves up while placing an IED.

4

═◇═

NOVEMBER

Tarin Kot (Uruzgan), 1 November

Morning Black Hawk flight to Tarin Kot. Stopped briefly at base in Arghandab to drop off Sergeant Major Watson for his battlefield rotation. The scenery was beautiful in every direction, most especially because it is fall and the leaves are turning yellow, orange, and red.

On days like this the contrast between the dull brown of the mountains and desert and the bright splashes of color in the river valleys below is especially lovely. Looking down on villages in the mountains of Uruzgan, I also saw piles of orange apricots on distant rooftops, drying in the sun.

Attended change-of-command at Camp Holland in Tarin Kot—Commander Geoffrey James is giving way to Commander Ronald Piret. In keeping with Navy tradition, a small brass bell was rung at various points. The ceremony took place in an airplane hangar decorated with flags from Afghanistan, Australia, Singapore, Slovakia, and the United States.

Met John Philp, the new Australian ambassador in Afghanistan who was previously his country's ambassador in Turkey. Governor Akhundzada also attended, small but irrepressible. For all the baggage he carries, it is hard not to like him. I keep thinking of him as the leprechaun of Uruzgan.

Talked to Adrian Lochrin, senior civilian from Australia. He mentioned that four members of the PRT including an Australian civilian had been badly wounded last summer when a ten-year-old detonated a suicide bomb near where they were standing—amazingly, all four survived.

Rob Sipe told me more about the two American soldiers killed last week in Uruzgan, including Sergeant Memon from Houston. He said the soldiers were serving as guardian angels to protect others. Someone offered them a cup of tea, and a disgruntled Afghan policeman shot them both in the back of the head. The policeman managed to escape.

Kandahar, 2 November

Catriona's eighteenth birthday—I called Ulaanbaatar and we talked for a few minutes. She has been waiting for this moment for a long time—but said she now feels "old."

Morning discussion among the generals about General Hamid. He is a Pushtun from Wardak but demonstrates remarkable effectiveness as a corps commander in southern Afghanistan. I wonder what happens to someone like him after 2014. Most of the senior American officers admire him a lot.

Evening ramp ceremony for Navy Seal killed earlier today near Shah Joy. He was born in 1990 and graduated from high school in 2008—the same age as Iain, the same class as Iain, and now dead at twenty-two following a Taliban ambush in a desolate part of Afghanistan near Ghazni.

Once again the ceremony involved a reading from Psalms, a recorded version of "Amazing Grace" on the bagpipes, and a lone trumpeter playing taps. General Abrams accompanied the coffin into the airplane, borne by six Navy Seals. Sergio, Jesse, and Bonnie attended—Bonnie was in tears afterward. She says it happens every time.

I learned later the soldier who had died was from New Jersey. His family was not happy with his decision to join the military and was even less thrilled when he became a Seal.

Kandahar, 3 November

All-day commanders' conference—a program backed by a thick package of more than two hundred slides. If it wasn't already clear enough, our campaign is winding down, though actual disengagement is still two years away. Troop levels have dropped 20 percent since summer. The number of bases is also in steep decline.

Increasingly, Afghan security forces are in the lead, though certain red lines are being drawn. According to General Abrams, "We won't accept Afghans dragging bodies attached to bumpers through the bazaars of southern Afghanistan." One recent report from Zabul following an assassination did say locals are calling for captured Taliban to be executed immediately.

According to Colonel Huggins, "Progress is being made [but] sometimes we get in the way." The Arghandab was held up as an example of relative success. One participant suggested decisions on when to engage should be based on three criteria: Is there hope? Is there need? And does anything useful come out of it?

Lunch and dinner at DFAC VIP room with four generals (Abrams, White, Hughes, and Brewer) and three colonels commanding brigades (Stuart, Webster, and Huggins). Riding to the DFAC in a van, one officer commented, "So far this war has cost enough to give every Afghan one million dollars," a debatable and even highly dubious figure that nonetheless reflects the high level of frustration at certain moments.

Learned that Mullah Torjan, member of the Kandahar Peace Committee, was arrested by the Afghan security services. A crowd of perhaps a hundred locals protested his arrest, saying this is no way to treat a mullah that chooses to reintegrate. The demonstrators also said they would urge their children to join the Taliban. Meanwhile NDS claims Torjan was picked up for trafficking guns to the Taliban. In other news, the district police chief in Dhand was just assassinated.

Attended late-evening Purple Heart ceremony for American soldier who broke his arm when his MRAP hit an IED on a morning trip from Tarin Kot to Choray. He was on his second patrol in Afghanistan. He was in the fourth car in the convoy rather than the first or second one. The driver was also injured, along with an Australian civilian working at the Uruzgan PRT.

Kandahar, 4 November

The rumor mill continues—the latest one is that ten Taliban disguised in police uniforms have infiltrated Kandahar Air Field and are waiting to launch an attack.

Sakari Karez, 5 November

Morning trip to Sakari Karez with General White. The base has largely been dismantled and will be turned over to the Afghan Department of Agriculture and Irrigation by the end of the month. Items of interest include two wells, a fire station, several storage buildings, and an incinerator plant. The wooden chapel is still in place, complete with a small steeple and windows painted to look like stained glass.

Lunch with Philip Dayal, USAID development officer serving at the Arghandab DST. He grew up in Punjab, attended school in Mussoorie, and got a degree from the Harvard School of Public Health. He is well into his second year in Afghanistan. He enjoys his work and respects the soldiers, but is pessimistic about what will happen when ISAF departs. Although the Arghandab has been peaceful in recent months he thinks sentiment there largely favors the Taliban. Yet he also mentioned that each Friday tens of thousands of Kandaharis picnic at a shrine just outside the Arghandab DST, a sign of the kind of peace that most Afghans long for.

Afternoon video conference with KPRT. Mullah Torjan is about to be released, having spent the past couple of days in NDS custody in Kabul. One thing seems clear: ISAF has few true partners in Afghanistan and almost nobody they can trust.

Late evening ramp ceremony at Kandahar Air Field for nineteen-year-old soldier from Iowa who committed suicide in Panjwai last night. He arrived two months ago and shot himself while on guard duty, creating such a mess his fellow soldiers burned the guard tower down rather than attempting to clean it up.

This time it was the five-person Third Infantry Division band that played a dirge-like version of "Amazing Grace" rather than the recorded sound of a piper. While waiting for the ceremony to begin, General Abrams mentioned the soldier who killed himself spent most of his childhood in foster homes. According to Colonel Webster, his Facebook page says he was happy in the Army.

Shah Wali Kot, 6 November

Morning Black Hawk to Shah Wali Kot north of Kandahar. We passed above Dahla Dam en route. Beyond Dahla Dam the Arghandab River is quite full. Just below Shah Wali Kot we crossed thick undergrowth. I later learned that this area is called the jungle—a place where Taliban fighters go for refuge.

Met district governor Haji Shah Abaidullah Popal, childhood friend of the Karzai family. He has been governor for seven years—perhaps the longest of any district governor anywhere in Afghanistan. He mentioned that his brother had been murdered by the Taliban.

Popal has a pleasant and outgoing personality, somewhat like Akhundzada in Uruzgan. He travels often and thinks security has improved. At one point he showed photos of a cache of Taliban arms that included IEDs and AK-47s. "America is a superpower," he said. "Our soldiers should be at least as well armed as the Taliban."

Participated in gathering of tribal elders next door. At least forty elders attended, all with long beards and black turbans. We sat on thick red carpets and were served naan, dahl, and potato curry. I talked with several people, including Haji Gul Badin (head of the district council), Abdul Karem (line director from the Ministry of Rural Rehabilitation and Development), and one of the local police chiefs, who, I later learned, is viewed by some as effective but reviled by others as a reputed pedophile who "keeps" young boys.

Several *maliks* made strong statements about Pakistan, focusing especially on the recent shelling at Khost. Someone mentioned with disdain Pakistanis who come to Afghanistan to wage war and conduct suicide attacks. Afghans don't much like any of their neighbors—but dislike Pakistan most of all.

The DST commander said at least 165 Taliban have been killed in Shah Wali Kot since last spring. As a sign of better security, he mentioned that each weekend more than 5,000 Kandaharis picnic at Dahla Dam. He commands a hundred soldiers in a district that has been the scene of much fighting, some of it quite intense, given the Taliban rat lines cutting across the district.

Visited USG-funded justice building with nice views toward the mountains. This is one of the better DST settings I've seen—or, perhaps, it is simply the lighting at this time of year and this time of day with brown mountains, golden trees, and a clear blue sky overhead.

I noticed a young man riding by on a horse—the first horse I've seen since leaving Mongolia several months ago. "Oh, that," someone standing next to me commented. "We use horses as mine sweepers."

Returned to Kandahar Air Field in time to attend another weekly briefing. According to estimates, at least forty Taliban IED emplacers have been killed in recent weeks across the battle zone. The feeling is that the Taliban are getting hammered tactically—but not necessarily strategically, given their continued belief that they are destined to rule a post-2014 Afghanistan.

Went to bed at midnight, before the first U.S. election results become available. Recent polls and predictions point to a narrow Obama win. It will be interesting to see what happens. I am not a political animal—and remain mostly ambivalent as far as this year's election results are concerned.

Kandahar, 7 November

Obama wins and it isn't even close. There is a different feeling this time around, lacking the hope, promise, and excitement of four years ago. The final results seem almost anticlimactic, as if everyone is just going through the motions.

Morning briefing for new British brigadier who will serve as chief of staff for IJC in Kabul. General Abrams is getting very good at these briefings—by now I've nearly memorized them myself.

Evening briefing for Graham Bowley from the *New York Times,* Jeremy Kelly from *London Times,* Kevin Sieff from the *Washington Post,* and Patrick Quinn from AP. They will visit Kandahar and Zaray tomorrow. They are skeptical about everything—and especially anyone representing the USG.

Late night dinner with General White to discuss tomorrow's meeting with Shah Wali Karzai in Kandahar. Colonel Mick King and SDO Sergio Guzman joined us, mainly to talk about the upcoming PRT/DST *shura.* We focused largely on the glide path that will result in a much smaller ISAF presence across southern Afghanistan in the months ahead.

Shah Wali Karzai's Residence, 8 November

Met USAID mission director Ken Yamashita on Kandahar Air Field flight line both coming and going to Kandahar PRT. He said it was a good day and that the Kabul group was especially impressed with the RAMP-UP project focused on urban Afghanistan.

Met Australian ambassador visiting Kandahar for the day. He is still waiting to present his credentials to President Karzai. We talked about the future of Uruzgan and the need to make sure Australia and the U.S. coordinate closely as they move to close the Tarin Kot PRT.

Met Shah Wali Karzai in Kandahar, travelling there in a convoy with General White, as well as with Rich and Kush. The hospitality was wonderful—a terrific lunch featuring *kabuli pilau* and various squash, pumpkin, and meat dishes. We were given boxes of pomegranates to take back to Kandahar Air Field.

Our extended conversation covered many areas, including Mullah Torjan's recent "arrest," the Kandahar Ulema Council, 2014 elections, upcoming actions focused on Panjwai, and the economic future of southern Afghanistan.

Shah Wali Karzai mentioned that his kids are clamoring to visit Dubai. The children attend the Turkish school, which he described as "very good." As a personality, Shah Wali Karzai remains somewhat diffident. At times he seems to go through the motions as tribal leader of the Popalzai—in his heart of hearts, he would rather be anywhere else, leading a different life. He is very concerned about the future of the many children in his care, both his and those of his murdered brother.

Joined General Abrams for meeting with the four international journalists. They spent their day in Kandahar, meeting Governor Wesa and visiting the new solar power system at Kandahar University. They also visited Zaray, reporting back on the improving Afghan army performance there.

General Abrams did most of the talking, conveying authority, sincerity, and knowledge of the facts. At one point he was asked what he felt during ramp ceremonies when dead soldiers start their long journey home. What would he tell the parents? He said he would say they were true professionals who gave everything.

According to General Abrams, "Afghan soldiers know how to fight" and will do "better than people expect." Recognizing that Afghanistan may not succeed once ISAF departs, he echoes the view of many in the military that the biggest deficiency may be the "governance gap" that in his view is failing to deliver essential services to the Afghan people.

Tarin Kot (Uruzgan), 9 November

Morning trip to Tarin Kot to attend memorial service for Kashif Mohammad Memon and Clinton Ruiz as well as a third soldier from the same base, Matthew Kantor. An Australian piper played several Scottish laments.

The order of service included Psalm 23 as well as a Koranic reading, reflecting Staff Sergeant Memom's Muslim background. As for Sergeant Ruiz who was killed in the same incident, his commanding officer read a letter from the father expressing appreciation for support from his fellow soldiers: "We have lost a son but gained a battalion."

Afterward learned more about the very disturbing green-on-blue attack from a couple of weeks ago that led to the deaths of Kashif Memon and Clinton Ruiz. Apparently, it was a Taliban implant, not a disgruntled policeman. He had shared a cup of tea with Sergeant Memon for twenty minutes before turning his gun on him.

Returned to Kandahar Air Field and attended another ramp ceremony, this one involving a twenty-one-year-old helicopter maintenance operator who shot himself earlier this morning. This is the second suicide in a week. His female platoon commander looked very cut up over it.

Afterward I talked briefly with Sergeant Major Watson about suicide in the military. He says most stem from relationship issues, financial problems, or disciplinary actions.

Boarded Black Hawk for second time today to visit Gecko. General Abrams thinks the Taliban are surprised at what they face, given that ISAF is reducing its presence—and will be even more surprised at the level of force ANSF will display next year. He thinks we are always skeptical about meeting our objectives—but wonders if perhaps we are doing better than we think.

Leaving the compound that once belonged to Mullah Omar, the sky seemed especially brilliant tonight, bright stars shining in every direction. We then made our way back to Kandahar Air Field, flying at low altitude in a darkened helicopter with wind rushing through the open windows, the lights of Kandahar shining brilliantly below. The electricity in Kandahar is now subsidized by ISAF, but this won't continue forever.

Camp Nathan Smith, 10 November

Attended KPRT change-of-command ceremony at Camp Nathan Smith— Commander Heath Starvis giving way to Commander Ashburn, both from the U.S. Navy. Colonel Huggins attended as battle space owner. He joined the Army at seventeen and has a lot of combat experience, including in Iraq. David Sias, Erin Tariot, and others from KPRT participated, along with several provincial dignitaries including Governor Wesa, Deputy Governor Qadim Patyal, and Mayor Qazi Mohammed Omer.

We talked briefly, Wesa expressing astonishment at the scandal that precipitated General Petraeus' sudden departure from the CIA. In reality, human nature trumps everything and even the most brilliant fall prey to it. Ironically, General Petraeus was fond of saying, "Character is what we do when no one is looking—and someone is always looking."

Attended evening ramp ceremony for twenty-five-year-old sergeant killed earlier today by an IED in Panjwai. He was from California and his job was to disarm IEDs. He was part of a dismounted patrol, sent to assist an Afghan checkpoint that had been fired upon the day before. Hundreds of people attended despite short notice. One soldier followed the flag-covered coffin as it was borne into the airplane, holding the leash of the late sergeant's black sniffer dog.

Qalat (Zabul), 11 November

Morning flight to Qalat to attend Zabul PRT change-of-command ceremony at FOB Smart—in this case, Lieutenant Colonel Marc Sheie is giving way to Lieutenant Colonel Justin Kraft, both from the U.S. Air Force.

Sheie received a bronze star from Colonel Chuck Webster, the battle space owner. Sheie told me later he will return to Tampa and then retire.

As at KPRT yesterday, the ceremony was held in the open sun and included two service songs: "The Army Goes Rolling Along" and the impossible-to-sing "Air Force Song." Local dignitaries were again out in force, including Governor Naseri. He seems distracted and distant. Almost certainly the Zabul PRT will close by July 2014. Our Afghan counterparts will be disappointed when they finally hear that news officially.

Today was especially beautiful with cloudless blue skies in every direction. Highway One north to Kabul was crowded with long lines of trucks. We also flew over Alexander's Castle—providing a connection to Afghanistan's ancient past and underscoring the reality that the American engagement is but one episode in a much longer history.

Kandahar Airport, 12 November

Morning meeting with Kandahar Airport director Faizi, recently returned from New York and Washington where he experienced Hurricane Sandy in all its fury. We talked about airport security, hajj returnees, and the upcoming FAA visit. I asked what he would think if the U.S. Embassy built offices and a small *shura* hall near the civilian terminal—an idea he greeted with enthusiasm.

Kandahar, 13 November

Opening remarks at *shura* involving staff from our PRTs and DSTs. I concluded with two Afghan proverbs: "When you've jumped across a stream once, the second time is easier." And, "The mountain may be high but there is always a path to the top of it."

Kandahar, 14 November

Anecdote from 8:00 a.m. staff meeting: One of the Afghan senior officers asked General Hughes if it is true that General Petraeus had an affair with a married woman.

On hearing the answer, he stated, "She should be taken to a room, placed on a prayer rug, and stoned to death."

What about General Petraeus? "He is a good man. He should be left alone."

Briefing for James Stavridis, the four-star admiral who heads NATO. We had not seen each other since graduate school at Fletcher more than three decades ago. Can that be possible? He is shorter than I remember and, like me, has lost most of his hair. As he eyes retirement, he congratulated me on "a good career."

The PRT/DST *shura* ended more or less successfully. For some of the military people present—including at least one and possibly two of the three PRT commanders—this is it, and there will be no successors. By next fall most of the civilians will also have departed from Afghanistan.

One statistic gives some measure of hope: there are 18,000 ISAF soldiers in southern Afghanistan right now, along with 57,000 from ANSF. Surely that number of Afghans will be sufficient to prevent the Taliban from taking total control. Already ANSF accounts for nearly nine out of every ten of the casualties in southern Afghanistan.

Attended memorial service at Mustang Ramp hangar for a soldier from California who killed himself five days ago. The program included the profile of a kneeling soldier and words of comfort from Psalm 23.

The soldier's commanding lieutenant colonel and captain spoke, along with a fellow specialist who remembered him covered in grease, hunting for a loose screw that had somehow fallen into the engine of one of the Chinooks he was repairing. He remembered that the fallen soldier liked to watch movies and planned to move to Canada in 2016, "because I want to."

Afterward signed the condolence book while a series of photographs flashed up on a nearby television screen—family, friends, his wife, a picture of a Thanksgiving celebration from long ago.

Kandahar, 15 November

Afternoon ramp ceremony for Sergeant Battle from North Carolina, killed in the ammunition dump explosion at Zangabad yesterday. General Abrams followed the flag-draped coffin into the airplane.

Sat in on evening briefing that suggested that the Taliban leadership in Quetta is confident about their ultimate success—when ISAF leaves in 2014, they expect to drive up Highway Four through Spin Boldak and immediately take control.

Kandahar Airport, 16 November

Morning meeting at Kandahar Airport with Haji Mohammad Hashim Agha, governor of Spin Boldak District bordering Pakistan. He assumed his responsibilities six months ago. His brother served there previously but was transferred to Panjwai District, where he was assassinated by the Taliban.

Hashim Agha is modest and unassuming—but by all accounts is a major landowner with lots of money. He said ten of his relatives have been killed by the Taliban. He also said he has eighteen children, twelve of whom survive. I later learned Hashim Agha has two wives—one Achakzai, the other Noorzai, each representing one of the main tribes living in Spin Boldak.

Agha likes to talk and he covered many topics, including elections, transition, and corruption. He mentioned that his brother visited the White House and met Obama. He requested international assistance to ensure fair elections. He bemoaned corruption. He expressed a wish for peace and reconciliation. He acknowledged that security issues prevent him from travelling to outlying villages—but said he hopes to travel much more often in the future.

On the assignment front it looks like USAID will support my nomination as political adviser at CENTCOM in Tampa after all. Almaty for a second time is also appealing. But CENTCOM has its attractions, including proximity to parents and other family. After more than twenty-five years abroad it is perhaps finally time to live in a new country—the fraying but somehow still United States of America.

Kabul, 17 November

Departed Kandahar Air Field at 9:00 a.m. on Embassy Air. The plane emptied at Tarin Kot, leaving a dozen of us to proceed to Kabul—including a young Afghan with a Koran who spent the rest of the flight reading quietly, nodding his head vigorously to the cadence of the Arabic text.

Met on arrival by embassy driver, a talkative Tajik from Panjshir. As always there is a sense of unspoken relief when we finally pull into the well-protected embassy compound with its several layers of security.

It is strange to be at the embassy and use real silver and real plates. Walking to our CHUs afterward, Karen Decker related her early experiences as SCR in Bagram. "It's sort of weird, isn't it?" she said, partly describing what all of us feel.

Kabul, 18 November

All day SCR *shura,* though with a cast of dozens of extras. Transition is the topic of the day, dominating every discussion. On corruption, one SCR commented that Afghans are only concerned about it if they are not actually participating in it.

Masha Hamilton arranged evening meeting for SCRs with several journalists including Patrick Quinn (AP), Michael Georgy (Reuters), Connor Powell (Fox), Maria Abi-Habib (*Wall Street Journal*), and Alissa Rubin (*New York Times*). They mostly seem cynical about what they see around them every day.

Kabul, 19 November

Afternoon meeting at parliament with two members from lower house—Khalid Pushtun from Kandahar who lived in New Mexico for twenty years and is associated with Gul Agha Sherzai, former governor of Kandahar and current governor of Nangahar; and Obaidullah Barakzai, a member of Hezb-e-Islami Afghanistan from Uruzgan.

I last met Barakzai a few weeks ago at the governor's *shura* in Tarin Kot. He has a dark beard, wears a black turban, and was holding two cell phones while fingering a set of worry beads. According to the briefing notes, he has twenty-five children.

We drove to parliament one way and came back by another, providing a rare opportunity to see street life in Kabul. The shops are full, the streets are crowded, and there is a lot of new construction. I noticed many mosques, some new but others recognizable from those I saw in my childhood visits during the late 1960s and early 1970s.

Driving along the polluted Kabul River, we must have been very near the place where Dad was photographed during his first visit to Afghanistan in 1958—age twenty-nine, he is wearing a white shirt and gray sweater. His hair is black, his gaze is steady, and he looks handsome and very young. I would have been a one-year-old.

I stare back at the photograph, at my father as a young man, at a peaceful Kabul street scene, mud houses in the background, three Afghan men walking beside a clean and swiftly flowing river lined with fruit trees. What became of the three Afghan men? What became of their families?

Pensive and nostalgic as I am right now, I have a feeling of sadness combined with a deep longing to somehow return to that long-forgotten scene for even a few minutes—to go back in time and reenter the place shown in that photograph as an invisible older adult, looking at my young parents and then at my one-year-old self, holding on even briefly to that moment of time that has already disappeared and by now is lost forever.

Kandahar Airport, 20 November

Up at 5:30 a.m. for early morning flight to Kandahar via Bastion in a Dash 8. Our flight south was full—Ambassador Cunningham is headed to Helmand and the younger Rabbani, head of the Afghanistan Peace Committee following the assassination of his father last year, is travelling with him.

I remember meeting the senior Rabbani in Kabul several years ago, when I visited Afghanistan from Islamabad to meet with USAID mission directors from South and Central Asia. For all the baggage he carried, he also had a lot of gravitas.

Now I am waiting in the airplane at Bastion, impatiently looking forward to our takeoff. I am supposed to meet the Pakistani consul in Kandahar in an hour but it looks like I will be late, possibly missing the appointment altogether.

We are flying now and I am looking down on the desert landscape that surrounds Helmand. I notice a couple of Strykers and a small convoy of MRAPs, the lead vehicle equipped with a roller to blow up pressure plate mines.

Where there is irrigation in the Helmand, there are plenty of Afghans who cultivate poppy. As we departed Bastion, I also noticed a myriad of aircraft—F-16s, Sea Stallions, Ospreys, and Apaches, though none of the Marine Harriers, a number of which were destroyed in a Taliban attack several weeks ago, killing two Marines.

Arrived at Kandahar Air Field thirty minutes late—time enough to drive to the Kandahar Airport terminal to meet two visiting diplomats from the Pakistani consulate. In an odd way, their physical appearance tells the story of Pakistan over the past generation: one, a Pathan from Peshawar, dressed like a *maulvi,* sporting a long beard and with a distinct black mark on his forehead, signifying that he prays regularly; the other, either a Punjabi or a *muhajir* from Islamabad, looking more like an old-school diplomat and dressed in suit and tie.

Both diplomats noted the sacrifices Pakistan has made since 9/11, including the deaths of 35,000 civilians and at least 5,000 soldiers. They expressed concern about what an unstable Afghanistan might mean for Pakistan.

They twisted the knife in a couple of places, stating that security in southern Afghanistan had never been worse, suggesting that the international forces have little to show for their decade-long effort in Afghanistan, and making the case that Afghans expect and deserve much more. Yet they also acknowledged Pakistan's own thirty-five-year interaction with Afghanistan had won neither love nor friendship.

Kandahar, 21 November

Ninety-fifth birthday celebrations for Third Infantry Division, organized in North Carolina in November 1917 at the onset of World War I. General Abrams spoke, and then the youngest and oldest in the division together cut the cake with a sword.

The Third Division band provided music, including the usual rendition of "Dog Face Soldiers" with its expression of relief at not being a "fancy pants Marine" and the claim that soldiers in the Third Division "eat raw meat for breakfast every day." American, Afghan, and NATO flags fluttered overhead against a backdrop of clouds and the occasional military plane heading off on its next mission.

Afterward I talked with several Belgian airmen and soldiers. They come on four-month rotations. Those present included a Belgian F-16 pilot and a Belgian military officer who spent several weeks at Five Hills outside Ulaanbaatar, preparing Mongolian soldiers for service in Afghanistan.

Regular evening briefing. The meeting this time took two hours and was very detailed. General Abrams is not convinced that a security agreement will be in place by the end of 2014, suggesting that it is likely to founder over immunity issues associated with ISAF soldiers.

Kandahar, Thanksgiving Day, 22 November

Thanksgiving Day. Work is lighter than usual—still, the day started at 9:00 a.m. with a contact brief for General Austin and the undersecretary of the Army, both visiting from the Pentagon to spend the holiday with soldiers. After the meeting they departed for their helicopters and the forward bases at which they will dish out turkey and mashed potatoes to the troops.

Ate dinner at north DFAC with twenty other civilians. The mess hall was crowded and included a detachment of cavalry with cowboy hats and spurs. The lines are long but the food isn't bad. It is cold and rainy in Kandahar—winter has finally arrived.

Talked to Fiona and Catriona in Mongolia, Iain in Texas, and Mom in Georgia by phone. Meanwhile, Dad and Cameron are heading to Central America on this long weekend for a glimpse of the jungles and Mayan pyramids of Guatemala. Cameron has been talking about taking this trip with his grandfather since high school and now he is finally doing it.

Gecko, 23 November

Slept until 10:00 a.m., then woke to a crisp, clear day with barren brown hills visible in the distance—southern Afghanistan at its best. Attended informal noon lunch with Generals Abrams, Brewer, Hughes, and White. No subject is off limits and we talk freely about anything.

One general mentioned Captain Brian Kitchings who was awarded a silver star in Panjwai yesterday. He stepped forward in a firefight when the situation was dire, risking his life to mobilize his platoon as well as a neighboring one. This was the same engagement in which two American soldiers stepped on IEDs, causing one to lose both legs.

Friday evening trip by Black Hawk to Gecko. We started the evening by feasting on the best food in southern Afghanistan—fresh fruit, fish, shrimp, steak, chicken, and pork chops. Apart from a good mess hall, there is a rose garden in full bloom and a roaring fire nearby, a sign that winter really has arrived. Mullah Omar would be appalled at what has become of his old compound, not to mention the fact that tonight's menu included pork chops.

This evening's conversation was more interesting than usual. Is Mullah Omar still alive? Would a split in the Taliban be good or bad for stability in Afghanistan? Will the Taliban immediately take over when ISAF departs—or will security be sufficient and Afghan society sufficiently changed that their plans may yet be thwarted?

At least one of the senior officers present subscribes wholeheartedly to the cell phone theory of economics as well as politics—Afghans have become so attached to their cell phones that they will resist any attempts on the part of the Taliban to take them away.

I see three possibilities: The Afghan government holds. The Taliban take over. Or the country fractures along regional and ethnic lines, with warlords once again filling all the vacuums that emerge. I have to think the Taliban are the spoilers. If they negotiate, the first scenario becomes more likely; if not, the third scenario will prevail.

Mosum Ghar, 24 November

Morning Black Hawk to Mosum Ghar for change-of-command ceremony—Colonel Webster from Second Stryker Brigade giving way to Colonel Getchell from Fourth Stryker Brigade. The ceremony included an opening prayer, a couple of speeches, and the furling and unfurling of flags. General Habibi attended along with Panjwai district governor Haji Mohammad, who greeted me warmly.

Afterward we walked to a nearby tent for lunch. General Abrams asked General Habibi about his battle plan in the Horn of Panjwai. Increasingly Afghans are in the lead—as they will be on this one.

Habibi expressed disappointment that American air power isn't used to full effect. General Abrams reviewed the rules of engagement, purposefully put into place to reduce civilian casualties. More than most people realize, lawyers play an important role in the conduct of this seemingly endless war.

Governor Haji Faisal Mohammad expressed appreciation to Colonel Webster for the very few civilian casualties during his tenure—virtually all of them have been inflicted by the Taliban.

Returning to Kandahar Air Field, the helicopter pilot chose a route that brought us briefly over the Registan Desert—nothing but sand dunes and a solitary mountain in the distance, as far as the eye could see.

Mosum Ghar ranks among the most scenic of forward bases in southern Afghanistan, surrounded on two sides by small mountains and on a third side by grape orchards. A large American flag has been created on one slope—red bricks for red stripes; white gravel for white stripes; and fifty large boulders painted white, each representing one star.

Kandahar, 25 November

Woke at 3:00 a.m. to attend ramp ceremony for Special Forces soldier killed in Uruzgan yesterday—only to find out it had been rescheduled for 2:00 a.m. Learned later that my planned trip to Daikundi was cancelled yet again, this time because of snow.

Shah Wali Karzai's Residence, 26 November

Office meetings with two departing KPRT staff—Yonas Hamda and Curt Wolters. Originally from Ethiopia, Yonas came to the U.S. at age eighteen and years later became a Peace Corps volunteer. Curt reminded me that he was one of my first bosses when I joined USAID in 1984. About to turn seventy-five, he is now looking for more USAID work somewhere else, perhaps in Pakistan.

Early evening flight to FOB Walton followed by convoy to Shah Wali Karzai's house on the eastern edge of Kandahar.

General Abrams wanted to talk about the Panjwai campaign—and the importance of ensuring that he Afghan government follows up any gains on the ground with a more permanent presence. He also talked about the immunity issue as it relates to a prospective BSA between ISAF and Afghanistan, suggesting that it remains a key issue that still needs to be worked out.

Governor's Palace, 27 November

Morning meeting with Governor Wesa in Kandahar. The roses in his garden are in full bloom and quite magnificent. General Abrams covered all his main points, including seeking civilian support for post-security operations in Panjwai.

Riding to the governor's palace in one of the large Oshkosh MRAPs, the bazaars of Kandahar and the traffic flowing through them were as busy as I've ever seen. Perhaps security is improving after all, perhaps Afghans will maintain it when ISAF departs. It is already largely their city and the foreign footprint diminishes further every day.

Returned to busy afternoon—always there are more e-mails from Kabul, always there are more fires to put out.

The latest word is that our DSTs in Panjwai, Maiwand, and Shah Wali Kot will close forthwith because they don't meet security requirements. Our hoped-for glide path is fast becoming a steep slide down a mountain.

FOB Apache (Zabul), 28 November

Morning flight to FOB Apache—we travelled in two Black Hawks followed by two Chinooks carrying Afghan guests from Kabul, all headed to the tranche three handover ceremony in Qalat. Essentially, that means security for Zabul is being turned over to Afghans.

The ceremony took place at Eagle, a small ANSF military base. Governor Naseri and General Hamid attended. The speeches dragged on for a long time—I was the only foreigner to speak and made sure my remarks were brief.

I used Arabic in a couple of places and read out in Pushto the motto of the Afghan army: "God, Homeland, Duty." Afterward the deputy minister of education who has a PhD in Islamic history from Saudi Arabia asked if I spoke Arabic.

The ceremony concluded with a drawing down of the NATO flag and the flying of the Afghan one. A small Afghan military band dressed in red uniforms struck up a tune while various members of the ANSF—policy, army, commandoes—stood at attention.

We walked to the Afghan army mess hall—several hundred of us, packed around long tables laden with mutton, *kabuli pilau,* spinach curry, and assorted fruits, including apples and bananas. Probably this was the most Afghans I have yet seen gathered in one room.

General Abrams pointed to someone on the Peace Council who spent three years in detention at Bagram. I've met him on previous visits to Qalat—he speaks a little English and we get on famously. His remarks reflected a disdain for the Taliban. Either he was grandstanding for the audience or he had a dramatic change in heart somewhere along the way.

A storm arrived just as we prepared to leave—rain first, then sleet, and finally small hailstones. Zabul is much colder than Kandahar and this storm will bring snow to the nearby mountains. Waiting out the rain, we spent three hours in the ISAF battalion headquarters, a new building built of plywood. The Afghan delegation from Kabul joined us and I met a couple of them.

I spoke at length with "Hollywood," interpreter for General Abrams. He has applied for an American visa and wants to move to the U.S. as soon as possible. He is from Nuristan and was appalled that it has become a largely Taliban province along the lines of Waziristan. He said Nuristan once placed a premium on education, including education of females. "Now everyone has been brainwashed by mullahs from Pakistan."

By 7:00 p.m. the sky cleared sufficiently for us to leave. The flight line was very dark, as was our trip back. Very occasionally I noticed the small fires of *kutchi* camps below us. At times I made out the headlights of brave drivers traversing Highway One from Qalat to Kandahar at night. And then we arrived at Kandahar Air Field, brilliantly lit up, a city in its own right, temporary home to nearly 30,000 lost souls from many different countries—me being numbered among them.

Tarin Kot (Uruzgan), 29 November

Quick trip to Tarin Kot—up on Black Hawk, back on C-130 flown by the Texas National Guard. It was a clear day with nice views toward distant mountains already covered in snow. At times like this parts of southern Afghanistan look a lot like Mongolia.

Attended memorial ceremony at Camp Ripley for Navy Seal Kevin Ebbert, killed last week by gunfire in Uruzgan while attempting to help others. A medical corpsman, he was thirty-two years old and leaves a wife named Ursula behind. He was from California. According to the eulogies, he was very organized, loved his wife, and wanted to be a doctor.

He must have checked "Atheist" on his religious preference card—no scripture or chaplain was involved, though a poem called "Ode to a Wandering Warrior" was recited with its various references to Valhalla. A comrade recalled that they were together on Thanksgiving Day—and then held up an artistic-looking turkey Kevin had drawn only a few days before.

A detachment of Afghan commandos attended, a welcome change from the last such event in which the Afghan military was entirely absent, two Special Forces soldiers having been killed in a green-on-blue attack.

I talked to General Mark Brewer and Colonel Ian Stuart from Australia. They said the entire Australian army numbers 30,000—somewhat larger than the Third Infantry Division when it is at its home base in Fort Stewart, Georgia.

Kandahar, 30 November

Attended change-of-command ceremony at Kandahar Air Field—655th Regional Support Group giving way to 652nd Regional Support Group. Both are Reserve units. The outgoing one has ties to New England, the incoming one to Montana and neighboring states. The worst part of their job will be organizing ramp ceremonies.

Met Colonel Considene from Oklahoma, visiting Kandahar Air Field from Kandahar for the day. He introduced me to his two sons, both in the Army. His brother's son, also a soldier, will drop by later in the day.

Lunch with Generals Abrams, Brewer, Hughes, and White. I mentioned that our DSTs and PRTs are now on a path toward quick closure. General Brewer referred to an incident in Zabul yesterday where an Afghan soldier "jokingly" pointed his rifle at several Americans. No one is amused—mostly they are shocked and appalled by it.

Afternoon remarks to thirty female soldiers from the United States, Australia, and Romania as they complete their Female Engagement Team training. None had heard of Malala of Maiwand or her connections with Malala of Mingora in Swat.

Dad is celebrating his eighty-third birthday in Macon, Georgia—time is moving much too fast. We were at least able to connect by phone. I never expect to reach that age—on the contrary, I have often thought my parents would outlive me.

5

—◇—

DECEMBER

Kandahar, 1 December

Visited Saturday morning market at Kandahar Air Field for the first time, crowded with dozens of stalls displaying a mix of handicrafts and pirated videos. There is a large pond nearby, providing Kandahar Air Field with an expanse of wetlands. At this time of year, it is filled with ducks—a wonderful sight.

Kandahar, 2 December

Usual Sunday schedule—country team via video with Kabul, stand-up meeting with civilian staff, and key leader engagement discussion involving the general command. Attended evening partnership dinner hosted by General Abrams for General Hamid. Generals Brewer, White, and Hughes attended, along with Afghan counterparts.

I enjoyed dinner—but General Hughes said afterward that he heard complaints from his table that dessert involved only a poor pudding and the drinks on offer did not include wine.

The company at my table—General Abrams, General Hamid, Sergeant Major Kefayataullah, and Colonel Shanahan from Australia—was more congenial. I can see why Hamid has earned the respect of the American military.

During the late 1980s Hamid was a military cadet in Moscow. He was briefly a prisoner of the Taliban during the 1990s, returning to active duty only in post-9/11 Afghanistan. He has four sons and six grandsons, all living in an extended family household in Kabul.

General Hamid's final remarks to end the evening were quite touching. He thanked the international community for building the Afghan army, describing it as "the best ever." He also expressed appreciation for American blood that has been shed in Afghanistan, saying it would "never be forgotten" and it had now become "part of Afghan history."

Panjwai, 4 December

Left at noon in two Black Hawks for Panjwai. The plan was to keep this DST open until summer 2014. It will now close eighteen months early because there aren't enough ISAF soldiers to properly protect the perimeter.

District governor Haji Faisal Mohammad (Ishaqzai) is not very hopeful, and neither are the other two people with whom we spoke, Haji Mahmood (Alakozai) and Haji Naik Mohammad (Noorzai). All three described a provincial government that is clueless and distant.

"It wouldn't matter if the senior politicians visited us," one of them said. "Even if they did, their promises will never be fulfilled."

Governor Mohammad's predecessor Haji Fazluddin Agha—brother of the current governor of Spin Boldak—was killed in Panjwai earlier this year.

One of the Afghans present stated Afghanistan fails because Afghans are bad Muslims. He complained that Afghan soldiers eat in public during Ramadan, setting a bad example. He said Afghanistan is riddled with corruption. He mentioned that many Taliban had once been his friends and were simply misguided. He added that ISAF should stay at least through elections to ensure that they are fair.

Haji Mahmood talked less and is reported to be shy and reserved. He looks striking with his long black beard and Taliban-style turban. The unofficial mayor of Bazaar-e-Panjwai, he heads the local shopkeepers' association. He said 120 shops have opened and a thousand new homes have been built in recent years.

I don't know why people such as the three hajis subject themselves to biometric tests to enter the DST compound and meet with us. Perhaps they are curious or like to talk to or hear foreigners talk. Or perhaps it is the drama of it all, the lingering hope that our conversations may actually lead to something.

Attended evening briefing. Several insurgents have managed to blow themselves up attempting to build or emplace IEDs and others have been killed by drones—yet IEDs remain the leading cause of death among ISAF and Afghan security forces.

Governor's Palace, 5 December

Ambassador David Pierce, acting special representative for Afghanistan and Pakistan, arrived from Kabul with a party of eighteen, half of them security guards. Formerly U.S. ambassador to Algeria, he spent a year as assistant ambassador to Ryan Crocker, but this was actually his first visit to Kandahar.

General Abrams provided the usual early morning briefing, presenting a fairly upbeat perspective on security but noting big gaps in governance. He professed optimism about the future.

We then took a brief tour of the command center as a potential U.S. consulate a couple of years from now. After that we boarded helicopters for KPRT, embarking on a series of meetings that lasted the rest of the day.

Governor Wesa's rose garden has never looked nicer. Two cranes walked across the grass. Possibly they have just arrived from Mongolia or Siberia, having flown over the Himalayas and Hindu Kush to make Kandahar their winter home.

Finally got accurate account of the two attractive blue structures outside the governor's palace. The larger building is the tomb of Ahmed Shah Durrani, founder of the Afghan state. The smaller building in front of it is the shrine where the cloak of the prophet is kept.

Wesa presented an optimistic view of Kandahar, highlighting security gains and school enrollment rates that now exceed 200,000. Increasingly, senior Afghan leaders accept that ISAF is leaving.

The governor served green tea with a selection of almonds, pistachios, and raisins, all from Kandahar. He said Shah Wali Kot is especially famous for its figs.

Met several members of Kandahar Provincial Council headed by Ehsan Noorzai. Dastageeri spoke at length, reserved but formidable with his long beard and Taliban-style turban. He reflects the old-style Pushtun personality, one that is being replaced by a younger generation such as Deputy Governor Qadim Patyal and Kandahar mayor Qazi Mohammed Omer. Everyone seems sincere and well-meaning, though the reality behind the smile is in some cases an ocean of corruption.

Wesa hosted lunch for his guests, both Afghan and American. Ambassador Pierce sat next to twenty-eight-year-old Maryam Durani, a Shia Muslim born and raised in Kandahar who is on the provincial council, was one of the State Department's International Women of Courage Award winners in 2012—and last year made *Time* magazine's list of the hundred most influential people in the world.

She talks fast and is fearless, having survived multiple attacks. She was also the only Afghan at lunch to make the case for a U.S. consulate in Kandahar.

After lunch met several members of the Kandahar Ulema Council, all men, all with long beards, all wearing turbans. The council is headed by Qari Bashir Ahmad, Mullah Toior Jan having lost his position. Both are re-integrees who previously identified with the Taliban. Both emphasized that Afghanistan is an Islamic society and the precepts of Islam should pervade every aspect of it.

Making his initial remarks in Arabic, Ambassador Pierce acknowledged the importance of the ulema and said religious leaders from Pakistan and Afghanistan should join together to promote peace. "It takes courage to make peace," he said. "As much courage as to fight a war."

Walked to KMIC for brief press conference limited to two questions. We then boarded MRAPs for the drive back to KPRT. The bazaars and streets of Kandahar seem more crowded each passing week.

Returning to Kandahar Air Field by helicopter, stopped briefly to look at Gecko as possible enduring presence site. It is scenically situated among the hills of northern Kandahar.

Amazingly, Gecko is still the default position for a consulate in Kandahar and OBO is preparing plans to construct an expensive new building there. Kandahar Air Field is the better location, hands-down—if there is ever a Kandahar consulate at all.

Kandahar, 6 December

Lunch with interpreter from Australia. He left Afghanistan in the early 1980s at the age of twenty-eight. Working for the Afghan Ministry of Agriculture, Irrigation and Livestock, he refused to sign an oath of loyalty to the Parcham Party. He later ran a small cassette shop in Islamabad before making his way to Australia.

Joined a few hundred others from Kandahar Air Field to greet eight wounded warriors returning to Afghanistan to exit it properly and on their own terms. All were badly wounded over the past couple of years, including one heavily burned across his face and body and several who had lost limbs in IED explosions. Each one was cheered loudly when stepping off the plane.

Kandahar, 7 December

Another day that was supposed to be quiet—but it is past midnight and I am just now getting to bed.

Governor's Palace, 8 December

Left early for Kandahar PRT in Black Hawk to attend media development conference involving various groups funded by the USG who don't always talk to each other.

Most Afghans receive information via radio, although the number of television viewers is growing. Almost no one reads newspapers. New media is gaining a foothold: one of the biggest changes in Afghanistan over the past ten years is the rapid expansion in cell phones and cell phone service.

Travelled by different route to governor's office. Wesa was subdued this morning and we moved quickly through our agenda. He has an impossible job. Rumors continue about his pending departure—fired, back to Canada, to Kabul to become a minister, none of the above—no one really knows for sure, probably not even the governor himself.

Attended media roundtable at KMIC involving Afghan journalists, including one working for BBC. They presented a bleak view of Afghan media—and an even bleaker view of what the media will look like after 2014.

Returning to my quarters I noticed several soldiers from a cavalry unit huddling together against the cold of a Kandahar December to smoke cigars. They looked dashing in their cowboy hats and spurs, like something out of the American West.

I ordered coffee and talked briefly in Hindi with the Nepalis manning the Green Bean. Taking a last look at the late night sky, I saw stars in every direction—and also the twinkling lights of the observation balloon with its night vision cameras tethered protectively a few hundred feet above us.

Indian Consulate/Camp Nathan Smith, 9 December

Breakfast at DFAC with Colonel Huggins. He leaves in January. He mentioned that as a battalion commander in Iraq he lost eighteen soldiers out of the five hundred assigned to his command; this time in Afghanistan he has lost nine out of the five thousand for whom he is responsible. He is optimistic that he is leaving Zaray in a better place. According to Colonel Huggins, the situation in Zaray had improved so much that it was becoming "like Arghandab, almost."

Joined Kabul embassy country team via video, followed by weekly KPRT staff meeting. Most civilians in southern Afghanistan are concerned about their jobs. I wish I could offer hope—but I really can't. The plan issued by Washington and Kabul is to draw down as quickly as possible.

Joined MRAP convoy for trip to Indian consulate to meet the Indian consul general in Kandahar. Three members of his staff joined us. Eleven Indian diplomats are assigned to the consulate—plus several dozen Indian security guards.

Members of the consulate staff live and work in a warren of buildings decorated with barbed wire and sandbags, located next to the Iranian consulate that is similarly protected. The Indian diplomats don't get out much and are not optimistic about what will happen next.

After our formal discussion we were served an excellent Indian lunch—peas *pilau,* curry, naan, and much else. I talked with a tall Sikh diplomat, originally from Punjab but now living in Delhi. His son and daughter study in Maryland.

Enjoyed relatively long trip back to KPRT via several crowded bazaars. Having grown used to some sense of normalcy, it is hard to believe Kandaharis will easily revert to either Taliban rule or civil war.

Joined local staff for lunch along with new detachment of SFATs from Hawaii and several members of our military protection team. Our eighteen Afghan employees seem committed. Some have noticed positive changes, though they surely have deep fears about the future.

Most are from Kandahar or Jalalabad. One is female—she lives on the PRT. She said she has adapted well and enjoys the food. It is hard to imagine the pressures that she must face every day.

Met Haji Noorullah Aziz, former Taliban commander and shadow governor of Kunduz and now Kandahar's director for the Ministry of Hajj and Religious Affairs. For part of the time there were just four of us sitting together on the floor—Erin Tariot, our translator, Noorullah Aziz, and me.

Noorullah Aziz just returned from hajj where he led a group of 1,500 Kandaharis. He mentioned meeting three of his former Taliban friends, also on the hajj. "They averted their eyes but eventually we talked. They asked me why I had joined the infidels. I told them, 'No, that's not right, we are all Muslims.'"

He said he was born in 1972, placing him in his early twenties when the Taliban arrived. He mentioned the successful Taliban effort to remove checkpoints manned by warlords and then take control of the entire south. He added that Mullah Omar wasn't the first Taliban leader; rather the first leader was another mullah who now lives in Karachi and is largely forgotten.

I asked if he saw Mullah Omar retrieve the prophet's cloak and wave it above the crowd. He said he remembered it to this day.

He mentioned he last saw Mullah Omar two and a half years ago—his health was poor then and it seems to have declined further every time he appears on a new video. According to Haji Aziz, "Eighty percent of us believe that he is now dead."

Our conversation briefly turned in a theological direction when I asked what the Taliban mean when they recite "Bismallah al-Rahman al-Rahim" [In the name of God, the compassionate and merciful], beautiful words that resonate across many cultures and religions. However, he went off on a tangent and didn't really answer the question.

One Afghan visitor who joined us stated that his country would be in a different place if only ISAF had talked to the ulema ten years ago. When asked why some Afghans left the Taliban to join the Afghan government, he said that some left because it was perceived that the Taliban had become the puppets of Iran and Pakistan.

As we departed, Haji Aziz gave me a small ring with a plastic stone that he had bought in a bazaar in Medina. "It isn't much," he said, "but it is given as a sign of respect." Instantly I thought of the Pushto proverb often evoked when referring to the importance of hospitality, even when given in the poorest of homes: "Let it be only an onion, but let it be given with love."

Returned to Kandahar Air Field on Black Hawk at sunset, watching the red sky turn dark against the distant hills. Met by Bonnie on arrival. She passed on the latest news about the fallout from the latest rumors on personnel cuts that are now having a corrosive effect on everybody.

Joined Generals Abrams, White, Brewer, and Hughes for dinner with a visiting senior general from Romania along with several other officers. Only the Americans, Australians, and Romanians still have sizeable forces in RC-South.

Arghandab, 10 December

Early morning Black Hawk flight to Arghandab DST, scheduled to close in April. The vegetation is getting browner but there are still plenty of shades of yellow and orange—without doubt, fall is my favorite time of year.

The initial briefing before we boarded our Strykers was very thorough, as was the case several weeks ago when the Canadian ambassador visited. We then drove through the Arghandab, which after years of violence is now safe by Afghan standards—safe enough that I spent the entire trip standing through an open back turret, admiring the passing views.

In better times Arghandab could easily have become a tourist attraction, given its river, jagged mountains, and fields of grapes and pomegranates. Most houses, even new ones, are built in a traditional mud-brick style, sometimes with small mud-plastered domes.

Michael Cygramus from the DST provided a running commentary. He mentioned that two years ago those travelling within a few hundred yards of the DST could expect to hear gunfire.

We made several stops including at a couple of bridges, at a mini hydro scheme due for renovations, and at an agricultural collection point that isn't used at all. Probably the most interesting part was to see two schools, one full and one empty.

The first school met in a warren of small mud rooms, one devoted entirely to girls. The third-grade classroom included several older children learning to read. Other classes were led by the brightest student, given a shortage of teachers. The teachers haven't been paid in four months.

I talked briefly in three classrooms, writing my name in English and Pushto on a small white board. Looking out over the sea of bright faces, both girls and boys, it is hard not to wonder what tragedies lie ahead. Afghanistan has seen little but war for more than three decades. Most people just want the long nightmare to finally end.

The second school a few miles farther on was once a large and magnificent structure with blackboards, classrooms, a well, and a latrine block. It was funded by Japan and officially opened in a large ceremony a couple of years ago. Now it is a derelict wreck—all the glass windows have been broken and the classrooms are in shambles, a sad commentary on good intentions gone awry.

Yet driving through the small villages and bazaars of Arghandab with its canal networks and orchards, gardens, and fruit trees I've managed to revive, at least for a while, my interest and even enthusiasm for this unexpected assignment in Afghanistan. I need to take what I can from it; it will end soon enough.

Returned to DST for lunch, leaving our gear at the small base chapel built in a tent. We then visited the government office next door to meet Governor Haji Shah Ahmadi, along with several tribal elders, bearded and barefoot with black turbans and the look of the old-style mujahideen who in their youth had kept the Soviets at bay. One elder, one eye shot out, looked vaguely like Mullah Omar.

At least one of those Afghan elders seated in the small room is numbered among those who dread the day when ISAF finally departs. Despite good security in Arghandab, he painted a pessimistic view about the future, believing Afghan security forces can't replace international ones. He also had a long litany of complaints about the provincial government.

Afterward we had about half an hour to enjoy the late afternoon view toward the Arghandab valley from a rooftop in the DST, the fading orange light from the sun reflecting off the brilliant fall colors below.

To the south a barren mountain offers protection to one side of the DST. To the east is the shrine of Baba Sahib, modernized now and visited by thousands of Kandaharis each Friday afternoon. To the west is another military outpost. And to the north is the Arghandab Valley in all its splendor, the browns mixing beautifully with the yellows and golds.

After more conversations and a few photos, we heard the sound of helicopters and saw a swirl of dust, the signal for us to climb up a nearby hill to the helipad for our short flight home.

Attended evening Purple Heart ceremony for three soldiers wounded in two separate incidents in Panjwai. One was shot in a firefight and the other two injured in an IED blast that killed their platoon leader. The one good thing about this ceremony is that each of those who received the Purple Heart still have their limbs intact and can expect a complete recovery.

Kandahar, 11 December

Ramp ceremony for Sergeant Wesley Williams from Ohio, killed yesterday in an IED explosion in Panjwai. Heroic efforts were made to save him at the Kandahar Air Field trauma center, including cracking open his chest and applying a desperate heart massage. But it just wasn't to be. He was twenty-five years old and leaves behind a one-year-old daughter and a wife who is eight weeks pregnant.

Once again hundreds of soldiers of all nationalities lined up on the tarmac to see off the casket. Once again the chaplain read a Bible passage and paid tribute to the fallen soldier. Once again there was a taped recording of "Amazing Grace" on the pipes followed by a lone trumpeter playing "Day Is Done."

Kandahar, 12 December

Received confirmation that Camp Nathan Smith will close by summer 2013, forcing an early KPRT move to somewhere else. The so-called glide path is fast becoming a cliff. I hate the idea that the Taliban will eventually inherit Afghanistan. More than a few Afghans also dread that moment and hope it never comes.

There is a feeling of Christmas in the air, evoked by lights, trees, and cards. Care packages arrive in a steady stream, sent by sympathetic Americans to their soldiers in Afghanistan. The homemade brownies arriving in one of them were delicious. Colonel King from Australia is amazed at the generosity of Americans toward their troops.

Winter has finally arrived in Kandahar. The sky is gray and it is cold and cloudy outside. As I prepare for bed a small storm is gathering and I hear the pleasant sound of raindrops splashing on the thin metal roof above me, reminding me nostalgically of lines from Faulkner that I have often repeated over the years, recalling the splashing tin roofs of my childhood when experiencing the late summer monsoon in the mountains of northern Pakistan: "How often have I lain beneath the rain on a strange roof, thinking of home."

Kandahar, 13 December

Cloudy and very cold—the rain last night has turned the dust that usually envelops Kandahar Air Field into mud.

Attended morning Purple Heart ceremony for Lieutenant Jason Pak. He survived an IED blast in Panjwai yesterday. He had been leading a dismounted patrol to track down an insurgent placing IEDs.

I learned later that Pak was born in South Korea and graduated from West Point, class of 2011. He lost both legs and three fingers on one hand. His father was in the Army and it must have been very hard to tell him the news.

Secretary of Defense Panetta arrived from Kabul at 11:00 a.m. with an entourage of nearly forty. His day at Kandahar Air Field started with a briefing in the command center over lunch.

General Abrams provided opening remarks but mostly let his soldiers speak—Colonel Getchell, Colonel Michaelis, and a young lieutenant posted in Maiwand west of Kandahar, along with their respective sergeants major. They seem optimistic and on-message on the quality and skills of the ANSF.

Afterward the secretary spoke to 250 gathered soldiers, mostly from the U.S., but also from Belgium, Luxembourg, Romania, Britain, and elsewhere. The sound system was so bad I couldn't hear much. He was asked several questions about Afghanistan and the future of the U.S. military. He was then interviewed by CNN before heading back to Kabul.

At around 5:00 p.m. I heard an explosion in the distance—the Kandahar Air Field rocket attack alarm quickly sounded and we were placed on lockdown. As I was told later, an American convoy had been struck by a suicide bomber shortly after leaving Kandahar Air Field. One American driving the front MRAP was killed and the soldier next to him was badly wounded several Afghans were killed and wounded as well.

Farewell for two departing staff, two of many that will be leaving during the coming weeks and months. About thirty people gathered in our big *shura* room for Afghan food, including naan and *kabuli pilau*. We don't do this often enough—occasionally, it is nice to have small gatherings outside work such as this.

Kandahar, 14 December

Missed 3:00 a.m. ramp ceremony for sergeant killed by suicide bomber outside Kandahar Air Field last night—I wasn't told about it in time. He was thirty-seven and a member of the Texas National Guard. His wife is posted elsewhere in Afghanistan and they have two children back in the United States. How sad, how very sad.

Four-star Marine general Dunford arrived in Kandahar at 11:00 a.m.—he will take over the Afghanistan command from General Allen in the new year. He will inherit a tough job with little chance of success.

Spent part of evening on boardwalk, ordering curry, chappatis, and Indian chai. Also got a haircut as I prepare to depart tomorrow. Christmas trees have been set up outside some of the shops. I stopped briefly to watch several female soldiers play flag football.

Dubai, 15 December

Bonnie Weaver dropped me off at the flight line at 11:00 a.m., all of us waiting patiently like exhausted sheep for the next part of our journey. I am very tired mentally, as tired as I have ever been in my life.

The chartered flight to Dubai, piloted by a Scottish captain, was crowded but uneventful. Thirty minutes into the journey, a stewardess from Eastern Europe came down the aisle to offer a beer to anyone who wanted one.

Atlanta, Georgia, 16 December

Delta from Dubai to Atlanta, a fifteen-hour flight. Very tired on account of jet lag.

Macon, Georgia, 17 December

Still tired, still sleeping irregularly. Outside it is raining steadily.

Attended weekly talk involving the dozen fellow retirees Dad meets with regularly. Mostly they discuss the dismal state of the world as well as shocking events such as the recent Sandy Hook school shooting in Connecticut.

My presence prompted a discussion on Afghanistan. Americans are sick and tired of it and want to move on. Afghanistan is seen as a colossal waste that never should have happened.

Fort Stewart, Georgia, 18 December

Left Ben Hill Drive at 9:30 a.m. for Fort Stewart near Savannah. After some difficulty, found Gate One and Warrior's Way with its rows of trees, each one planted for a Third Infantry Division soldier who made the ultimate sacrifice, mostly in Iraq but lately in Afghanistan as well. The number of trees already exceeds four hundred.

Given the season, green wreaths decorated with red ribbons have been set at the bottom of each tree. Some family members place small trinkets around "their" tree as a form of remembrance, as a way to somehow grasp memories and hold on to them for a little longer. The objects include photos and poems, baseball hats and license plates, plastic toys and insignia, soft toys and shoes.

We met one other person, a retired soldier straightening wreaths knocked askew by the wind. He said his son serves with Special Forces in Kandahar.

The first of the trees for Afghanistan has only recently been planted—the rest will come later.

Also toured the small Third Infantry Division museum with its artifacts from two world wars and conflicts that followed, including Iraq and Afghanistan. One gallery recognizes Medal of Honor awardees, including Audie Murphy—and Sergeant Smith, one of four American soldiers awarded the medal during fighting in Iraq.

Headed to Savannah for the night, Cameron and Catriona taking one room at the Mulberry Inn near the waterfront, Fiona and I another one. Kandahar seems far away but also very close.

I enjoyed the river walk, the view toward the bridge and the ships, the color of the sky as it changes from orange to pink and then light purple before the coming dark. I'm glad we are here during Christmas season when there are fewer visitors than usual. I wish this particular night did not have to end.

One good thing about four months in Afghanistan is that I try to hold on to such moments for as long as possible.

Savannah/Tybee Island, 19 December

Walked around old Savannah for most of morning before heading to Tybee Island for lunch. There is family history here—Dad's father worked for the railways and the entire family was given a train ticket to visit Tybee annually.

Macon, Georgia, 21 December

Clear but cold—spent much of the day sorting through books.

Macon, Georgia, 22 December

Iain arrived from Goodfellow Air Force Base in Texas—all of us attended the annual Addleton Christmas party, an event that by now has been going on for at least seventy years. Only three of Dad's thirteen brothers and sisters are still living.

Macon, Georgia, 23 December

Got up early to go to Atlanta Airport with Iain and his almost-fiancée Andrea Becerra—she is heading to Miami to spend Christmas with her family. Accompanied parents to Vineville Baptist Church and then spent quiet day on Ben Hill Drive.

On occasion my mind still wanders to Afghanistan. Bonnie is working on a small celebration for those who will be in Kandahar on Christmas Day. News reports from Uruzgan report that Commander Price, a Navy Seal, has just taken his own life.

Macon, Georgia, 24 December

Christmas Eve. Attended two services—5:00 p.m. at Vineville Baptist with Mom and Dad and 11:00 p.m. at Christ Episcopal with Nancy and her husband Jeff. After the midnight service at Christ Church, spoke briefly with Rabbi Schlesinger who serves with Nancy on the Macon City Council. He asked about Afghanistan and I said things are difficult there right now.

Macon, Georgia, Christmas Day, 25 December

Christmas Day—it rained for most of it. Unusually we are all together—Mom, Dad, and all the siblings and grandchildren. Mom spent a lot of time preparing for this day and Dad composed a prayer especially for the occasion—the house looks lovely, the food was fantastic, and people seem to enjoy each other.

But time is taking its relentless and unforgiving toll on all of us. When does the hammer drop, when does catastrophe strike? The Pushtun proverb has it right when it says that much happiness is inevitably followed by much sorrow. In my heart of hearts, I have to wonder—Will there be a family night like this ever again?

Macon, Georgia, 26 December

Latest news from Kandahar is that Kabul has just retracted its extension of Bart Major's tour only two weeks after informing him that he could stay through November 2013 rather than May 2013. Public Affairs called him the day after Christmas to break the news.

Spent part of day shopping with Fiona, Catriona, and Iain. I bought a couple of books. Cameron joined us for dinner. This was our last meal together in a long time—perhaps ever. I hate the idea that our family life is fast drawing to a close, that we are all about to spin into our different orbits that will only rarely intersect.

Iain's comments reflect some misgivings about the Air Force, based partly on the realization that he has joined a large and rigid bureaucracy. I can't see him staying beyond his required four years and even that may prove too hard for him to bear.

I briefly tried to raise the issue of what it might take to maintain a sense of family togetherness in the months and years ahead, despite the tyranny of time and distance. But in the end I couldn't quite manage it—inexplicably our most difficult conversations are all too often with those we love most.

Macon, Georgia, 27 December

Quiet day, all of it spent at home. Cameron and Iain left at the end of it—Cameron on his snowboarding trip to West Virginia, Iain to Miami where he will briefly meet Andrea before returning to Texas. Iain realizes our meetings are becoming rarer and more difficult to organize—he gave Fiona and me an especially long embrace as he headed out the door.

Macon, Georgia, 29 December

Spent morning doing errands, then drove Fiona and Catriona to Atlanta Airport for their 1:00 a.m. flight to Seoul and then onward to Ulaanbaatar. Goodbyes don't get easier as we get older. Perhaps it is because of our sure knowledge that, at some point, there will be that final hug, that final embrace, that final farewell.

Macon, Georgia, 30 December

Celebrated my brother David's fifty-eighth birthday on Ben Hill Drive. Toward the end our conversation focused mostly on Afghanistan. I told David all the reasons why life in Kandahar is hard and often frustrating. From here on out the goal is mostly to be an observer, content to watch life as it is lived in its extremes, trying in some small way to make sense of human nature and even human folly as it unfolds.

Macon, Georgia, 31 December

New Year's Eve. Accompanied Mom and Dad on brief downtown trip to see how Macon celebrates, then returned home to watch the New York version on television.

It is just now after midnight. Fireworks are going off in the distance, making loud noises. The year 2012 is a closed book at this point, but the first pages of this new year will be opened soon enough—if only I had even an inkling of what it might bring.

6

—♦—

JANUARY

Macon, Georgia, New Year's Day, 1 January

New Year's Day. Watched *Les Misérables* with Mom and Dad—a tear jerker with a strong cast; for all the twists and turns, it is fundamentally a story about redemption, a concept that this age has mostly rejected.

Macon, Georgia, 2 January

Early-morning doctor's visit—had small growth on my left cheek removed. Spent rest of morning sorting through boxes. Iain called from Miami, en route to San Angelo via Atlanta and San Antonio.

Afternoon visit with Ralph Stokes and his daughter Ann Grace in their new assisted living home off Zebulon Road. Ann and I are the same age and she was born with spina bifida. Her family did not expect her to live this long.

Ralph is now in his mid-eighties and wants to make sure she is taken care of; his wife Dot died last year. We've known the family for decades—Ann has had a hard life yet somehow remains mostly cheerful and even inspiring, having come to terms long ago with the limitations imposed on her from birth.

Macon, Georgia, 3 January

Morning appointment with Dr. Esnard. Everything looks fine on the cardiology front—my heart is still beating; my artificial heart valve is still doing its job.

Zack and Hilda Young dropped by in the afternoon. Zack is one of a diminishing number of World War II veterans, and he briefly recalled his part in the Battle of the Bulge that took place during the final winter of the war.

Macon, Georgia, 4 January

Farewell phone calls from Iain and David—also talked with Fiona and Catriona in Ulaanbaatar via Skype.

Listened to NPR report from a military rehab center in Rawalpindi. More than 3,000 Pakistani soldiers have been killed along the border with Afghanistan over the past 10 years, many as a result of IEDs; another 10,000 have been severely wounded, in many cases losing one or more limbs. Their stories are as heart-rending as the ones I've heard from Walter Reed.

Macon, Georgia, 5 January

Last day in Macon. Cameron drove to Georgia Tech early. David came for lunch. I accompanied Dad on his weekly walk through Ocmulgee National Historic Monument with Molly—we came across a white egret and two large deer.

Wrote "final instructions" in case I do not survive the rest of my time in Kandahar—something I was unable to do in August. Then headed to Atlanta Airport for the late night Delta flight to Dubai.

Dubai, 6 January

Landed at Dubai Airport at 9:00 p.m. local time. The flight was full, mostly with young males headed to Afghanistan. On arrival noticed latest news from Kandahar—at least four Afghans killed by three suicide bombers at a local *shura* in Spin Boldak near the border with Pakistan.

Enjoyed long conversation in Urdu en route to Flora Creek Apartment Hotel with my taxi driver, Mohammad Farooq from Jhelum. He arrived in Dubai from Pakistan eight years ago and finds life hard but lucrative. "The city is no place for human existence," he said, waving his hand at the traffic and tall buildings. "The best life is in a small village."

Dubai, 7 January

Spent day in Dubai recovering from jet lag. Walked along Dubai creek and briefly visited Deira City Center. Dubai is amazing—not least because it is built on the backs of workers from South Asia and the Philippines.

Kandahar, 8 January

Departed at 7:00 a.m. on Fly Dubai flight, first to Camp Bastion, and then to Kandahar. The flight was two-thirds full, reflecting diminishing numbers of civilian contractors.

I noticed only one female, an attractive young lady from Philippines with dark eyes. My seat companion was an African American airplane mechanic from Atlanta. He has worked at Kandahar Air Field for two years and will be leaving for good in May.

It was cold and raining when we finally reached Kandahar. Every bag was inspected for alcohol and pornography.

The ghosts of the Taliban would have liked that—the inspection, after all, took place in the old terminal building with thick walls and bullet holes, the place where the *talibs* of Kandahar made their last stand in late 2001.

Noticed a PIA Fokker Friendship sitting on the tarmac outside the civilian terminal when we arrived—the direct air link between Kandahar and Quetta must now be in place.

Bonnie Weaver was there to meet me and everyone at headquarters said hello. General White said it had been relatively quiet—but I don't doubt life has been hard for the past couple of weeks during the holiday season.

Now I have to go through hundreds of e-mails. Trudging to the DFAC at 8:30 p.m., I was once again reminded how quickly the dust of Kandahar that we used to kick up every day can be turned into the mud of Kandahar by the winter rains.

Kandahar, 9 January

Attended afternoon transfer, Task Force Wings out of Hawaii commanded by Colonel Tate giving way to Task Force Falcon from Hunter Air Field near Savannah commanded by Colonel Peppin. During their twelve months in Afghanistan, Task Force Wings clocked nearly 140,000 hours in the air.

Atmospheric reports in recent days mention local concern that ISAF vehicles are driving too fast in Kandahar—and today an American Stryker plowed into a rickshaw, killing one Afghan civilian and injuring three others.

Kandahar, 10 January

Morning meeting with chargé from Australian Embassy, visiting from Kabul to meet Australians at Kandahar Air Field. Uruzgan is on track for a better closing scenario than most places—probably we will be working together there until late 2013.

Afternoon video conference with Tina Kaidanow in Kabul as well as the various fellow SCRs from across Afghanistan. She presented a bleak drawdown picture and is deeply pessimistic about any USG presence outside Kabul beyond 2014.

Early evening CUA. I'm still jet-lagged and almost fell asleep as the various reports come in. I did wake up when I heard this, though: the IED casualty figure across southern Afghanistan for December 2012 was eighty; one year ago the comparable figure was more than twice that.

Kandahar, 11 January

Relatively quiet day. Spent part of it walking along the boardwalk, stopping briefly for masala chai. Also joined Generals Abrams, White, and Hughes for weekly lunch to catch up on events over the past month.

General Abrams talked briefly about Job Price, the SEAL commander in Uruzgan who took his own life in December. It shocked everyone, confirming that suicide is an issue across all ranks, including senior officers.

"It was very hard," Abrams said, recalling the memorial service that involved many stories about times both good and bad.

Chris Hughes recalled a phone call from Commander Price the day he left on leave. "It was sort of strange," he said. "He didn't really have an agenda, he just wanted to talk."

Several of the senior officers are skeptical about an ISAF presence at Kandahar Air Field beyond 2014. That means there won't be a civilian presence either—something that will be widely seen by local Afghans as a signal that we really have given up on southern Afghanistan.

For some reason this week's deep dive was especially interesting. I am impressed by the tactical strength of ISAF, but if I say that I have to add that I am also impressed with the resiliency of the Taliban. They keep getting hammered—but keep coming back for more.

Stayed in office late enough to see Obama-Karzai press conference on television. The body language between the two seems better than usual. Karzai is quite well spoken and finally accepts the idea that the Americans won't stay unless the immunity issue is resolved.

President Obama confirmed that U.S. involvement in Afghanistan really is ending—the task now is nation-building at home, not abroad. We will remain engaged in Afghanistan but in a much more circumscribed way.

Shah Wali Karzai's Residence, 12 January

Dinner with Shah Wali Karzai; Rich Pacheco and Lewis Gitter accompanied me along with Nasemi, my new translator from New York.

Shah Wali Karzai just returned from India where he had gone for a health checkup. He mentioned the Moghul monuments he visited in Delhi linked to Afghan kings. He also mentioned that Afghans far prefer India to Pakistan, adding that the new PIA flight from Quetta to Kandahar attracts almost no passengers.

According to Shah Wali Karzai, Afghans have gotten used to his brother as president and many would prefer that he stay on for another term. He also appealed to traditional modes of governance in Afghanistan, in this case citing especially the old Afghan *jirga* system based on consensus as a widely accepted approach.

He described the Taliban as "brutal," adding that many Afghans "fear" their return. He repeated several times a phrase that I have often heard in recent days: "The biggest mistake Americans can make is to leave Afghanistan too soon."

The protection detail for the forty-five-minute drive to Shah Wali Karzai's house involved a new set of soldiers. We travelled mostly in the dark—the roadside shops are largely closed right now. One car runs interference, protecting us from incoming traffic.

On arrival we go through several checkpoints before reaching Shah Wali Karzai's residence. As always we ate well—*kabuli pilau,* roast chicken, roast mutton, and various squash dishes. The tea, raisins, figs, and pistachios served at the beginning of the evening aren't bad either.

Shah Wali Karzai still hasn't warmed to his title as titular head of the Popalzai—there are a million places he would rather be than Kandahar. He is quiet, soft-spoken, and unfailingly polite. He appears to appreciate these occasional discussions. An introvert by nature, in another lifetime he might have been a professor living anonymously in a small and quiet college town.

Kandahar, 13 January

The ongoing discussion on potentially placing a Pakistan Army liaison officer at Kandahar Air Field seems to be getting nowhere. "Another sprinkling of fairy dust from Kabul," according to one senior officer who doesn't much like the idea.

Listened to presentation on final campaign before drastic troop drawdowns preclude further combat operations. The plan is to finally clear the Horn of Panjwai. Concluding remarks by General Abrams were on target, among other things noting that what most Afghans want is some sort of ISAF presence, even a small and symbolic one, after 2014.

Yet Deputy Governor Patyal is one official who hopes all foreign soldiers leave as soon as possible. He may have a point when he says if all foreign soldiers leave, the Taliban's rationale for fighting a war will also disappear.

Stayed up late to watch Atlanta Falcons finally win a playoff game—30–28 against Seattle. They started with an early lead but almost blew it in the fourth quarter. Now they will play San Francisco for the NFC title. Called Iain and Cameron at half time—both are doing well.

Kandahar, 14 January

Context brief for Senator Mitch McConnell (Kentucky) and four new Republican senators—John Barasso (Wyoming), Jeff Flake (Arizona), Deb Fischer (Nebraska), and Ted Cruz (Texas). The briefing by General Abrams was exceptional. I'm sure the senators will be happy to tell their constituents that they visited Kandahar—and just missed one of our occasional rocket attacks.

Otherwise a busy day, though I didn't accomplish much: morning meetings, afternoon conference call with KPRT, and evening dinner with Charlie Wintermeyer, who was up for a couple of days from KPRT. The rapid drawdown we face in the coming weeks will be very difficult.

Kandahar, 15 January

Morning presentation by visitors from Kabul embassy on updated Civil-Military Strategic Framework for Afghanistan. Already it is being overtaken by events. Very quaintly, it still includes references to the four plus one approach—an embassy in Kabul and consulates in Kandahar, Herat, Jalalabad, and Mazar-Sharif. That was the plan a few months ago. Now we will probably not have a presence in the south at all.

Two conference calls, first with Kabul on countering violent extremism and then with the Zabul PRT headed by Tim Bashor. The call with Kabul focused on outreach to key religious leaders, something that is being launched even though our ability to undertake such a program is severely diminished. Meanwhile, the Zabul PRT is moving rapidly toward closure.

Talked briefly to General Hughes after the evening CUA. I asked about the rocket attack at noon on an empty safe house storing munitions for the Taliban. He said an American soldier had lost his legs when he stepped on an IED prior to the attack; the soldier had been fulfilling an obligation to close off the target beforehand to make sure no civilians wandered by.

Hughes said another American soldier was killed under similar circumstances a few weeks ago. "We are required to have these soldiers on the ground beforehand," he said. "But it just isn't worth it. After what happened twice, I don't think we should order any more attacks on empty buildings again."

Kandahar Airport, 16 January

Lunch with Lynne Tracy, deputy assistant secretary for Central Asia at State—she is en route from Kabul to Bishkek via military aircraft from Kandahar. We had dahl, chappatis, and masala chai at the Indian stall on the boardwalk.

We first met years ago in Pakistan when she was the consul general in Peshawar. After I left Islamabad she was attacked outside the consulate—her driver did all the right things and she escaped unscathed. Stephen Vance, a USAID contractor whom I knew in Mongolia, wasn't so lucky—he was attacked outside his house in Peshawar and killed.

Lynne also served in Bishkek and Ashgabat where she was DCM. She was enthusiastic about my pending assignment in Almaty, offering positive comments. Once again I find myself excited about the prospects of a more normal life—not to mention views of the snow-covered Tien Shan outside my office window.

Drove to Kandahar Airport to meet Haji Dastageeri, member of the Kandahar Provincial Council from Panjwai. He was wearing his usual Taliban-style turban. He is fairly large but speaks in an appealing, soft-spoken manner.

I asked many questions and he did not push back on any of them. Like several others, he is ambivalent and even skeptical about elections. He understands the need for an immunity agreement for U.S. soldiers after 2014—but acknowledged that many Afghans would oppose it, despite similar agreements in other countries such as Turkey, Germany, and South Korea.

Dastageeri thinks southern Afghans will accept only a Pushtun as president. He also thinks Gul Agha Sherzai, previous governor of Kandahar and now governor of Nangahar, is popular across the region. He describes views of the people of Panjwai as mixed—they are hedging their bets and are neither fully for the Taliban nor fully for the government of Afghanistan.

He didn't accuse the United States of abandoning Afghanistan—though I sometimes find myself struggling to describe in even general terms what our presence in southern Afghanistan will look like a couple of years from now.

Kandahar Airport, 17 January

Morning meeting at Kandahar Airport with one of the members of the Kandahar Provincial Council. His comments included the following: "You are not leaving us, are you?" And, "If you leave, there will be civil war."

He also expressed concern about President Karzai's recent performance in Washington and doesn't support the idea of convening a *loya jirga* to discuss immunity issues—in his view, that is a decision Karzai should take himself.

Like more than a few tribal leaders (and in keeping with long-established Pushtun tradition), he takes a dim view of local mullahs, commenting that the actions of the Taliban have completely discredited them. He thinks mullahs can be easily bought with an occasional monetary contribution or new set of clothes: "They aren't like a motorcycle that needs gas. They are more like a bicycle that just needs air."

Afternoon ramp ceremony for Sergeant David Chambers from Virginia, age twenty-five. His legs were blown off a couple of days ago and he never recovered. These scenes are becoming all too familiar—the somber line-up of chaplains on one side, the general staff on the other; the longer line of enlisted men farther up the tarmac; the muffled band playing "Amazing Grace" and then the lone trumpeter playing a mournful version of "Day Is Done," each note more melancholy than the last.

We watch silently as the flag-covered metal box containing the last mortal remains of the departing soldier are hefted into the belly of the airplane, followed by General Abrams, Sergeant Major Watson, and their counterparts from Task Force Dragoon. The air crew meanwhile stands at attention outside their plane, watching silently as the ceremony runs its course.

Gecko, 18 January

Evening Black Hawk flight to Gecko—my first helicopter flight since returning to Kandahar ten days ago. As always the food at Gecko is excellent. I talked briefly to the chef. He said he was from Cape Town and has been in Afghanistan for eighteen months.

There were several new faces at the Gecko briefing this time around, including a tall and striking blonde. It was hard not to look in her direction—for a moment it seemed as if she had just wandered in from a James Bond movie set.

This evening's conversation was especially interesting and included speculation about what happens next. ISAF has been heavily involved for years, but we still have a hard time understanding important aspects of this place and it is even more difficult to make predictions about the future.

Qalat (Zabul), 19 January

Early-afternoon Black Hawk flight to Zabul. Met on arrival by Tim Bashor and others from the PRT. Tim showed me my small but cozy room and then we departed for Apache, the new brigade headquarters—although in terms of numbers the new arrivals are more the size of a battalion than a brigade.

We looked quickly around the base and then started the briefings. The new military team will be in Afghanistan for nine months, not one year. They will be undertaking an assignment for which they did not originally prepare—mostly in the background and mostly involving training.

"But if I do it myself, the result will be much better." "Don't think you can win this war single-handedly in only a few months." Perhaps such lines are repeated with each rotation. As has so often been said, we aren't fighting a ten-year war; rather, we are fighting a one-year war ten times. Surprisingly the new colonel welcomes civilian advice and the other new officers don't mind hearing the civilian perspective either.

Walking around Apache afterward, the colonel said his soldiers recently destroyed an empty house containing weapons. An Excalibur artillery piece was used. He said the ordnance was fired from many miles away—a record for this particular device.

Returned three miles to Zabul PRT by road, passing again through a crowded Qalat bazaar. I saw what looked like a lighted Christmas tree in the distance—Tim said it was where a couple of new hotels have been built, all bathed in neon.

By 7:00 p.m. we were making our way across a dark road from the PRT to Governor Naseri's compound. He lives next door to an ornate *shura* room—and across the hall from a small dining hall. Our dinner included mutton, rice, lady fingers, and naan, along with fresh apples, oranges, and bananas for dessert.

We talked for three hours, more or less covering the universe. As always, some of the talk drifted toward Pakistan where Naseri and so many other Afghans once lived as refugees. He recalled the time, centuries ago, when Afghans ruled from Central Asia to India. The Afghan nationalist narrative also claims that some of the leading poets from the classic Persian literary tradition were actually Afghan.

At heart Naseri is a frustrated academic. Like Shah Wali Karzai, in another life he might have been a professor in a small college town. His facts and figures sometimes border on the fictitious and even ludicrous. At the start of the evening he was optimistic about Afghanistan's future—but by the end of it his words reflected a sense of dread and even despair, views shared by many Afghans who teeter between extremes when thinking about what comes next.

He is not happy to see the PRT close in May. Yet he realizes it is inevitable. Now he wants to approach all the donors in Kabul in an almost certainly futile effort to increase foreign aid. He thinks Zabul is isolated and remote, far from the centers of power, with little chance of figuring prominently in any Kabul development plan—and he almost certainly is right.

Qalat (Zabul), 20 January

Morning meeting at Zabul PRT. It is hard for our employees who have to leave early. Wesley Nguyen will probably have to leave in May, and will return to Mongolia where his wife is from; he is already looking for work. He asked why staff at the DSTs and PRTs can't finish out their assignments at Kandahar Air Field, continuing to provide coverage from a distance. That is my preferred approach, too—but the mandate from Kabul and Washington is to draw down much more quickly than that.

The return trip to Kandahar Air Field took exactly thirty minutes, all of it over a chilly and mostly brown winter terrain, though some distant mountains do have a dusting of snow. Most *kutchis* have now set up their winter camps along the bases of mountains and above dry riverbeds. All things considered, I would much rather be a nomad in Mongolia than a *kutchi* in Afghanistan, though Mongolia is far colder.

Dinner at Asian DFAC. I talked briefly in Hindi to a server from Goa and then settled down with a large group of Asian and African contract employees to watch Chelsea eke out a 2–1 victory over Arsenal.

Watching such games, I think often of Iain and Cameron and how much I loved to see them play soccer; my feelings are tinged with regret for those games that I missed. Once again I have this overwhelming desire to relive the past, if only for a moment. Yet even at the time when I watched those games I knew that such moments of joy would be fleeting. I realized, even then, that all I saw in front of me would all too quickly pass away.

Kandahar Airport, 21 January

Morning meeting at Kandahar Airport with an old and frail village elder from Panjwai. He owns land in the area, having survived first the Russians and then the Taliban. One of his several sons, a major in the Afghan army, was killed by the Taliban a couple of years ago. His father and Ahmed Karzai's father were friends.

Our meeting made me think of the way that Afghanistan used to be, the village elder having been a witness to decades of Afghan history. He recalled that he once attended a primary school in Panjwai during the King Zahir Shah era.

On several occasions he grabbed Nasemi's hand to explain a point. He had a tattoo on one wrist, a common practice here and especially among the Taliban. He had a white turban and white beard and he occasionally cleaned his ears, even as he talked in his animated and lively style.

He often repeated himself, noting on several occasions that he welcomed an American presence in Afghanistan. Perhaps he was trying too hard. He kept saying we should avoid letting anyone know about this conversation, for fear ISI or Iran or the Taliban would find out about it.

On a couple of occasions, he offered information and contacts in exchange for money, perhaps thinking I was a security agent. Before parting he introduced his two nephews and asked that I find work for them.

Afternoon meeting with John Sopko, head of investigations for USG programs in Afghanistan. Sopko worked for several years on Capitol Hill with Senator Sam Nunn. This was mainly a get-acquainted session. Although one article in the American media has described Sopko as having one of the hardest jobs in the country, what is even harder is to design an effective project and then implement it in the middle of a war.

Attended evening Martin Luther King Jr. Day celebrations at nearby entertainment tent. A couple hundred people attended, most soldiers and most African American.

General Hughes was guest of honor and made a few remarks. A Caucasian sergeant with a southern accent and a gift for the dramatic recited the "I Have a Dream" speech without notes and almost brought the house down—he was very, very good. I'm a sucker for rhetoric and was moved by the incongruity of it all.

The evening included a poetry reading and gospel choir. Perhaps the "I Have a Dream" speech seemed contrived and over the top at the time. Now, fifty years later, it has a powerful ring to it, as if it were truly being recited for the ages.

The current political discourse in the United States seems pedestrian by comparison, with its litany of trite references meant to appeal to the hearts and minds of the endless list of special interest groups that fuel both political parties. That said, President Obama did tap into something in his inaugural speech when he evoked Abraham Lincoln and his references to the fact that "blood drawn with the lash shall be paid by another drawn with the sword," a moving rhetorical flourish that I somehow wish were true.

It is hard to believe that four years ago I was on the Mall watching President Obama being sworn in for the first time. Everyone hoped for healing at the time—but, four years on, we seem to be growing more rather than less polarized with every passing year.

Kandahar, 22 January

Missed yesterday's farewell lunch for General Allen. However, part of the conversation among the senior officers revolved around the challenges that he had faced over the past nineteen months, along with the exhaustion that inevitably accompanies it.

Met General Dolan, commanding U.S. Air Force officer at Kandahar Air Field. He is dealing with many problems—including contractors who leave third country employees behind, forcing them to fend for themselves; a few resort to prostitution. I asked about nationalities represented at Kandahar Air Field—he said that the largest single contingent, well over two thousand, comes from India.

Spent most of the day in the office finishing three separate papers, including my quarterly report for Ambassador Cunningham.

I am concerned about what happens next to Dale Kramer, one of our departing civilians who did amazing things a couple of years ago. He was stationed in the north and his convoy came under attack after an IED killed three ANSF soldiers in the lead vehicle. When the gunner in Dale's MRAP stepped down to call for air support, Dale—a former Marine—stepped up, firing at the dozens of Taliban who had surrounded the convoy.

The gunfight lasted twenty minutes and several RPGs exploded nearby. Dale is credited with saving many lives and was awarded the State Department's Valor Award.

The story should have been reported at the time—but has never been picked up by any international media anywhere. I support his request for an eight-month extension but he probably won't get it, a casualty of our steep drawdown in staff.

Kandahar, 23 January

A quiet day. My main task was to open the economic conference at Kandahar Air Field involving staff from our PRTs and DSTs. It was a sober gathering given that most of our locations will close during the coming months.

A couple of people from Kabul attended and one of them hinted that the latest word is that our drawdown may be happening too quickly. What a mess. It is impossible to get our story straight!

In other news the IG is dropping the investigation of General Allen. Meanwhile Governor Wesa is furious because UNAMA is publicly accusing him of keeping a private prison at the governor's palace in Kandahar, something he vehemently denies.

Kandahar, 24 January

Morning context brief for Hans-Lothar Domröse, visiting German general from NATO—he was accompanied by General Yakovleff (France) and General Gaskin (United States).

General Abrams rattled off several interesting statistics: 80 percent of ANSF patrols in southern Afghanistan were independent during 2012 and ANSF units bore more than 85 percent of the casualties.

Recalling that the Arghandab was a killing ground only a couple of years ago, the German general was quick to note that the Soviets never controlled either Arghandab or Panjwai.

Morning briefing on the future of Kandahar Air Field. General Dolan also attended, commenting on the uncertainty that clouds everything. He noted that one option might be to return all of Kandahar Air Field to its former civilian status. On a lighter note, he mentioned that a few days ago a private plane belonging to the UAE royal family unexpectedly arrived at Kandahar Air Field to go bird hunting—the visiting party had not requested advance clearance and no one knew what to do with them.

Briefing on KPRT followed by lunch with Commander Ashburn and Brian Bachman. It was amicable enough but the topic is disappointing for all of us—KPRT will have to vacate Camp Nathan Smith in summer 2013, not 2014 as originally planned; that means KPRT will probably also have to close, shortening tours for many working there now.

Kandahar, 25 January

Spent a couple of hours on the boardwalk, first looking at shops, then drinking a cup of masala chai, and finally reading most of the pirated book I just bought—Peter Marsden's *Afghanistan: Aid, Armies and Empires,* a scathing take on U.S. efforts in Afghanistan.

For some reason I took time to linger and reflect on the many scenes in front of me throughout the day, including the crowds of people in the DFAC. I usually sit by myself and I need that time—alone but with dozens nearby.

My nearest neighbors were from Macedonia. A detachment of Bosnians has recently arrived. The kitchen crew largely comes from India, Nepal, and various places in Africa. And, everywhere, American soldiers. I love looking at the names on uniforms—whatever else might be said about the American military, the soldiers come from every tribe and nation, from every part of the United States and from the far ends of the earth.

Tomorrow I fly by helicopter to Kandahar for the national day reception at the Indian consulate. It will be interesting to see if Pakistani and Iranian diplomats show up.

I usually take a brief moment for reflection each time I board a helicopter or MRAP. Is this the last time, should I pray that somehow this cup is taken from me, should I wish for some other fate? In the end I'm fine with whatever happens. I don't regret being here. I've had a wonderful life. I'm ambivalent about some aspects of this mission—but not about my moments on this good earth, the human drama I've been given to witness, the life I've been privileged to have.

Indian Consulate, 26 January

Morning flight to KPRT, crossing many fields where *kutchis* are setting up their tents; it is during the winter months that they want to live closer to Kandahar.

As we landed I noticed a couple of kids crouching to escape the wash of the helicopter rotors and the dust that they kick up. One small boy was knocked off his bicycle. Farther away a couple of other children waved in our direction.

MRAP convoy to the Indian consulate through crowded streets and a bazaar alive with activity. People mostly just ignore us. Some traffic circles in Kandahar have been renovated, including one commemorating the battle of Maiwand in 1880. It is surrounded by several nineteenth-century cannons, each of them painted green.

The Indian Constitution Day celebrations were about as normal as it ever gets in Kandahar. About eighty invitations had been sent out and almost everyone invited showed up.

Several distinct groups were represented, including consuls general from India, Pakistan, and Iran; Governor Wesa; General Razziq and other security officials; a crowd of Afghan businessmen; and a couple of international representatives including the head of UNAMA (an Uzbek) and two others from the ICRC (one from Senegal, the other from France). Erin Tariot and Ellen de Guzman from KPRT attended, otherwise the guests were entirely male.

I sat next to General Kandahari, the new head of the Afghan National Army's Fourth Brigade in Uruzgan. He is from Arghandab and as a young man fought the Soviets there.

Introducing myself to one talkative Afghan officer attending the event, I pointed out the consuls general from Pakistan and Iran, whereupon he looked at me and quickly said, "I don't like either one of them."

General Razziq also attended, seemingly recovered from his wounds though still a prime target for the Taliban. He looked like one of the youngest Afghans present—but all the other Afghans seemed to defer to him.

Had interesting encounter with businessman from Panjwai who said he never left Afghanistan, even during the Taliban era when business was 10 percent of what it is today. He said he imported two construction cranes from Dubai, but the Taliban didn't know what to do with them. Unusually, he is upbeat on Afghanistan, saying that if the international community offers support and ISAF remains in the background the country will prosper.

He operates a private school in his home village near Panjwai, enrolling four hundred boys and girls. He pays six teachers, recent high school graduates, $300 a month. He also opened a computer room. His school starts in the afternoon, after government schools finish—many students attend both.

The Indian food provided by a local restaurant was very good. Looking around under the hot sun of the early afternoon, it was possible to see some brief sense of normalcy somehow taking root here, a different side of Kandahar that may one day become more commonplace.

Kandahar, 27 January

Stayed at Kandahar Air Field all day. It was cloudy in the morning; by evening a full moon was visible. The weather is also warming up, at least for now.

Late night phone call to family in the United States. Cameron mentioned he was wearing his Kandahar sweatshirt when he visited Starbucks in Atlanta recently. Someone saw him, asked about his shirt—and ended buying him coffee and a cinnamon roll because of it.

Governor's Palace, 28 January

Short flight to KPRT followed by convoy to governor's palace. We had a long agenda but Wesa doesn't give much away. He has been asked to visit Kabul to meet President Karzai—perhaps about the president's pending visit to Kandahar, perhaps about transition, perhaps about the Aino Mina development project in which Mahmood Karzai plays a central role.

Even as we talked, Wesa commented that a meeting was going on next door to discuss what happens after ISAF leaves. Attendees included Haji Dastageeri, among others.

According to Wesa, people in Kandahar are preparing for the transition and some are even optimistic about it. One of the Afghans sitting at the table repeated some of the scathing comments we have been hearing recently about the greed of the mullahs—combined with the suggestion that it doesn't take much to "buy them off," as he put it.

Returned to Kandahar Air Field to face avalanche of e-mails. There are so many unknowns it is hard to know where to begin. Under any scenario the next few months will be difficult.

Received e-mail late in the day from an FSO in Kabul whose parents had passed along a request from a friend of theirs. An American family lived in Kandahar during the early 1950s, and the father had worked for Morrison-Knudsen. While in Kandahar, their daughter, aged ten, died of polio. She was buried there almost immediately, in a small plot on the edge of town.

The e-mail from Kansas included a photograph of the gravestone:

Marilyn Jean McBee
Born June 8, 1944
Dratwer, Missouri, USA
Died June 17, 1954
Manzil Bagh, Kandahar, Afghanistan
Loving Daughter of
Charles and Ruby McBee

What a sad and lonely grave site—and now I have been asked to see if it somehow still exists.

Zaray, 29 January

Black Hawk to FOB Pasab in Zaray for all-day meetings in governor's office— first with district governor Niaz Mohammad Sarhadi and later with many of his officials including the district police chief, education director, chief prosecutor, and others.

The chief prosecutor had chubby fingers adorned with big rings, while the governor had a jovial face and white beard, making him look like an Afghan version of Santa Claus.

We were served tea by a young soldier in uniform who appeared Mongolian—he must have been a Hazara from central Afghanistan. One American major bowed his head and said a silent prayer before starting his lunch.

Sarhadi has been governor for two years and was in good form. The local police force has grown from zero to more than four hundred. He thinks security has improved dramatically and is proud of his accomplishments in education.

During the 1980s Sarhadi taught at a refugee school in Pakistan but his Urdu is lousy. An Achakzai, he staged an unsuccessful run for parliament in the last elections. Yet he still wields influence, presenting himself as a canny senior statesman.

We stayed for lunch—rice, naan, lamb, meatballs, dahl. While we were talking, word came that an Afghan policeman had stepped on an IED a few miles south of Pasab. He was brought into the medical station next to where we were meeting. Sadly, the medics were unable to save his leg.

Returned to Kandahar Air Field in the late afternoon, crossing a landscape that has not yet emerged from winter. Toward evening a huge moon emerged out of the darkness.

Spin Boldak, 30 January

Woke early to meet Deputy Special Representative for Afghanistan and Pakistan James Warlick. A former ambassador to Bulgaria, he was leaving Fletcher as I was arriving back in 1980. His wife was ambassador to Serbia and is now our consul general in Melbourne.

When the Kabul group arrived we immediately departed for the Joint Border Coordination group in Spin Boldak. It involves officers from Afghanistan, Pakistan, and ISAF, and the main intent is to avoid border incidents such as the one a couple of days ago that killed two Afghan policemen. Colonel Shahid on the Pakistani side was very articulate, and his presentation made me wonder if I will ever again serve in Pakistan.

After the briefing General Hughes accompanied us on a helicopter tour of the border. It was a fairly dismal day with an overcast sky and clouds of dust blowing in from the Registan Desert.

Yet views toward the border were nice enough—the large Pakistani flag waving at Dosti Darvaza; the red fort-like outposts belonging to Pakistan's Frontier Corps; the small berm marking the actual border; and the frenetic activity in Wesh, with its maze of cars, trucks, and storage yards.

A quarter million people plus three thousand trucks and two hundred private vehicles cross the border each week. A few months ago General Hughes took this same trip—and his helicopter accidentally wandered nearly half a mile into Pakistan. He said he now has the "best pilot in the division." He added that the previous pilot who wandered into Pakistan had been sent home.

Returned to Kandahar Air Field for lunch and ribbon-cutting ceremony marking completion of new tarmac on the civilian side of the airport. Director Faizi and the minister of transportation attended.

Governor Wesa joined us after lunch, catered by a hotel in Kandahar. Finally, Faizi can say the minister has visited his airport. But it will be a long time before the Afghans can take over and run it properly.

Spent an hour talking to Governor Wesa. Ambassador Warlick covered much of what we talked about in Kandahar a couple of days ago—transition, elections, reconciliation, etc. Wesa was very optimistic, I hope not unduly so.

Wesa thinks the ANSF can handle whatever the Taliban send in their direction. But he assumes that ISAF will be there to back up their efforts—something that may not actually happen.

He brought two of his three Canadian daughters with him—one is a lawyer and another is a recent graduate of the London School of Economics. Perhaps not surprisingly, both are thoroughly Canadian, including in the way in which they dress.

Kandahar, 31 January

Finally, a quiet day on Kandahar Air Field without much happening other than meetings and report writing. One commentary from Kabul made an amusing reference to the "Kandahari way," referring to people who change their political allegiances in ways that are quick and unexpected.

The weekly SCR video conference with IPA in Kabul lasted longer than usual. A lot is happening, most of it not good. The drawdown is difficult—we are so involved in personnel and management issues there isn't enough time left over to do our "real" mission. Or perhaps that is our "real" mission, to calmly undertake the administrative requirements to draw down even more quickly than we had originally planned.

7

⟷

FEBRUARY

Gecko, 1 February

Cloudy day with steady rain for part of afternoon, providing Kandahar with the water it so desperately needs.

Talked with military colleagues involved in civil affairs. One said recent meetings between the Afghan government and the Taliban in Qatar point to a mutual desire to reduce the rhetoric on both sides; GIRoA will refrain from using the word "terrorists" to describe the Taliban and the Taliban will avoid using the word "puppet" to describe the government. They think reconciliation may be possible under a new Afghan government, after elections in April 2014.

Read survey on religiosity in Kandahar. Almost half the Afghans living in Kandahar pray regularly—but half almost never attend the Friday sermon. Most say they are "conflicted" about the Taliban, viewing them as "good Muslims," but are appalled when they kill civilians, turning them into "bad Muslims." Many locals think peace will be possible after ISAF leaves, removing the target that has kept the war going for so long.

Black Hawk to Gecko for Friday evening briefing. Six Pakistanis were picked up by Afghan security forces earlier in the day for taking photos. Our discussion focused partly on Razziq, the Kandahar police chief who terrifies the Taliban. Already several attempts have been made on his life—and the effort is continuing.

Aino Mina, 2 February

Visited Mahmood Karzai in his home in Aino Mina where he hosted the best Afghan meal I've ever eaten. No wonder the Karzai family has done well running restaurants in the United States. He recently relinquished his American passport, possibly paving the way for a role within the Afghan government.

Although plagued by media allegations of corruption for his land dealings at Aino Mina, his focus on economics as a pathway forward for Afghanistan is quite reasonable. He thinks his brother Qayum might be a good candidate for president, describing him as "ten times a better politician than me." He also thinks President Karzai has missed important opportunities during his term of office, isn't well versed in the realities of the business world, and lacks substance in important areas of foreign policy.

When asked about another brother, Shah Wali Karzai, he responded without enthusiasm. The two of them live only a few hundred yards away from each other—yet very rarely visit and hardly ever talk.

Mahmood mentioned first coming to the U.S. in the mid-1970s when his father urged him to leave because Afghanistan was moving toward the Soviet camp. He had studied medicine in Kabul but never practiced it in the United States, taking a business path instead.

He arrived with nothing—but came to appreciate the opportunities given to him and during the next few years became a millionaire. Now he expects to spend the rest of his life in Afghanistan.

He is quite upbeat about Afghanistan's future, believing a peace deal will eventually be struck with the Taliban. He has known Governor Wesa since childhood but isn't always impressed. He mentioned corruption at the border crossing at Wesh. Perhaps the only political figure in southern Afghanistan he really warms to is the mayor of Kandahar.

Aino Mina houses 25,000 people—but should eventually have a population of more than 250,000. Only a small corner is built up; most of the rest consists of wide avenues, street lights, and empty plots of land. There are a few fountains. A large restaurant is under construction, built in Italian style near a small lake. It is currently empty, surrounded by several small cabanas for family picnics.

Mahmood said he supports various small businesses that produce furniture, metal gates, and slabs of cut marble for tabletops. The marble project is managed by a young Asian American from California who has been living alone in Kandahar for the past ten months.

Driving back to Kandahar Air Field it was interesting to see a landscape I usually view only at night. There is a lot of business activity, much of it associated with debris left behind by departing American soldiers—wood pallets, stacks of mattresses, piles of Styrofoam, mountains of tin cans—all relics of a twelve-year military campaign that is finally drawing to an unhappy close.

Attended evening Purple Heart ceremony for Private First Class Kevin Win from California, age twenty. Earlier today he stepped on an IED while on dismounted patrol in Panjwai. Remarkably the second, larger explosion did not go off—he broke a leg but escaped having his legs blown off.

General Abrams described Win as "the luckiest soldier in the Third Infantry Division," adding he must have a "good guardian angel." He attributed the ineffectual mine to an incompetent Taliban IED maker. Win looked very young, very Asian—and very sheepish about all the attention.

Three American soldiers were killed in Afghanistan during the entire month of January, one of them in RC-South. That must be some kind of record.

Worked until after midnight. Walking the few yards from my office to my CHU. It was raining heavily—just what Kandahar needs, and just what I need to sleep well tonight, the rain making a pleasant sound as it pours down in torrents on the thin metal roof above my bed.

Kandahar, 3 February

Cloudy and rainy most of day, making it impossible for helicopters to fly. Spent most of day catching up on reading e-mails and reports. At evening briefer one colonel mentioned an unusually gifted Afghan sergeant who had identified sixty-eight IEDs in less than forty-eight hours, locating hidden explosives in the same way an exceptionally skilled dowser finds water.

Camp Nathan Smith/Sariposa Prison, 4 February

Late morning flight to KPRT followed by lunch with two Afghans representing human rights groups in Kandahar—Mohammad Zaman Rufi from the Afghan Human Rights Organization and Shamsuddin Tanweer from the Afghan Independent Human Rights Commission. They vehemently dispute claims made by more skeptical and more cynical Afghans that their organizations are Western implants.

One case we discussed involved Zahra, a young woman from Nimroz whose parents moved to Kandahar and sold her as a child bride at age twelve to pay a drug debt. She ran away and now seeks a permanent divorce. She will almost certainly get it because she was too young to get married in the first place—unless her mother-in-law and husband manage to prove that she is actually nineteen and that the torture marks all over her body date from before her wedding.

Joined MRAP convoy to visit provincial courts and meet Dil Aga Himat, chief judge of Kandahar; Khaliq Khan, attorney general for Kandahar; Seleh Mohammad, NDS chief prosecutor; and Mohammad Anwar, chief prosecutor for Kandahar. The milky cardamom tea was wonderful.

Members of the judicial staff are pleasant enough—but it is often hard to know what lies behind the smiles. The chief judge stated that when someone comes to his court, that person gets a fair trial. But he went on to imply that the wealthy and powerful in Afghanistan ensure that their cases never advance that far. By definition, the cases he sees involve defendants with neither money nor power.

Also visited Sariposa Prison, site of a mass Taliban escape involving more than four hundred prisoners a couple of years ago. One account says the Taliban tunneled underneath the walls, another that they fled through an open gate.

A tunnel was actually dug but there is some debate as to whether hundreds of inmates could have fled through it in a very short period of time. Perhaps it was a combination of both—some prisoners escaped via the tunnel, causing a distraction that allowed others to flee through the front gate.

Colonel Farooq, the new head warden, was brought in to clean up the mess. He is a calm, soft, grandfatherly type with a gray beard and a reassuring presence. Previously he was in Zabul where the prison has only two hundred inmates.

The prisoner population at Sariposa exceeds two thousand, causing severe overcrowding. Only one section of Sariposa is sparsely populated—the women's section containing only a handful of inmates.

Sariposa is smaller than I expected and at least seventy years old. We climbed up to the roof to look out into the open courtyards of the two main sections, one for regular criminals, another for insurgents. It is hard to tell one section from the other.

Clothes were spread out on bushes and on flimsy rope lines in the courtyard below us to dry. The prisoners wear ordinary Afghan street clothes and most have beards and turbans. They looked in our direction, seemingly more out of curiosity and bemusement rather than hatred. Still, prisons always have a feeling of strangeness and foreboding and I was not sorry to leave.

Returning to KPRT we stopped briefly at the governor's palace where I noticed a pair of cranes loitering on the grass, no doubt resting after their long journey south from Mongolia. The Kandahar bazaar was well stocked and we saw more of it than usual, everything from bodybuilding gyms to computer stores, from video vendors to car repair shops.

Arrived at KPRT at 5:00 p.m., just in time for our return helicopters—only to find that flights back to Kandahar Air Field had been cancelled because of clouds and rain.

Walked instead to the DFAC for Mongolian barbeque night featuring shrimp, chicken, and beef, mixed together on a hot plate with lots of garlic and curry powder. It was a wonderful meal. Had coffee at Green Bean before returning to my room for the night.

Camp Nathan Smith, 5 February

Cloudy morning, further delaying flights. Spoke at 9:00 a.m. weekly KPRT staff meeting, mostly to respond to questions about the path ahead. Many bitterly resent the fact that KPRT is being closed one year early.

At around 11:00 a.m. the two Black Hawks finally arrived, taking us on the short flight home. By afternoon, the skies were completely clear—it should be this way for the next several days though the temperature in Kandahar has also plummeted.

Kandahar Airport, 6 February

Morning meeting at Kandahar Airport with six ulema, brought together by Haji Dastageeri. One was Masood Akhundzada, the keeper of the cloak reputedly worn by the prophet Mohammad long ago and by Mullah Omar more recently.

Several of Akhundzada's relatives have been killed. He said he could do nothing when Mullah Omar grabbed the cloak from him and started waving it around. President Karzai was the last to see the cloak and that was ten years ago. Now it is kept under lock and key in three successively smaller boxes.

It was an interesting meeting and Dastageeri made sure everyone had their say. The recurring complaint is that the Afghan government doesn't listen to the clergy, support them, or take them seriously.

One mullah was especially animated when talking about Taliban suicide bombers, making the point that nothing can be done to stop them. Someone else said a 300,000-strong Afghan army should be sufficient to withstand the Taliban—but expressed concern that it will lack air support. All the ulema recalled the days of King Zahir Shah when religious leaders received respect as well as stipends.

Akhundzada runs a madrassah with five thousand students—three thousand boys and two thousand girls. He claims Iran pays students attending the Shia madrassah in Kandahar as much as he can pay his teachers.

I mentioned that in the United States a minister might lose his congregation if they believed he no longer reflects their faith. One of the ulema laughed, adding that if an Afghan mullah doesn't reflect true Islam he should be stoned. I heard later that more than sixty members of the Kandahar ulema have been killed in the past several years, including the keeper of the cloak's brother.

Afternoon town hall video with former senator John Kerry, our new secretary of state. He made opening comments about the importance of our mission.

There was time for three questions—one from Bagram, another from Herat, and a third from Kabul.

Kerry said staffing numbers for Afghanistan should be available soon—but it is clear that there will be a big drawdown. He suggested we are paying for mistakes made by others who planned for a much bigger presence in Afghanistan than was ever warranted.

I strongly agree that the story should be left for Afghans to write. I also agree that the number of ISAF soldiers should be greatly reduced. But the slope for our departure is too steep—we might have had it right a few months ago, but now it is becoming an unseemly rush for the exit, one that is all the more pitiful because arguably at one point we came close to actually getting it right.

Kandahar, 8 February

Another day spent entirely on Kandahar Air Field. Spoke to forty female soldiers from the U.S. and Romania completing their training week on female engagement in southern Afghanistan.

Spent part of day finalizing the first dissent cable I have ever written. It is supposed to go directly to Secretary Kerry though I wonder if he will ever actually read it. It mostly critiques our overly cautious approach to public outreach, using the spiking of the Malala story from last fall as an example of the problem in microcosm. Sent courtesy copy to Ambassador Cunningham who replied that he had "no problem with it."

Rereading e-mail input from Islamabad and Washington in October that ended any hope of publishing the Malala article in Pushto in the Afghan local media, if anything, makes me more determined. Washington stated at the time via e-mail that "we prefer to be more low profile," adding "please no USG op-ed." And all this is because of a misplaced concern that conspiracy theorists in Pakistan would go into overdrive if we commented on the Malala case, blaming us for organizing the attack.

Kandahar, 9 February

All-day commander's conference at Kandahar Air Field. Finally, I am beginning to understand military terminology and the military way of doing things.

There is a growing recognition that the Fourth Infantry Division will have a far more circumscribed assignment than ours. General Abrams says that with time slipping away he wants to focus on transactional relationships—if we give something, we should expect something in return.

The retrograde process is daunting and thousands of vehicles, containers, and other items are already waiting to be loaded up and sent back home. There is also a plan for the various memorials commemorating soldiers who have been killed. Such items will be dismantled and sent back to the U.S. The chapels built for soldiers on various bases also have to be taken down rather than turned over to Afghans.

Sat with Colonel Shanahan at lunch—he is the Australian adviser to General Hamid. Like General Abrams, he is impressed with General Hamid, one of many trained by the Soviets. Years later they number among the most professional of military officers in Afghanistan.

I asked Shanahan how Afghan officers are assigned. He said senior Afghan officers typically want to avoid service in Kandahar: "It is like German officers during World War II. None of them wanted to serve on the eastern front."

Attended evening barbeque for battlefield commanders—shrimp, chicken, sausages, and steak. The verandah outside our quarters is now finished. We served ourselves there, walking to nearby tables and warming ourselves beside a small wood fire. It is still quite cold in Kandahar.

Kandahar, 10 February

Relatively quiet day. General Abrams was in Kabul to attend the change-of-command ceremony, General Allen giving way to General Dunford who will preside over a sharp drawdown in forces as well as the transition to noncombat roles.

Edited mangled cable on Mahmood Karzai's development project at Aino Mina. Also discussed our drawdown plans. This is the hardest part of this assignment—to preside over the curtailment of tours for so many people who expected to be here much longer. Evening phone call with Fiona—one of the few good moments of the day.

Kandahar, 11 February

Another quiet day—this is probably the longest stretch I've ever been on Kandahar Air Field without leaving it. I mostly caught up on personnel evaluations. Also wrote another cable, this one based on a recent and unclassified DoD survey shedding light on religious affairs in Kandahar.

An overwhelming majority of Kandaharis describe the Taliban as "good Muslims," explaining away Taliban atrocities by saying they couldn't possibly have been committed by "true" Muslims or "real" Taliban. Most Kandaharis want ISAF troops to leave—but most hope an agreement is reached so ISAF backs up GIRoA. Nearly 60 percent want continued U.S. support.

Read more news reports on Haji Dastageeri. Rumor has it that he is in touch with everybody including the Taliban, but rejects their entreaties to join them. He is on friendly terms with almost every powerbroker in Kandahar, an impressive achievement.

Meanwhile, Shah Wali Karzai's candidate—described by his opponents as an illiterate Popalzai who rarely attends meetings—was elected chairman of the Kandahar Provincial Council, ensuring support for Karzai family interests during upcoming elections. Current chairman Noorzai and four of his colleagues boycotted the event to show their disapproval.

The Taliban keep getting hammered in southern Afghanistan. Most recently one of their commanders was killed by a Hellfire missile in Maiwand. Others involved in various IED networks are picked up from their compounds almost every day. There are also increasing media reports of Taliban infighting in Quetta and elsewhere.

It is hard to know if this is only a temporary setback—or if things really are somehow trending GIRoA's way. Many Afghans are tired after thirty years of war and perhaps that is enough to shift things in favor of the government.

Attended Purple Heart ceremony for Joshua O'Neill from Maryland. He and six others were riding in a minesweeper in Maiwand earlier this morning that got blown up by an IED. It ended up sideways and the gun turret was blown completely off. Remarkably no one was killed and no one lost limbs. O'Neill will be sent to Germany for further treatment but everyone else suffered only light wounds.

One slightly wounded soldier was eighteen years old and looked even younger. I wanted to ask him, "Do you have a note from your parents giving you permission to participate in this war?"

Kandahar, 12 February

Another day at Kandahar Air Field. Heard about demonstration against the Taliban involving at least a hundred people in the Horn of Panjwai, possibly organized by someone whose three grandchildren were kidnapped by the Taliban; others say it is because a local villager was cruelly treated. Perhaps this will become the belated Panjwai Uprising, similar to what happened in Ghazni several months ago.

Briefed on visa referral process from Kabul, giving me authorization to provide type A and type B referrals. Obtaining an American visa is very difficult. Yet Haji Dastageeri and the keeper of the cloak have both asked for one, wanting to visit Asadullah Khalid, the head of NSD recovering at Walter Reed.

It would be fascinating if we could somehow support their request and give them a chance to finally visit the United States. Probably Dastageeri would be viewed as a highly problematic case by Homeland Security, given his prior associations with the Taliban. I doubt if our military would support a visa for him, either.

Evening briefing. There is much interest in the Panjwai uprising. There is also a sense or at least a hope that the Taliban are finally fracturing—their leadership seems increasingly disunited. According to some accounts, certain members of the inner circle are fighting each other, and it has been a long time since Mullah Omar has shown his face to anyone.

The wind began to pick up as I walked toward my quarters late at night. It is cold and the weather forecast for tomorrow is dismal. I am scheduled to leave early and will hopefully reach Tarin Kot before the storm sets in.

Tarin Kot (Uruzgan), 13 February

General Abrams arrived at morning staff meeting with a black mark on his head for Ash Wednesday—the only officer I noticed attending early-morning mass.

Afterward Bonnie drove me to the flight line for a Texas National Guard C-130 flight to Tarin Kot. It is cloudy and the route took us close to mountains. The rivers below are as full as we will ever see them. Nasemi and John Dunlap, one of our civilian officers, are coming with me on this trip.

Departed by armored Australian Bushmasters to meet Dr. Abdul Ghafar Stanikzai, director of the Uruzgan branch of the Afghan Independent Human Rights Commission. He briefed us on several issues, many centered on violence against women.

One case involves a husband who first crippled his wife and later poured hot water on her legs, injuring her further. The husband and his brother are now in jail. Stanikzai claims Afghans are becoming more aware of these issues and are increasingly repulsed by them.

Afterward Stanikzai hosted us for lunch—not only the usual *kabuli pilau*, mutton curry, and naan, but also a platter of small fried fish cooked whole that were delicious. I talked to the cooks afterward—I thought the fish might have been bought in the bazaar but they said they had been netted in the river yesterday.

Our small convoy then headed to the governor's office to meet the Uruzgan deputy provincial governor along with heads of various line departments. Governor Akhundzada's special assistant attended, no doubt to make sure the deputy governor sticks to the official script.

The provincial head of finance looked very traditional and lacks education in a formal sense. But he was also almost certainly the smartest person in the room. By contrast, the young man who heads the economic department can boast of some education but was quite glib when it came to real life experience, trading mostly in platitudes.

Returned to PRT for dinner—the reputation of the Uruzgan DFAC is legendary across RC-South. That said, two whole suckling pigs carved up for everyone to see is going too far, especially in Afghanistan. For the Afghan translators who eat in the DFAC it must be like seeing rats roasted on a spit.

After dinner I looked through some of the shops on the base—a mix of electronic items, pirated videos, and handicrafts, some going back to when Uruzgan was a Dutch PRT. The snow-covered mountains to the north look nice.

Lights off by 11:00 p.m., an early night. I was assigned to a temporary hooch with two bunk beds and not much else. I am very happy about any night in which I get eight hours of sleep.

Tarin Kot (Uruzgan), Valentine's Day, 14 February

Valentine's Day—Catriona bought white lilies and chocolate for Fiona in Ulaanbaatar; she also made tea and cooked pancakes for her.

Early-morning meeting with the mayor of Tarin Kot, a former mujahideen who seems competent and committed. He was reproachful and expressed fear concerning the pending ISAF departure, asking that at least a small number of soldiers be left behind: "You are leaving while some fires are still burning."

Returned to PRT gym for official change-of-command ceremony—Adrian Lochrin giving way to his Australian Foreign Service colleague John Feakes.

The proceedings started with four national anthems—Afghan, Slovak, Australian, and American. This was followed by six speeches. A part of Australia will always be in Tarin Kot, given the Australian blood and treasure that has been expended here.

Colonel Stuart is a good commander and will certainly be a general someday. The reporting from Uruzgan is excellent—once again I have this hope that it will be archived somewhere in Australia, documenting everything that happened during their years in Afghanistan.

Talked with Governor Akhundzada who had flown down from Kabul with the Australian ambassador. He is portly and cheerful and seems in good health following medical consultations in Delhi. At lunch I sat with him as well as Member of Parliament Barakzai. They were both upbeat, perhaps because the recent budget news from Kabul is encouraging.

Talked briefly with the leader of the Barakzais of Uruzgan. He was much less circumspect, pleading for ISAF troops to stay longer. He had a turban, thick glasses, missing teeth, wrinkled skin, and a long white beard.

He too fought the Soviets during the 1980s. He has six sons—one killed by the Soviets, another by a Taliban IED. He said four of his grandsons have also been killed by the Taliban. He was especially perturbed by the brutality of the murders; they were killed while he was on a trip to Kabul, without even having any weapons to fight back.

I offered condolences but he just waved his hand and said unfortunately there was nothing unique or unusual about his story; it is a common occurrence across Afghanistan.

Returned to Kandahar Air Field at 2:30 on a C-130 belonging to the Texas National Guard. I slept for most of the thirty-minute journey, managing a few minutes of rest wherever I can find it.

Left almost immediately from flight line to late afternoon and early evening meetings—4:30, 6:00, 7:00, and 8:00. It never ends. The advance guard of the Fourth Infantry Division from Colorado is at Kandahar Air Field for one week, preparing for their upcoming deployment in the summer.

Kandahar, 15 February

Overheard two British contractors talking at breakfast. The most voluble one referred to the two small beach houses he owns in the Philippines. "In Sin City," he said. "Philippines is like Thailand twenty years ago, which is why I like it much better." If his contract is extended for one more year, he will buy a small hotel.

Talked briefly with an American contractor doing his laundry. He departs tomorrow after three years in Afghanistan. He will meet his Ukrainian girlfriend in Dubai and then head with her to Nebraska to see if she likes it there.

Shah Wali Karzai's Residence, 16 February

At morning staff meeting heard references to one Afghan soldier hitting another on the head with a boulder in Chora. ISAF medevaced him to the military hospital at Kandahar Air Field where he later died.

Dinner with Shah Wali Karzai. As at Mahmood Karzai's lunch a couple of weeks ago, the meal started with pistachios and raisins from Kandahar and finished with oranges and guavas from Pakistan. Shah Wali Karzai was in a pessimistic mood, mostly because of falling real estate prices. He said that when U.S. soldiers leave, the Afghan business community will also depart.

The conversation started with a discussion on religious outreach. Shah Wali Karzai thinks mullahs who register should receive small government stipends as was often the case in the past, enough to influence their sermons or at least ensure that they don't become inflammatory.

Shah Wali Karzai remains skeptical about national elections and continues to think his brother is the one politician who can hold the country together. He touched on recent provincial council elections, blaming Kabul for interfering with them. He was upbeat about the new provincial council chairman who others have sometimes described as illiterate. He hopes that the five disgruntled members who boycotted elections last week can be persuaded to return.

The head of the cadastral office in Kandahar joined us for dinner. He thanked KPRT for building a new office—only to have a Taliban suicide bomber destroy it nearly a year ago. His seven-year-old son had been visiting and died in the blast. He showed us photographs of the destruction as well as a color picture of his late son in a helicopter. The awful memory of that day nearly reduced him to tears: "Even when the Soviets invaded Afghanistan, such actions were not permitted."

Our security detail was led by Lieutenant Brad Cohn, West Point class of 2010. He is delighted to be a platoon leader, stating that most of his graduating class has already served in Afghanistan; he had been afraid that he might not have the chance.

He majored in history at West Point and wrote his thesis on the Israeli army, specifically their no-surrender policy—a view stretched to the limits in the 1973 Yom Kippur war when commanders on the Bar Lev Line phoned Tel Aviv to ask if it was "okay" to surrender to the Egyptians. The Israeli commanders who got this message were unable to frame an answer, torn between wanting to save the lives of their soldiers and the no-surrender ethos forged at Masada.

Returned to Kandahar Air Field with time enough to look up at a brilliant star-strewn sky and then spend a few minutes going through e-mails. Some personal responses to my dissent cable have arrived, all favorable. I know it has been passed around senior levels at State—but whether it will have impact or elicit a response is an entirely different matter.

Kandahar, 17 February

Attended morning service at Fraise Chapel. The congregation was large and diverse and included soldiers as well as civilians. The sermon was on the sins of King David and the text for the day was drawn from Psalm 51: "Have mercy on me, O God."

During weekly security meeting Brandon Padillo mentioned Cydney Mizell, an American NGO worker kidnapped in Kandahar in early 2008, briefly held for ransom, and then killed. Periodically, someone claims to have found her remains and wants to return them for a reward.

The latest episode involved a phone call to KPRT by a local Afghan who said he found bones in Panjwai—but yesterday he failed to turn up and did not deliver them as promised. Some years ago remains were actually turned in.

However, when tested in the U.S. they proved to belong to a Caucasian male—leading everyone to assume they must have been the remains of a Soviet soldier killed in Panjwai during the 1980s.

Other missing people our RSO has on his watch list include Colin Rutherford, a tourist who disappeared in Kandahar in 2010; and Warren Weinstein, a USAID contractor who I know well and, if alive, is more likely in Pakistan.

Brandon mentioned that yesterday an Afghan American was briefly detained for filming an ISAF convoy in Arghandab. He claimed to be visiting from California and further claimed he was looking for retirement property—a far-fetched explanation that actually proved to be true.

Evening briefing on Panjwai. There is hope in some quarters that the uprising among the Noorzai in three villages in western Panjwai may become a tipping point, though others are concerned that GIRoA has been too slow to respond. The last district governor had initial success in convincing local Taliban to change their allegiances but was subsequently assassinated.

Dinner at Echoes with Colonel Thompson, soon be a general. He now works at the Pentagon but will arrive in Kandahar with the Fourth Infantry Division in the summer. Afghanistan will be a first-time experience for him. Like many others he previously served in Iraq.

Arghandab, 18 February

Morning Black Hawk flight to Arghandab accompanied by Ed Birsner and Colonel Valhola from our civil affairs team. Nasemi is with us as well to provide translation. I have long wanted a more detailed conversation with some of the religious leadership in Arghandab and finally it is starting to happen. While perhaps a bit late, the embassy also wants us to increase our religious engagement, though it is very hard for either diplomats or soldiers to "do" theology in any way that matters.

The view across the Arghandab valley is wonderful, even in the midst of winter. We met briefly in the canvas tent that serves as the DST office and then walked to the governor's compound, meeting first with district governor Shah Mohammad.

The district governor has been in place for two years, bringing about much change. But he also faces corruption charges and may soon have to resign. He was very talkative, holding forth on the failings of Afghanistan and how to remedy them. He has always claimed that when ISAF leaves, he will also leave. Referring to the ulema, he said, "They are in a position to make fires—but they can also put fires out."

Talked to a succession of religious leaders starting with one from Mansurabad near Shah Wali Kot. He was upbeat, especially given that his area is contested territory and the Taliban there remain quite strong.

Also met with a *maulvi* from Loy Minara. Age thirty-three, he received his early education under the Taliban. An imam in a local village mosque since 2010, he too professed optimism about the future, tinged with nervousness about what happens when ISAF soldiers leave. "Everything that ISAF has done is like a big block of ice," he said. "When ISAF leaves, it will all melt into nothing."

Spent time talking to a third religious leader who served as a land and property officer in Kandahar during the time of the Taliban. He is more like a businessman than a spiritual leader and imports oranges and bananas from Pakistan. He too was fairly upbeat, confident that a path to peace will somehow be found. After three decades, he thinks Afghans are sick of violence and want it to finally end. "The war is over," he said, though I am not at all convinced.

Finished afternoon with a long and disjointed conversation with a fourth *maulvi*. In his late forties and from Langar, he fought with the mujahideen during the 1980s and later studied in Quetta. His eyes flashed with anger and he sometimes seethed with rage toward the Afghan government, dismissing it as grossly corrupt. He said Afghanistan will never be peaceful unless it addresses the most important issue of all—justice.

Unexpectedly, he embraced me when he departed, asking that I be his voice. "I am a nobody," he said. "I have no voice and nobody listens to me. But please tell people there will never be peace in Afghanistan without justice."

Most of the *maulvis* seem sympathetic to parts of the Taliban narrative while acknowledging that the Taliban have failed to live up to their early ideals. One of them said that rural farmers dropped their scythes and joined in the thousands the first time the Taliban asked them to rally for a battle in Farah. Later people became disenchanted and much less willing to fight.

Some conversations became more personal and I mentioned the seven-year-old child killed by a suicide bomber in Kandahar last year.

"What will the suicide bomber say to God when he is asked to account for his life on judgement day?" I asked. "And what about the mullah who convinced him to do it?"

Some mullahs said they speak out against suicide bombers in their Friday sermons. But the last one I spoke to was unmoved, stating that this was just one among thousands of tragedies befalling his country over the past thirty years.

Participated in two video conferences at Kandahar Air Field—one early in the morning as part of embassy country team, the other late in the afternoon with our PRT in Zabul. For the fourth consecutive week there are no American deaths to mention and to mourn.

Ambassador Cunningham said he met Governor Naseri in Kabul on Saturday, hearing the usual concerns about the closure of the PRT in early May—though Tim Bashor believes it is time to finally shut it down.

Late in the day heard indirectly from IPA in Kabul that the embassy wants to turn off meetings in Kandahar with certain members of the extended Karzai clan, presumably because President Karzai doesn't want foreign diplomats talking to his relatives. Here, as elsewhere, continued allegations of corruption are probably part of the mix. Whatever the reasons, this is guidance that is hard to understand—family feuds matter in southern Afghanistan and we need to somehow know more about them.

The proofs for *Mongolia and the United States: A Diplomatic History* arrived from Hong Kong University Press. This book has many defects—but after all these months I'm happy and surprised that it will eventually see the light of day after all.

Kandahar, 19 February

Spent part of morning with visiting IG team from Kabul. They are looking at transition planning, an area in which we have much to talk about. The team leader has spent eight months in Kabul and this is his first time out, underscoring yet again how different our world is from those who live in the embassy.

The latest rumor is that a couple of the provincial and district governors that we engage with regularly are under investigation for corruption. Certain Afghan parliamentarians seem to be behind this effort. Corruption is so endemic that almost any accusation probably has at least some truth behind it. It is nonetheless surprising that the district governor concerned was so calm when I recently talked to him, given everything else hanging over his head right now.

Camp Nathan Smith/Pakistan Consulate, 20 February

Morning Black Hawk flight to Camp Nathan Smith followed by convoy to Pakistan consulate in Kandahar. The consul general and his deputy along with a vice consul from Khyber Agency were waiting to greet us, though the welcome was somewhat marred by an initial standoff with the U.S. soldiers accompanying us.

Unlike at the Indian consulate, the Pakistani diplomats stood firm in saying, "This is Pakistan territory," and "Guns aren't allowed inside." In the end, the soldiers remained in a waiting area while the rest of us were led to the consul general's large office.

The consulate walls are decorated with posters printed by the Pakistan Tourism Development Corporation. One showed a polo match at the Shandur Pass between Gilgit and Chitral, another the tomb of Quaid-i-Azam Jinnah in Karachi.

We stayed a couple of hours and were served small *chappli* kebabs, chicken tikka, and milk tea. All the Pakistani diplomats speak Pushto and were wearing Pakistani national dress. The consul general is a career diplomat, but I can't help but speculate that his more vocal deputy may be from the Pakistani intelligence services. He often dominated the conversation, though at one point the consul general told his deputy in Pushto, "Don't interrupt. I want to explain this."

The Pakistan narrative is that they have borne more sacrifices than anyone else in the long war on terrorism. They expressed fear about an unstable Afghanistan, combined with consternation at ISAF's failure to restore security. They also think that the Afghan army has yet to prove that it can fight by itself; they described the Afghan police in even more dismal terms.

The Pakistani diplomats mentioned that PIA now flies to Karachi twice a week via Quetta, adding that a one-way ticket costs $130. They criticized the international community for leaving so little behind despite spending billions of dollars. They also blamed Afghans for making trouble in Baluchistan.

Toward the end of the conversation one of the Pakistani diplomats mentioned that his country had offered refuge to "the Tal . . . I'm sorry, I mean the Afghans," a sort of Freudian slip that was quite telling. But I have enough lingering affection for the country of my birth that I enjoyed the conversation and the chance to engage with Pakistani diplomats in this fashion.

I mentioned at one point a *ghazal* from my favorite eighteenth-century Urdu poet Mir Taki Mir: "Kahin kya jo poochay koy hum se Mir, jihan main tum ayey the kya kar chaley," roughly translated as "What should I say, if anyone asks of me—what did you do while you lived on this earth?" It is a couplet that I think of whenever I am in a pensive mood, contemplating my purpose for being on this planet at all.

Returned home to read e-mail from the embassy in Kabul describing a meeting with President Karzai in which he referred to his "rogue cousin" in Kandahar who is "supported by the Americans." That seems like a stretch, though we did report a rift of sorts within the extended Karzai family led partly by a cousin who some have speculated became wealthy off ISAF contracts. It was probably this same cousin who disrupted the recent Kandahar Provincial Council elections—unsuccessfully, as it turns out, because in the end President Karzai's candidate won.

Kandahar, 21 February

Afternoon contact brief involving U.S. Army chief of staff Odierno. Viewed as an exceptionally able commander in Iraq, he is physically impressive—tall and with a large head shaved bald.

General Odierno has already visited Kandahar several times, always briefly. He was surprisingly soft-spoken yet very accessible to soldiers, including various sergeants major who came in from the field with their colonels to join the generals for dinner.

We talked briefly, comparing notes on his visit with Secretary Rice to Mongolia during the mid-2000s. I can see why he is considered an inspiring leader.

During the question-and-answer time after dinner, Odierno commented on the latest budget crisis, the upcoming Supreme Court decision on same-sex marriage, and the crisis of ethics and accountability in senior military ranks. He thinks the two qualities that any senior Army leader absolutely must have are competence and integrity.

One colonel asked about the number of American soldiers that might be deployed in a post-2014 Afghanistan and he suggested "around 9,500."

I asked if there would be an enduring U.S. presence in southern Afghanistan and he said Kandahar Air Field still remains a viable possibility. He added that Afghanistan needs a "robust State Department presence in the south."

Kandahar, 22 February

Afternoon briefing. One soldier in the field who interacts often with Afghans mentioned that they make every effort to learn the social and political terrain in which they work—to such an extent they exchange insults over the radio with local Taliban: "Oh, that's you over there. You're holding a set of binoculars, right? Please don't shoot."

Kabul, 23 February

Mike Sullivan mentioned the head of the cadastral office in Kandahar whose seven-year-old son was killed in a suicide bombing and whom I met at Shah Wali Karzai's last week. He recalled that the rule of law group was visiting Spin Boldak and the cadastral chief turned up, unexpectedly bringing his young son along for the ride.

After much consternation the cadastral officer and his son were allowed to board the helicopter together. It was during that trip that Mike took a picture of the proud father and his son, memorializing on film what was perhaps the most exciting moment of his short life. The father doted on this young son—it still makes me sick to think that one week later he was dead.

One of dozens of trips in a Black Hawk helicopter, somewhere above southern Afghanistan

The mountains of southern Afghanistan, as viewed from a Black Hawk helicopter en route from Uruzgan to Kandahar

Meeting with Afghan district officials in the Horn of Panjwai, west of Kandahar and on the main road to Helmand and Herat

Meeting with Afghan district official in Shah Wali Kot, north of Kandahar

Lunch in Tarin Kot with Dr. Abdul Ghafar Stanikzai, head of the Afghanistan Independent Human Rights Commission in Uruzgan

Chief engineer at Kajaki Dam—USAID installed the first two turbines in the late 1970s; he almost always kept the power running through the Soviet era, Taliban era, ISAF era, and even beyond

My heart aches whenever I look at this photograph, the last one taken of me with my translator Nasemi in a *shura* room in Tarin Kot (Uruzgan)

Afghan children surrounding our MRAP as we prepare to depart Alexander's Castle in Qalat (Zabul)

Afghan police protective unit outside Qalat (Zabul)

Field trip to the Arghandab Valley northwest of Kandahar, one of the more beautiful corners of southern Afghanistan

"Guardian Angel" providing force protection during a field trip to Arghandab, northwest of Kandahar

"Graveyard of Empires"—abandoned Soviet era tank in Qalat (Zabul)

Phil and Jesse, two colleagues who provided essential support during the year that I
spent in Afghanistan

With Colonel "Mick" King from Australia, a friend and colleague who served in the civil affairs unit for Regional Command South

View of Kandahar city from an MRAP

MRAP returning to its base in southern Afganistan

Farewell meeting with Haji Dastageeri, a local leader with important influence in parts of southern Afghanistan

Farewell meeting with Shah Wali Karzai, titular head of the Popalzai tribe and half brother to then-president Hamid Karzai

Final meeting with Afghan officials at the Governor's Palace in Kandahar

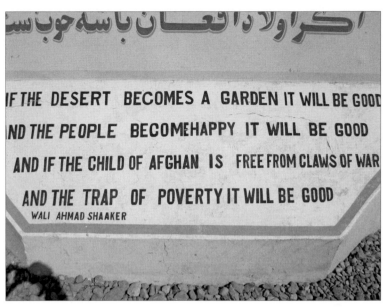

IF THE DESERT BECOMES A GARDEN IT WILL BE GOOD
ND THE PEOPLE BECOMEHAPPY IT WILL BE GOOD
AND IF THE CHILD OF AFGHAN IS FREE FROM CLAWS OF WAR
AND THE TRAP OF POVERTY IT WILL BE GOOD
WALI AHMAD SHAAKER

What all Afghans want to see—translation of Pushto verse, painted on a
wall at Camp Nathan Smith in Kandahar

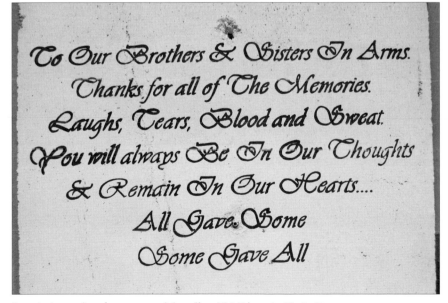

To Our Brothers & Sisters In Arms.
Thanks for all of The Memories.
Laughs, Tears, Blood and Sweat.
You will always Be In Our Thoughts
& Remain In Our Hearts....
All Gave Some
Some Gave All

Inscription painted on memorial wall at ISAF base in Tarin Kot

Dusty sunset in Tarin Kot (Uruzgan)

Afternoon Embassy Air flight to Kabul on Dash 8. There isn't much snow on the southern mountains—but, farther into the journey, the ice pack on the Hindu Kush looks much more promising.

Looking down in the midst of winter, the empty landscape below might well have been Mongolia. Population density picked up again near Kabul and the city from the air seems immense. As we landed, the highest mountains to the north were turning first orange and then purple. By the time we reached the embassy the sun had been swallowed by the night.

Driving toward the embassy the streets and bazaars were crowded while the wedding palaces were lit up in all their garish colors. Our driver was from Panjshir, had worked at the embassy for six months, and remained quite laconic despite Bonnie's best efforts to start a conversation with him. He did say he couldn't afford to have his wedding at one of the wedding halls that we drove by; they are much too expensive.

Walking around the compound at night I unexpectedly ran into a colleague. We talked briefly and as he departed I was astonished to hear him say, "I hate working here." Perhaps the stress levels are as high in Kabul as they are in Kandahar.

Attended wine and cheese reception hosted by Ambassador Cunningham for visiting SCRs. Wine is not allowed on Kandahar Air Field, but it was flowing freely here in Kabul tonight. Puritan that I am, I refrained from drinking—but did enjoy the cheese, shrimp, strawberries, and especially the mangoes, which I finished off almost single handedly.

Kabul, 24 February

Attended morning country team meeting in Kabul, starting with moment of silence for the one American soldier who died last week in Afghanistan. His name was Jonathan Davis, he was a Navajo Indian, he was thirty-four years old, and he was killed in Helmand.

As for the SCR *shura,* Ambassador Cunningham said we should not expect post-2014 troop numbers from President Obama anytime soon. ISAF will be in Afghanistan for the summer fighting season—but in the background. Prospects for a post-2014 consulate in Kandahar are very uncertain. At this point, "We just don't know where we are going."

Hearing descriptions from other parts of the country, northern Afghanistan really is a different place while the south lags way behind. At least one theme is consistently heard across the country: Afghans blame Pakistan for most of their troubles. As for post-2014 scenarios, Tina Kaidanow's advice is, "Prepare for the worst."

We covered many topics, including public outreach, religious engagement, and elections. We were told to "adjust" our "messaging." The operative phrase is not "free and fair elections." Rather, it is "credible and transparent elections." We should no longer talk about an "enduring presence" in our regions. Rather, we should refer to the importance of our "partnership."

We touched on the human aspects of our rapid drawdown. According to the State social worker who gave a presentation, the departing FSOs that he talks to when passing through Kabul on their way back to the United States often reflect "tremendous anger, anxiety and fear."

Joined other SCRs for evening meeting with several journalists at Masha Hamilton's apartment, including Michele Neubert from NBC and Shashank Bengali from the *Los Angeles Times*. It has been several years since any of them visited Kandahar.

One journalist asked how "we" could support Razziq, the well-known police chief in Kandahar. She thinks he is unredeemable and should be held accountable for his sins. Yet she also thinks I am doing the right thing by being willing to reach out to a broad range of Afghans, despite their possible prior ties to the Taliban and perhaps even al-Qaeda.

Kabul, 25 February

The halfway point of my time in Afghanistan. I can't say it has gone quickly. But, suddenly, six months are behind me and I am finally on the downward slope of this assignment.

Spent most of day at SCR *shura,* hearing from long line of speakers and occasionally entering into the discussion. It is somehow reassuring to hear differences of opinion and to realize that everyone in Kabul doesn't think alike. The ambassador retains some measure of optimism while his deputy takes a bleaker view on what happens next.

It was cold and rainy for most of the evening. Andrew Wilder came by for part of it, visiting for a few days from Washington, DC. He knows much more about Afghanistan than I ever will and laments what he describes as missed opportunities over the past ten years.

Andrew thinks most Afghans would welcome a sustained American presence beyond 2014. He also thinks Karzai is often erratic and wonders why the U.S. hasn't challenged him more often. Looking ahead to April 2014 elections, he mentioned possible candidates. The worst-case scenario would be for Karzai to extend his term or for another Karzai relative to run in his place.

Kabul, 26 February

Embassy Air flight to Kandahar cancelled due to rain and clouds. By late afternoon the rain had turned to sleet and then snow. By now the mountains surrounding Kabul will be covered in snow.

Walked to ISAF base, partly for a meeting on CERP projects but also to browse in the Afghan shops. The CERP meeting was a timely reminder of why I am happy not to be in Kabul—at times it bordered on excruciating.

Put out late-afternoon fire involving a governor in southern Afghanistan who supposedly left his marks on at least one IED. I don't believe it for a minute and am certain that there must be some mistake. While some governors may want to hedge their bets and play both sides, everything associated with this particular allegation is ludicrous.

Drinks with Aammon O'Shaughnessy, the New Zealand chargé d'affaires who recently served as New Zealand's ambassador to Tehran. He has an office in the British embassy and his staff consists of himself and a cat.

New Zealand's PRT in Bamiyan is about to close. They have been in place for nearly a decade and taken several casualties. What remains of their mission is focused entirely on training.

Kabul, 27 February

Woke early to walk into blanket of snow covering the embassy and all of Kabul. It was just before 6:00 a.m. and members of the Gurkha security forces were making their way to their posts, carrying guns and wearing helmets and protective gear. They emerged like ghosts through the falling snow and we nodded briefly in recognition as we passed each other in the dark.

Not surprisingly, the early-morning flight to Kandahar was cancelled. Planned trips to Zaray and Panjwai won't happen either. I returned to my CHU for a couple of extra hours of sleep and then took care of business at IPA before learning about a possible afternoon flight to Kandahar via Tarin Kot.

The cars left the embassy at 12:30, passing through mud and melting snow en route to Kabul Airport. The Air Embassy terminal was more crowded than usual, filled with passengers from previously cancelled flights wanting to make their way to Herat, Mazar-Sharif and Kandahar.

The flight south was quite lovely, especially the early part when we flew over ridge after ridge of newly fallen snow. It is in the midst of winter when central Afghanistan and the Hindu Kush are at their most beautiful.

Spent part of morning reading Richard Holbrooke's *To End a War* about the Balkans. One of his early chapters starts with a quote from *Moby-Dick*: "I am tormented with an everlasting itch for things remote. I love to sail forbidden seas, and land on barbarous coasts."

Returned to office facing mountains of work. General Abrams has now returned to Kandahar while General White just departed for leave in the United States. It is cold but clear at Kandahar Air Field. Walking to the DFAC for dinner I noticed a full moon overhead.

Kandahar, 28 February

Met USAID mission director Ken Yamashita at Valdez—he arrived from Kandahar via Helmand. We both listened to a conference call with USAID administrator Rajiv Shah, ostensibly to thank the Pakistan and Afghanistan missions for their hard work. I've been out of the USAID system for a long time and am no longer familiar with many of the issues involved.

Attended dinner at Lux VIP room along with guests attending citizenship swearing-in ceremony at Kandahar Air Field tomorrow. Most civilian staff also attended, some coming from our PRTs in Kandahar and Zabul. We don't often eat using real plates and real cutlery.

Responded to questions from the embassy in Kabul on Uruzgan police chief Matullah Khan, another problematic strong man who generates controversy and is sometimes mentioned in the media amidst allegations of corruption and human rights abuse.

8

—◇—

MARCH

Gecko, 1 March

Attended naturalization ceremony for thirty American soldiers, including several Marines who flew up from Helmand for the occasion. General Abrams introduced Ken Yamashita as guest of honor, and Ken's remarks briefly described his decision to leave Japan and become an American citizen thirty years ago.

The new Americans come from seventeen countries including several countries in the Caribbean and South Pacific. Two originally came from Canada and one, Aleksey Sasov, said he migrated from Uzbekistan to the United States seven years ago.

The youngest soldier—Cherry Ann Guevarra from Philippines—led everyone in the Pledge of Allegiance. Pius Bannis, an INS officer originally from Haiti, administered the oath. Chaplain Walker offered prayers at the beginning and end of the ceremony.

Lunch with Generals Abrams, Hughes, and Brewer; General White left a few days ago on leave. We covered many issues but ended with a discussion on Matullah Khan, the chief of police in Uruzgan who generates such controversy within both embassy and ISAF circles.

Kandahar, 2 March

Evening barbeque with Third Infantry Division generals, colonels, and sergeants major. It is just cold enough to warm ourselves beside an open fire. I sat next to a dog handler with an apt name—Sergeant Doggett. There is something brave yet terrible about the use of dogs in war, especially dogs trained to sniff out IEDs even if it kills them.

Kandahar, 3 March

Frustrating day. USAID pulled the plug on a community development program in Spin Boldak despite what we see as signs of progress. Elsewhere, the military plans to pull the plug on the Zabul Teacher Training College construction project despite a long succession of promises going back years. That decision breaks the "finish what we started" edict that has been evoked so often here in Kandahar.

Unusually, the senior officer handling development programs was frazzled when we launched into a discussion about the fate of the college in Zabul, probably because he spent most of his day investigating the case of two young Afghan boys inadvertently killed in Uruzgan. Meanwhile, news also arrived that the wash created by a helicopter landing east of Kandahar had blown a heavy gate on top of an American soldier standing nearby, seriously injuring him. Everyone seems to be facing more frustration than usual right now, perhaps magnified by accidents like this.

Exchanged e-mails with Masha Hamilton in Kabul on my draft op-ed on Marilyn McBee, the little American girl who died of polio in June 1954 and is buried in Manzil Bagh. At first I was annoyed about the extra work she set in motion—but I have to acknowledge the latest draft is better than the first one. Brian Bachman, head of the Kandahar PRT, thinks members of his local staff have located the cemetery where Marilyn McBee is buried.

Said goodbye to Dale Kramer, another of our departing civilians who has been in Afghanistan for a long time. He leaves tomorrow, disappointed because he was not extended for a further eight months. He will join his family in Michigan and seems resigned to it. I'm sorry we couldn't work out an extension, especially given his heroic deed in eastern Afghanistan. It is a remarkable story, contained only in the deposition of the officer who commanded the convoy. Dale said that perhaps his purpose in life was to be in eastern Afghanistan on that one day, saving the lives of several others.

I recognized Dale at the weekly all-hands meeting—and also recognized Keith Poe who departs a few days from now. Dale is Jewish, and a former Marine, who used a machine gun to great effect when his convoy was attacked. Keith is a practicing Mennonite from a pacifist tradition who must have been astounded to end up serving in one of the most kinetic districts in southern Afghanistan.

Kandahar, 4 March

Another frustrating day, prompted partly by further discussion with the Kabul embassy on Matullah Khan and General Razziq. It looks like our draft cable offering a perspective on continuing disagreements within the Karzai family as they are being played out in Loya Kandahar isn't going anywhere, either. We may not like some of the people who shape life and politics in southern Afghanistan—but we need to at least know about and understand them.

Met Ambassador Philp from Australia along with John Feakes from the Uruzgan KPRT. Philp discussed Matullah Khan with Ambassador Cunningham in Kabul last night and both Philp and Feakes had just come from a meeting with the senior ISAF officers here in Kandahar where the matter also came up.

The Australian perspective is closer to that of the military in both Kandahar and Uruzgan—while acknowledging deep concerns about Matullah Khan, they are skeptical that the alternative will be any better. We ask Afghans to do it their way—and we shouldn't be surprised when they do exactly that.

Provided brief remarks at conference bringing military staff from across Afghanistan to Kandahar Air Field to discuss base closure. That is their full-time job, to figure out how and when to do it. I evoked the Pushtun proverb about the man who "started to take off his trousers before he reached the river." There is a certain amount of that going on right now, a possibly premature haste to do some things too quickly.

Evening video conference with Fourth Infantry Division in Colorado as they prepare for their Kandahar deployment. Almost every soldier in the Colorado audience served previously in either Iraq or Afghanistan or both. General Abrams was quite brilliant—a forty-five-minute monologue laying out everything there is to know about the security situation in southern Afghanistan.

The views of the senior military leadership on ANSF are fairly optimistic, especially with respect to the leadership qualities of some of its colonels and generals. In their view, it is hard to imagine that the Taliban will defeat Afghan security forces on the battlefield, though governance remains as a central concern. One officer pointed specifically to recent ANSF actions during an attack in Uruzgan near Daikundi. In the end, a force of 150 insurgents was defeated in a battle in which there was no ISAF involvement at all.

Kandahar Airport, 5 March

Passed courtesy copy of e-mail exchange with Kabul to General Abrams, summarizing embassy concerns about both General Razziq in Kandahar and Matullah Khan in Uruzgan.

Noticed new T-shirt for sale at the PX: "Game Over, Afghanistan," capturing to some extent the views of more than a few soldiers in Kandahar as they prepare to depart.

Afternoon meeting with several Afghan business leaders in the VIP room at Kandahar Airport. The first involved Mohammad Yousuf Yousufi from the Kandahar Chamber of Commerce, accompanied by several others representing some of the leading entrepreneurs within the business community in Kandahar.

Asked about the future, four of the five businessmen described themselves as optimistic. A fifth said he is pessimistic, mainly because "70 percent of the rural areas" prefer the Taliban. He added that city dwellers are soft; ultimately, it is their tougher country cousins who will determine Afghanistan's fate.

One businessman wants to import oil from Turkmenistan rather than Iran. Everyone welcomes the recent verdict against those involved in corruption at Kabul Bank: "When justice is delivered, it is good for all of us."

A senior representative from the Babari Company does business with Brazil, India, the United States, and other countries—during a single month, he placed a $1.5 million order for American chickens. Engineer Baqi, another businessman, makes soft drinks (Kool Kola and Kool Dew), bakes cakes, and manufactures PVC pipes, employing more than five hundred Afghans.

The businessmen stated flatly that Afghanistan has changed and will never go back to the 1990s. Yet all of them firmly believe that the U.S. runs the world. When I said it is Afghans who should write their own history, one interrupted to say, "No, other countries will write it for us."

Our next guest was accompanied by an Afghan American friend, James Sidiqi, who was born and raised in Philadelphia. His father was Afghan and his mother was American. As a result, he grew up speaking neither Dari nor Pushto.

One of the businessmen recalled that he was in Kandahar when the Taliban first arrived, adding that they were initially seen as "heroes" at a time when there was a "checkpoint every hundred meters."

He later fled to Quetta with his family on six hours' notice, carrying only suitcases. He studied pharmacy at the University of Baluchistan, developing an affinity for the Baluch. "They are braver than Pushtuns," he said, holding out hope that Baluchistan will one day join Afghanistan, providing a badly needed outlet to the sea.

He returned to Kandahar in the early 2000s "because the arrival of foreign forces gave us hope." "We achieved a lot," he said, adding that "progress is unbelievable." He mentioned that ten years ago the road from Spin Boldak to Kandahar was a dirt track and "everything in Kandahar was destroyed." Having achieved success, he said with some passion, "I don't want to have to run away to Pakistan or Iran ever again."

He mentioned that he has six brothers and seven sisters. One uncle is the Afghan consul in Karachi. The family knew Karzai's father, who he described as a "great man." His own father was a "mullah without a mosque." A liberal Muslim, he became a staunch critic of the Taliban. He especially liked the quote, "If you save one life, it is as if you have saved the universe—and if you destroy one life, it is as if you have destroyed the universe."

His extracurricular activities include a school in his home village, just off Highway One in Panjwai. It has several hundred students, both boys and girls. He also helps support the national cricket team; the Kandahar cricket team that has won two straight national championships; and the Maiwand Heroes, the local soccer team that placed third in Afghanistan's new premier league last fall.

He was scathing about Iranians who employ Afghans to do their dirty work: "They are soft. They don't work hard and are not good farmers." In his words, "The Soviets destroyed my country." He claimed, "When the Soviets came, Afghans left the country; when the Americans came, they returned to it."

He concluded his reflections by making a strong case for at least a limited ISAF presence in Afghanistan after 2014, suggesting that "if even ten American soldiers stay behind, there will be confidence in southern Afghanistan."

Between meetings we wandered around Kandahar Airport. It looks good, Faizi having painted the corridors blue and installed new glass doors. The rose garden in front of the terminal is attractive, as is the bigger garden nearby.

Faizi's large birdcage is now covered with sheets of plastic, protecting the inmates from the cold. The doves, pigeons, parrots, and two brightly colored Australian cockatoos are all still alive. However, Faizi's peacock did not survive the winter.

Kandahar, 6 March

It seems that another name is being added to our "please don't visit" list, one of several Karzai relatives in southern Afghanistan who is simultaneously a cousin, black sheep, and a potential source of conflict within the family. Taken together, all these stories somehow make the Pushto proverb about family solidarity or lack thereof come alive with a vengeance: "Me against my brother; my brother and I against my cousin; me, my brother, and my cousin against the rest of the world."

Brief discussion at early-morning staff meeting on Panjwai. Ahmed Bari, aide to district police chief Sultan Mohammad, stepped on a pressure-plate mine and was killed. Bari was one of the braver police officers—he was known to ride on top of MRAPs, looking for IEDs.

Talked to one of the senior officers about his conversation with Colonel Crider in Qalat. The fate of Zabul Teacher Training College is still up in the air, though a couple of junior officers at Kandahar Air Field want to terminate it. Perhaps it won't be cancelled after all.

Evening video conference with Fourth Infantry Division. I'm amazed at the advance planning built into the U.S. military. I attended the MRX at Fort Stewart a year ago—but in reality had almost no idea what to expect until I arrived.

Kandahar, 7 March

Morning meeting with an American civilian working in Zabul. He mentioned Colonel Ashraf, a Jordanian who heads up the Jordanian effort in southern Afghanistan. His contingent includes two imams focused on village outreach.

Received e-mail stating that the governor whose fingerprints were allegedly traced to an IED has been cleared after all—it was simply a technical mistake. It is frustrating that things went this far, and it could easily have turned into something much more disastrous.

Meanwhile, there is a meeting in Zabul about the most recent fatwa from Pakistan justifying suicide bombing. The Afghans are convinced it is part of ongoing efforts to undermine their country. Always it is the Pakistanis who are viewed as the villains.

Early evening video conference with training group at Muscatatuck, Indiana, preparing for their Afghan assignment. Seventeen students are enrolled and four of them will end up in Kandahar—a huge reduction in size compared to the class I attended last summer. I may have alarmed them with my comments on our rapidly diminishing presence in southern Afghanistan.

Movie night—about two-thirds of our civilians at Kandahar Air Field attended. Both movies were depressing, the first (*Buzkashi Boys*) about the foiled dreams of a street urchin and blacksmith's son in Kabul, the second (*Mohtarama*) a documentary in black and white on women's issues in Afghanistan. One line will stay with me for a long time: "I eat poison and pretend that it is sugar."

Met Charles Yepa from KPRT as he prepares to depart. A Native American from New Mexico, he retired from the military last year after thirty-seven years of service. He met the senior General Abrams often in Vietnam, flying down occasionally as a courier from Pleiku.

The flags outside the command center were flying at half-mast as I headed to bed. Sergeant Rasool said it was a suicide and that the remains arrived at Kandahar Air Field two hours ago.

Kandahar, 8 March

Regular Friday lunch with the generals. My contribution included recent reporting cables and reflections on statements made by the district governor in

Chora (Uruzgan) that any Taliban found with weapons should be shot. Partly this reflects disillusionment with the Afghan judicial system. And partly it reflects dismay at the death of the governor's friend, the informal mayor of Chora, who was recently killed by an IED.

Attended ramp ceremony for a soldier from Ohio, a transportation specialist who shot himself in his room yesterday. He was born in August 1990. Contrary to what I thought, he was assigned to Kandahar Air Field, not one of the forward bases farther afield.

It is a dusty day in Kandahar—everything is covered in brown and the haze makes it impossible to see even the nearby mountains. Hundreds of people paid their respects, including soldiers and airmen from Romania, Britain, Belgium, Slovenia, and the United States.

I joined the senior officers to watch the dust-colored MRAP bearing the coffin drive slowly toward the ramp. The chaplain read from Psalms, a recorded piper played "Amazing Grace," and then the flag-draped silver box was borne toward the C-130, first through lines of enlisted men and then officers, everyone saluting this sad, final journey.

One young soldier was sobbing even as he shouldered his unbearable load. While this was happening two Belgian F-16s landed and a small dust devil whipped across the tarmac before disappearing into nothingness.

Following the evening briefing, a senior officer invited me to his office to see a chilling video taking from an observation balloon—the treatment of a captured Taliban meted out by members of the Afghan local police in Panjwai as an act of revenge. The government of Afghanistan is doing the right thing by investigating—but we're not yet sure how far the investigation will go.

Kajaki Dam, 9 March

Morning flight to Kajaki Dam on a contracted Russian helicopter. General Abrams was dubious about me taking this flight—he doesn't much like flying, especially in a Russian helicopter where there is no second helicopter in case something goes wrong. This was a tour for journalists including Shashank Bengali from the *Los Angeles Times*. The point was to see if progress is finally being made on this never-ending project that started when USAID installed the first two power turbines in 1975, just before Afghanistan started its death spiral. The bearded senior Afghan engineer who showed us around has been in place since the very beginning.

Drove to the top of the dam among a profusion of spring flowers—yellow, red, and purple. The view toward the reservoir was beautiful, the sun sparkling off the large expanse of deep blue water reflecting toward the clear blue sky above. Remarkably, even pine trees grow at Kajaki.

Met a couple of Scotsmen, one wearing a small blue and white Scottish flag on his body armor. One American has been in Afghanistan four years— and said Kajaki was his favorite place. The contractor Black & Veatch employs several young Afghans. They seem very Western, and at least a couple of them have joined yet another popular Afghan pastime—bodybuilding.

Kandahar, 11 March

Weekly call with Kabul dominated by a discussion of some of President Karzai's recent public statements, including the suggestion that the Taliban and the U.S. share similar goals and are both working together to destabilize Afghanistan. Increasingly, I appreciate a comment made by a friend at the United States Institute of Peace in Washington, DC, at the beginning of this assignment that we have somehow managed to become enablers in an increasingly dysfunctional relationship.

In other news, sixteen of the top twenty scores in Afghanistan's annual high school examination were registered by students from Daikundi. Other Afghans are shocked and claim fraud, believing that such things can't happen in a "backward" province that is mostly populated by Hazaras.

Kandahar, 12 March

Woke up to news of a fallen angel—a Black Hawk went down last night making its final turn a few hundred yards from Kandahar Air Field. Five people were killed, including the pilot, a West Point captain named Sara Knutson who was twenty-seven. Perhaps weather was a factor. The helicopter was completely burned, leaving only a small part of the tail. Attended ramp ceremony at 11:00 p.m., exactly twenty-four hours after the crash and a few hours after the last of the relatives in the U.S. had been notified. General Dunford came down from Kabul, joining General Abrams for the ceremony.

The crowd was very quiet and subdued throughout the fifteen-minute ceremony, though before and after we heard the sound of planes as well as a Chinook helicopter flying loudly overhead. The MRAPs bearing the coffins drove slowly out of the gloom, led by two soldiers and flashing yellow lights.

These events are always sad—and always result in moments of reflection afterward. As Bonnie said as we drove home through the dark, family members thousands of miles away have just gotten the news their loved one has died and are just now realizing their own lives have been changed utterly, completely, and forever.

Rob Sipe called just before midnight from Uruzgan to report an unsuccessful VBIED suicide attack earlier in the evening at an Afghan National

Army camp in Tarin Kot. Although the bomb didn't explode, the man driving the truck jumped out and escaped. Now everyone in Uruzgan is on lockdown until he is found.

Kandahar, 13 March

A disappointing day—the NATO SCR who planned to arrive from Kabul cancelled his trip to Kandahar and Uruzgan. Given events in Uruzgan last night, we could not have left the base in any case. The story about the truck laden with bombs turned out to be wrong. But the threat remains and our trip is off because of it.

Said farewell to two departing staff—one served at Arghandab, the other in Maiwand. Based on their comments, Arghandab has improved while Maiwand remains fragile. What amazes me is the extent to which our people pour their heart and soul into these small and isolated places.

Also said farewell to Paul McEarchern, the Australian liaison officer at Kandahar Air Field who is leaving to become DCM in Dublin. His successor, Rohan Titus, originally from Sri Lanka, just arrived.

Received e-mail from Ambassador Cunningham expressing grave concern about Karzai's recent statements linking the Taliban and the U.S., and declaring that both want his government to fail. Some think Karzai is posturing, perhaps wanting to avoid the same fate as Najibullah who became increasingly nationalistic in the final stages of Soviet rule. Or perhaps the stakes in his own mind are even higher as he tries to ensure a better place in Afghan history.

Haji Dastageeri's statements, as quoted in today's *New York Times,* say it all: "This is political talk. These kind of remarks being made by Karzai make people worry about the future of Afghanistan. . . . People are still hopeful for a better future in Afghanistan, but we need the world community, and we are a fragile country and vulnerable. So the relationship that has been built with the world community should not be broken."

Kandahar, 14 March

Morning briefing followed by lunch with visiting think-tank groups—Michael O'Hanlon (Brookings Institution), Anthony Cordesman (Center for Strategic and International Studies), Michele Flournoy (Center for a New American Security), Stephen Biddle (George Washington University), and former ambassador to Afghanistan Ron Neumann (American Academy of Diplomacy). The downsizing of our Army in Afghanistan is well under way—but the steady flow of visitors from Washington continues unabated.

The presentation by General Abrams went fine. He has increasing confidence in the ANSF and thinks the so-called Panjwai uprising is the start of something important. He said the same thing in a Pentagon press briefing yesterday, leading to a sudden spate of articles about the current situation in southern Afghanistan.

After the evening CUA Chris Hughes talked about his day with provincial police chiefs. The Afghan visitors were impressed with the command center including the video screens—but even more impressed with the forensics, including the ability to identify bomb-makers by their saliva and their fingerprints.

Managed to do laundry one day ahead of schedule. While waiting for my clothes to dry, talked briefly with an airplane mechanic who owns fourteen properties in Key West, Orlando and Rome, Georgia. He is a plumber and says he makes more money as a plumber than he does fixing planes.

Gecko, 15 March

Attended noon memorial ceremony for five soldiers aboard Black Hat 14 killed earlier this week while on a training mission just outside Kandahar Air Field. This is different from a ramp ceremony but no less moving. Large photos of each soldier were on display, placed just above their boots, rifles, and night vision–equipped flight helmets: Captain Sara Knutson, Chief Warrant Officer Bryan Henderson, Staff Sergeant Marc Scialdo, Staff Sergeant Steven Blass, and Specialist Zachary Shannon.

Memories from comrades were especially poignant. One officer remembered that Captain Knutson always smiled. He said he had given the framed wedding photo she always kept on her desk to her husband, also a helicopter pilot stationed at Kandahar Air Field, just before he departed to accompany her remains home.

Another soldier recalled the cookout he shared with the Blass family including their young son Hayden in Georgia, just before the two of them deployed. Yet another soldier mentioned he met Specialist Zachary Shannon's parents prior to departing. Zachary, age twenty-one, was their youngest son, and they were reluctant to see him leave for Afghanistan. As he remembered it, he assured the family he would look after Zach while in Kandahar, promising that their son would make it home alive.

The last roll call followed by the firing of the volley and the sounding of taps were the saddest moments of all. Five names were called out followed by five different variants of "He has left us, sir," "She is no longer with us."

I sat in the front row and when I finally looked back at the large hangar behind me all I could see was a sea of green uniforms. Almost everyone from the Third Combat Aviation Brigade, Task Force Falcon, must have been there on this heartbreaking day.

Kandahar Airport, 16 March

Morning meeting with a tribal leader from Panjwai at Kandahar Airport. We mostly talked about the Panjwai uprising. He thinks it is a real movement, precipitated by locals who can no longer tolerate the behavior of the Taliban. He also thinks it needs continued ANSF support to succeed.

As the meeting ended, our distinguished visitor suddenly turned to me and said, "Afghanistan needs change." A long-time supporter of the Karzai family (and before that a mujahideen commander and then a Taliban supporter), I took his brief comment to mean the next Afghan president should not be a Karzai. As best I can tell he will likely support Zalmay Khalilzad or Nangahar governor Sherzai, both of whom he said would be good for Kandahar.

Morning MRAP to governor's palace in Kandahar. We started with a press conference to launch the My Afghan Library program with a selection of high-quality books in Pushto and Dari for children. About fifteen journalists showed up. The article on Marilyn McBee in Pushto has just been published in two local newspapers.

Afterward we walked to Governor Wesa's office. He was scathing in his criticism of one of our local development projects. In his view, we are not communicating enough.

Excruciatingly, the day ended with another helicopter crash, this one near FOB Walton. It was a small, two-person helicopter and probably went down for mechanical reasons. One crew member is dead and the other, now in ICU, is not expected to survive. I hate it when flags at Kandahar Air Field fly at half-mast.

Dubai, St. Patrick's Day, 17 March

St. Patrick's Day. Morning country team with Kabul via video conference followed by all-hands meetings at Kandahar Air Field. I then headed to the flight line for the two-hour journey to Dubai.

The Fly Dubai captain was a woman from Europe and the cabin crew included a young man from South Africa. It is always a relief to take off toward the south, first crossing the Registan Desert and then heading over Iran. Snow still persists on some of the peaks in southern Iran.

Robert Smith and Bonnie Weaver were both on the same flight from Kandahar, each heading in their different directions. I still don't know what to make of the story that Robert told as we waited to depart: A few days ago, Afghans and Americans were eating together at KPRT. One of the American females mentioned that it must be uncomfortable to wear a burka. Immediately the Afghan she was talking to launched into a bitter tirade: "The Koran requires it." "Westerners have forced their women to work." "All of you are going to hell. That's what it says in the Koran."

Singapore, 18 March

All day in Singapore, time enough for a free two-hour city tour. The guide was young and very proud of her country and why not? As she described it, almost everyone in Singapore owns an apartment and almost everyone looking for a job finds one.

Christchurch, 19 March

Landed at Christchurch by the middle of the morning, even as Fiona was arriving from Ulaanbaatar.

Mount Cook, 20 March

Spent day in and around Mount Cook. Afghanistan is never far away. This time I noticed several New Zealand Army magazines lying around the restaurant, almost all of them featuring stories about New Zealand's military deployment in Afghanistan.

Lake Hawea, 21 March

Spent part of evening at Lake Hawea Hotel attempting to access Internet. The music included Otis Redding's "Sitting on the Dock of the Bay," very much capturing my mood right now.

Dunedin, 25 March

Drove from Roxborough to Dunedin before ending up at Portobello on the Otago Peninsula. In a few days all this will seem like a distant dream.

Milford Sound, 28 March

Finished William Dalrymple's *Return of a King* about Shah Shuja, Dost Mohammad, and the First Afghan War. He draws certain analogies with recent events in Afghanistan, some of them forced. Shikarpur figures in several places and Dalrymple also includes excerpts from Mirza Ata Mohammad's *Son of Battles,* a nineteenth-century work commissioned by E. B. Eastwick, the first English collector posted to Shikarpur, my childhood home. According to Mirza, "Telling the truth is bitter." As he also tells it, "The joys and griefs of this fleeting faithless world do not last. . . . The world is a dream. However you imagine it, it passes away until you pass away yourself."

9

❖

APRIL

Christchurch, 3 April

Breakfast with Fiona and then we together headed for the airport. She is returning to Ulaanbaatar via Auckland while I take Singapore Airlines to Dubai.
Watched *Zero Dark Thirty* en route. It was unexpectedly disappointing—the
feel of many of the scenes ostensibly set in Pakistan simply doesn't ring true.

Kandahar, 4 April

Arrived in Singapore late and then boarded midnight Singapore Airlines flight
to Dubai. Everything seemed to take a long time, especially the passport line—
but I did catch my Fly Dubai plane to Bastion and then Kandahar. Almost
everyone got out at Bastion, including a strong Danish contingent.

It is hard to believe that I am back in Kandahar, especially considering the
places we've been during the past two weeks. I missed the rain that is a blessing
in southern Afghanistan. The hot season hasn't yet arrived. I hardly had time
to catch my breath before reading e-mails on four different accounts and then
starting the first round of endless meetings.

Kandahar, 5 April

Noon lunch with the generals. Three Taliban shadow governors were killed on
Easter Sunday, including the shadow governors of Panjwai and Maruuf. The
Panjwai shadow governor was killed by a grenade thrown by an Army Ranger
as the governor tried to escape his compound while the Maruuf shadow governor died in an ambush organized entirely by Afghan security forces.

Rumor has it that a leading Taliban was attending the funeral for the
shadow governor from Panjwai when he heard about the death of his shadow

governor in Maruuf—he reportedly responded by angrily throwing his cell phone on the floor. From a Taliban perspective, the 2013 fighting season is not starting well. Many insurgents arriving this spring seem young and inexperienced. This year's poppy harvest is about to begin.

I am again struck by the guarded optimism of General Abrams—or, as he describes it, his preference for seeing the glass as half full. Some media accounts suggest that Taliban setbacks are adding to internal dissension in Quetta and Kandahar, and there are some signs that Taliban leaders are fearful of spies within their ranks.

Attended evening Purple Heart ceremony for Zachary Gore, badly injured by an IED near Shah Wali Kot earlier today. Two other soldiers were also wounded, though much less seriously. General Abrams praised the medical care at Kandahar Air Field, adding that we are "lucky" not to be attending a ramp ceremony tonight.

Qalat (Zabul), 6 April

Morning flight by Embassy Air to Zabul for book distribution at local school under the My Afghan Library program, followed by press conference and meeting with Governor Naseri. Two Afghan journalists from Kabul are accompanying us as part of a larger initiative organized weeks ago by the Public Affairs office in Kabul to distribute books, not only in southern Afghanistan, but in other parts of the country as well. The idea is to give the Afghan media a better sense for what is happening in the remoter regions of their own country. We went over plans yesterday, just after my return to Kandahar. But even before leaving for New Zealand, I had told Kelly Hunt who liaised with Kabul in organizing this trip that I would participate should this program be extended to include Zabul or anywhere else in southern Afghanistan.

While waiting for the helicopter I talked with Nasemi, who has served as my translator since December. He mentioned a nephew living in New Zealand with a wife and baby; the nephew and his family are having a hard time. Nasemi himself has never married though his own family has talked about arranging a marriage for him.

I said migrants move for the sake of their children, not themselves—it can be very difficult. We all live for our children, and it is the sacrifices made by those before us that make our own lives possible. Having been a refugee, he agreed completely. He added that his nephew had served as a translator for the U.S. Army but left after an IED killed a colleague. Nasemi supports several relatives in Kabul, New Zealand, and the United States.

Kelly was enthusiastic about the program in front of us. "This will be a great day," she said. "I really look forward to this event. It is going to be wonderful. You are going to like it a lot." She mentioned excitement about her next job in Washington. Anne Smedinghoff, a public affairs colleague from Kabul, said she arrived in Afghanistan in July last year—this was her first trip to Kandahar.

Met on arrival by Tim Bashor and his team. We were early so we sat in the PRT *shura* room for about half an hour, discussing the upcoming day as well as recent events in Zabul. He was optimistic, both about developments in recent weeks and the direction that Zabul seems to be going, even as ISAF begins to disengage.

The Zabul PRT has many empty spaces and most containers have by now been removed. The memorial stones have also been taken down.

We then put on our gear, met our military protection detail, had a final equipment check, and left by the south gate just before 11:00 a.m. As I walked out of the gate, I noticed a small sedan a few feet in front of me driven by an Afghan. He had attempted to park just outside the PRT but was being turned away, even as we stepped out of the compound.

This was a new exit for me—in every other visit to Zabul I have departed out the north gate, crossing the road to the governor's office and residence. I noticed two concrete guard towers on each side of our gate. The street in front of us was almost empty with almost no traffic and no people. Tim told me later that civilians in the Zabul PRT took this route from time to time, most often on foot—to visit the hospital, the agricultural office, the school for girls, and the school for boys, all of which have received ISAF assistance over many years. Today's destination was meant to be the school for boys, the government building closest to the PRT.

Most of the soldiers protecting us are in their last weeks and even days in Afghanistan. For some reason we took a left turn rather than a right turn when we left the PRT, heading toward the agricultural office about a hundred yards away, an alternative and less-direct back route to the school for boys that Tim said had on some occasions been used before. But this time the small metal door leading from the courtyard of the government agricultural office to the school was locked. There was a discussion among the Afghan soldiers guarding it and we were then asked to turn back.

Retracing our steps, we walked in front of the south gate for a second time, approaching the school from a different direction. A civilian car trailed by a police pickup truck raced by. I remember a policeman in the back of the truck shouting and pointing wildly.

And then there was an explosion.

I was walking at the front of the group along with Tim. We both fell immediately to the ground and then we both rolled into a shallow concrete-lined drainage ditch nearby. My first thought was that we faced a complex attack—what would happen if numbers of Taliban also made an appearance to attack the camp? I thought about my life as I prepared to die. I wondered what my family would be told.

I was told later that there was a second bomb—one was a VBIED suicide bomber about ten or fifteen yards from where I walked, the other an IED placed against the wall of the camp, near the front gate.

I was told later that the car I saw turned away as I left the PRT a few minutes before was driven by the suicide bomber. It is hard to understand why he didn't explode his vehicle when he saw me emerge from the PRT, even as he was being asked by the American soldiers not to park in front of the PRT.

The first minutes seemed very confused. When it became clear that there would be no further attack the soldiers asked Tim and me to return the short distance to the safety of the PRT. Three wounded soldiers were lying near the entrance. I made my way back inside with Tim, all the while trying to account for members of our party.

Kelly and Anne came by in stretchers looking very badly hurt as they were being taken by first responders to the small first aid station set up within the PRT, perhaps fifty yards from the south entrance—I briefly held each of their hands and said to hold on, that they would make it. Tim helped one of the American soldiers carry one of the stretchers to the first aid station. I wish I could say I put my first aid training into practice—but I did not. Others at the PRT were already moving into action and I felt as useless as I have ever felt in my life. There was a lot of blood on the floor. Nasemi was lying on the floor dead, his face gray, the lower part of both legs blown off. At first I did not recognize him, perhaps because I did not want to. Two American soldiers were also lying on the ground, already dead.

Eventually Kelly and Anne were taken to the helicopters, first to medical facilities at nearby Apache and then to Kandahar Air Field. Again, I held their hands for the short distance from the first aid station to the waiting helicopters. Both Kelly and Anne were unconscious and neither could hear me. Again, I urged them to hold on and somehow make it to Apache, where doctors were already waiting for them.

Shortly later a soldier from the PRT command center walked by and told me that both my colleagues were alive when they reached Apache, leaving me relieved and somehow happy, even elated. I do not know how long it was after that but another soldier then returned to where I was sitting beside the helicopter landing zone, this time to say that I was wanted at the PRT command center—there was something that I needed to know. There I was told that Anne had died despite the best efforts of the medical people at Apache to save her life, devastating news that made the rest of the day that much harder to bear.

Later I was told that another wounded American soldier died while being taken to Apache by MRAP. Kelly looked like the one least likely to survive. But she is hanging on despite severe head injuries.

Tim and I talked for a time beside the helicopter landing zone. Steve Overman from the Zabul PRT and Abbas Kamwand from Kabul were lucid but they too were medevaced to Apache and then to Kandahar Air Field. There was a long gaping wound down Abbas' thigh, visible through his torn trousers even as he walked around to look after others. Both the Afghan journalists from Kabul survived.

Lieutenant Colonel Kraft, commander of the PRT, had been out on another mission when we arrived; he now returned by MRAP, joining me briefly at the helicopter landing zone. Looking toward the flight line, he said I would remember this day for the rest of my life, that it would be impossible to ever forget it. He also said that no matter what we thought, "The enemy always has a vote."

I talked to one of the American soldiers present at the scene, an experienced Afghan hand named Al Dozier. He had a bandage on his leg. He said he stepped in front of the car as he emerged out of the PRT gate, lifting a hand to stop it. It exploded in front of his face but it was those in the back and to the side who took most of the blast.

Tim said body parts from the suicide bomber were strewn across the road. "Nothing but meat along with a couple of bones," he said.

Colonel Jim Crider, commander of ISAF troops in Zabul, arrived from FOB Davis by helicopter to start his preliminary investigation. Four FBI agents will fly down from Kabul in the evening.

The casualty count for the day was three U.S. soldiers dead, Nasemi dead, FSO Anne Smedinghoff dead, an Afghan doctor who happened to be walking by dead. Ten others were wounded, Kelly critically.

At 3:00 p.m. the Embassy Air helicopter came back for me as scheduled— our party had started off in the morning with such promise and now I returned home entirely alone, the saddest and loneliest flight I have ever made.

The crew chief jumped out of the helicopter and looked at the flight manifest with its several names when he arrived. He then looked at me and asked, "Is that it? Are you the only one?"

The flight back to Kandahar Air Field seemed longer than usual. Occasionally I looked out the window at the dusty landscape below; at the several Romanian military outposts looking out over Highway One connecting

Kabul with Kandahar, a thin ribbon of asphalt stretching across an ocean of brown; at the barren mountains variously colored brown, red, and black; at the occasional green fields and gray gravel river beds below. I looked across toward the empty space where Anne had been sitting a few hours earlier, on our flight to Zabul. I wished that I had taken a photograph then, I wished that she were sitting there now, I wished that she were still alive.

I wanted to accompany Nasemi's body back to Kandahar Air Field in one of the Black Hawks—but Army protocol did not allow it. I can never forget that last glimpse of Nasemi as the sheet was pulled back for me to make the identification. His face was gray, his arm and hand frozen above his forehead in an impossible effort to somehow deflect the explosion. I put my hand on his forehead, felt the stubble on his face—and said that I was sorry.

Bonnie was waiting for me on the flight line when I returned to Kandahar Air Field. Years ago she had witnessed a deadly explosion in Baghdad that damaged her ear drums. We made our way together to the hospital, eventually meeting Steve and Abbas who were being treated for their wounds. Masha, head of Public Affairs at the embassy in Kabul, had already arrived.

Eventually Kelly reached Kandahar Air Field in a helicopter ambulance, already in an induced coma. Secretary Kerry called Anne's parents to tell them the devastating news. I called Kelly's father and then handed the phone to Dr. Zinder, head of the hospital, to give Kelly's father his prognosis. What a difficult conversation.

I must have returned to Kandahar Air Field by mid-afternoon though it seemed that I was away for much longer. I talked to Diane Latham, our new RSO who had met me when I first arrived from Zabul. She said she had desperately wanted to fly up to Zabul so that I did not have to fly back alone—but her name was not on the flight manifest and it was too late to make any changes. I also talked to David Donahue twice, trying to convey something of what happened. General Abrams called to ask about my welfare. Sergeant Rasool gave me a brief hug. Later in the evening I talked with Ambassador Cunningham and Ambassador Llorens, another former ambassador who is part of the senior embassy team. I answered dozens of e-mails, most of them asking for updates, some of them asking for additional details, all of them expressing deep concern.

Everyone is devastated at the personal costs that at this point seem far too high. I was ready for it, I almost expected it—but were something like this to ever happen, I did not expect to be among the survivors. This was a day I visualized months ago—but with a different outcome as far as my own life is concerned.

I finally returned to the office late, first calling Fiona and Catriona (it is late in Mongolia and they must have been sleeping), then Mom and Dad in

Macon, and finally Iain in Texas and Cameron in Georgia. They were surprised and relieved.

For my parents especially this might have been the call they have been
dreading—it so easily could have been a call from the secretary of state delivering devastating news to them. Somehow and for reasons I can't begin to understand I survived almost unscathed.

Masha feels guilty about organizing this outreach program. I could easily
move in that direction too—Did I have a premonition? Should I have done
something completely out of character and somehow called the whole thing
off? Realistically, whatever I felt this morning when I left Kandahar Air Field
was the same thing that I have always felt whenever I have left the safety of the
barbed wire or the cement T-walls on numerous other occasions. This is part of
my service in Afghanistan, this is what I had prepared to do, this is part of the
risk that comes with this job. This beautiful morning that I am just now taking
in with all its wonder and splendor might very possibly be my last.

I remember Kelly's sunny smile in the morning as we waited on the tarmac;
she had been so enthusiastic about what the day ahead might hold for all of us.

I have this archaic and old-fashioned sense of duty that makes me do these
things though I sometimes don't know why. I volunteered and knew at the
outset that I would accept whatever happened.

When I first talked with Masha and Ambassador Cunningham, my first
words were, "I'm sorry. I did not take care of our people."

As I went to bed the media reporting started to appear on the Internet,
much of it wrong, including the statement that it was a convoy that had been
attacked. Governor Naseri's convoy did pass by just before the explosion and
early accounts suggest he was the target. I'm not so sure.

The postmortem of what happened will surely focus on the left turn made
at the start of our walk—and the fact that we were on an open street that had
not been closed off to traffic. It does seem to have been targeted, not random.

General Abrams said as I was leaving the office that the intent might
have been to kill a lot of people when the Afghans and the Americans walked
together to the school ceremony that never happened. The fact that we were
stretched out along the road rather than clumped together might have made
a difference.

Kandahar, 7 April

Participated in weekly embassy country team by video. I provided a quick
summary of yesterday's events. Went directly from there to our weekly stand-
up meeting, again focusing on what happened in Zabul. These were some of
the hardest remarks I have ever given.

Spent an hour with three FBI agents who are investigating the attack. I tried to recall what happened though not everything remains clear. Afterward, all three agents said I was being too hard on myself—I could not have prevented what happened and I should stop blaming myself.

Visited Kelly in the Kandahar Air Field hospital. She is still unconscious but there is hope she may yet pull through. One main concern is bleeding and pressure on the brain. Images from an ICU are never pretty—wires, machines, and tubes everywhere.

Our guests from Kabul arrived in the afternoon—Ambassadors Cunningham, Llorens, and McFarland and most of the Public Affairs section. We walked together to the ramp ceremony with its five metal boxes—Anne, Nasemi, Sergeant Ward, Sergeant Santos, Corporal Robles-Santa, all killed yesterday.

The PA system was off so I didn't hear much of what was said. I did make out the Third Infantry Division band playing "Amazing Grace" as well as "Day Is Done," one high note quivering briefly as if in sadness. I appreciate the solemnity of these ceremonies, the opportunity for moments of quiet reflection.

Afterward boarded C-17 carrying the five coffins and also ferrying dozens of soldiers to Bagram where we are changing planes en route to Germany and then Dover.

Remarkably, Kelly is now at the hospital in Bagram en route to Germany. I looked in on her at Kandahar Air Field before she departed—she is still unconscious but we are hopeful. Akemi Tinder is travelling with her. All of us so much want Kelly to live.

Bagram/Frankfurt/Dover, 8 April

The flight from Kandahar to Bagram was completely full. Nahdreh Lee and some of her RC-East staff met us on arrival—she gave me a small hug, we had a sandwich, and then I tried to catch a few moments of sleep before continuing on the worst journey of my life.

I am travelling with David Snepp from the Public Affairs office in Kabul, the two of us charged with escorting the civilian bodies home.

While looking in on Kelly at the Bagram hospital, we heard a baby crying—a strange sound in a military facility. I asked about it and was told, "That is not a good story." It must be connected with an air strike in the east yesterday that killed several insurgents—but also left several children dead or wounded. What a bloodletting and for so many years; surely there will somehow be a way to bring it to an end.

We are flying to Germany and then Dover on another C-17. There was an early-morning ramp ceremony at Bagram for another civilian killed somewhere in the east. The ceremony was similar to the one held earlier today in Kandahar though in this case the small Army brass band played "Abide with Me" rather than "Amazing Grace."

There are now nine ice-filled metal boxes from three different regions of Afghanistan in our aircraft making its way to Europe, the pitiful remains of the day from an especially brutal twenty-four hours.

Right now I am sitting next to the broken bodies of Anne and Nasemi and seven others and I can't help but think that there should be a tenth flag-draped box for me. Five of us from Kabul and Kandahar arrived in Zabul on Saturday morning to join our civilian colleagues for a program there—of those five, Anne and Nasemi are dead, Kelly is critically injured and her life hangs in the balance, and Abbas will be in the hospital for a long time. I am walking, though sore and bruised—and at this point I am having a hard time understanding how and why I survived at all.

It is a seven-and-a-half-hour flight and it is now very cold. I am sleeping fitfully, sometimes on the floor beside the coffins, sometimes on the improvised canvas seats that line each side of this C-17. Right now we are over the Black Sea, approaching Europe.

I briefly talked to the two pilots in the cockpit. Both are former ROTC cadets—one from the University of Oregon, the other from Brigham Young University. Both are stationed at McChord Air Force Base in Washington State.

They seem very young, slightly older than Iain. I mentioned his ROTC experience and the fact that he is now an Air Force second lieutenant at Goodfellow in Texas. I also mentioned that Cameron is studying aeronautical engineering at Georgia Tech.

We arrived at Ramstein Air Base in the morning and were met by the chaplain. The base commander also arrived along with our consul general in Frankfurt who previously spent two years as management officer in Kabul.

I took a quick shower and tried to prepare myself for what lies ahead. There was another small ceremony, this time inside the plane. This was a simple memorial moment, a short prayer followed by time for brief reflection. Standing and then kneeling next to where Anne and Nasemi lie, it is hard not to cry.

The new flight crew is as engaging as the last one. They love their work and fly all over the world—Africa, Asia, even several trips to Kandahar Air Field. All of them are former ROTC. They said that when they carry fallen heroes home, they try to learn something about them. They realize that news about the death of Anne, only twenty-five and with such a brilliant future, is by now making its way around the world.

Very kindly the pilots offered David and me their bunk beds behind the cockpit for the rest of this flight. "We appreciate the fact that you survived this attack and we know that you will have a lot to do when you arrive." This was an unexpected but wonderful gesture, giving me a few hours' sleep, albeit fitfully.

Early in the journey from Germany we crossed Scotland and then headed for Islay and Jura where George Orwell wrote *1984*. The clouds lifted and I could make out almost every feature of Islay, including Bruichladdich and Port Charlotte where Iain, Cameron, and Catriona used to go to school.

It will be hard to meet Anne's family, especially when I increasingly realize there were a thousand other ways this event might have unfolded, all of which might have given Anne, Nasemi, and the three soldiers who now lie here in front of me a better outcome.

If only the weather had been bad and we had been unable to fly. If only we had taken vehicles and not walked. If only we had turned right rather than left. If only we had departed a few minutes earlier.

When the bombs exploded, it was only a matter of seconds and yards—if only I had walked slower or faster, if only I had changed places and been in the back or middle rather than at the front of our small group. But at this point nothing, absolutely nothing, can be changed.

I think of our motivations also. Nasemi must have had his fears in working on the frontlines of Afghanistan—yet he was here, partly to support a large extended family. In less than four months we had formed a bond of appreciation and trust, occasionally discussing amongst ourselves what we heard and thought about Afghanistan.

I did not know Anne but am amazed to learn something of her past, including that she joined the Foreign Service immediately after college, almost certainly the youngest in her A-100 class. She took on tough assignments, wanted to see the world, wanted to make a difference, wanted to be involved.

For my part I somehow have this life-long call to service of some kind, something that stands way outside our involvement in Afghanistan. I can question it, I can shake my head, I can acknowledge big mistakes. But my calling isn't to this particular cause—rather it is to my country as it struggles, all too often incompetently, to make its way in a world where multiple decisions, some of them contradictory, shape future consequences.

I don't believe in utopias. I will always think that ultimately human nature, which doesn't much change, will trump ideology, no matter how enlightened and idealistic the cause. We live in the mud, not on the mountain top—though sometimes the clouds briefly lift and we can somehow see that mountain top in ways that amaze and astonish us.

Our window on the universe is small when set against the backdrop of eternity. We don't have much time. We do what we can, at our best offering small examples of sacrifice and tiny tokens of love in the brief moments allotted to us, moments that are precarious and can abruptly end at any time. Sometimes, if we are lucky, we can briefly redeem time.

"My grace is sufficient." "As the day, so shall your strength be." We will be landing at Dover shortly and I hope this parental advice that I have often heard will somehow prove accurate or at least provide something to cling to in the hours ahead.

One of the pilots told David that when asking for clearance to land at Dover, he announced that he was carrying nine American heroes home from Afghanistan. Our plane was granted clearance immediately with these words from the control tower: "Cleared for landing. American heroes coming home."

This is the longest day of my life. It started at 1:00 a.m. in Bagram—and it continues even now, more than twenty-four later, back in the United States.

We arrived at Dover where my chief of staff Phil Russell, now on leave in the United States, was waiting to greet me. We then drove to a hotel to change before returning to the base. This time we met Anne's family—Dad Tom, Mom Mary, and the youngest daughter, a sophomore at Dickinson College in Pennsylvania. It was a sad meeting but they wanted specific details from that horrific Saturday and I provided them. We then left for the tarmac for the heartbreaking ceremony there.

Afterward David and I spent a couple of hours at Fisher House where military family members stay for events like this. We heard an extended family being comforted and counseled on what to expect. I believe their brother, husband, or son was part of our force protection unit at Zabul, making everything I observe even harder for me to bear.

Then we went to the tarmac again, this time to receive Nasemi's remains. Under Secretary Patrick Kennedy and other senior State officials attended both ceremonies.

Nasemi's family is still in New Jersey. The representative from the company that hired Nasemi told me that he did not list any next of kin, though he was close to his parents who just arrived in the U.S. as refugees. They don't speak much English and perhaps he thought they couldn't handle such devastating news.

Some insurance may help. But lack of a continuous income will be harder for nephews and nieces in the U.S., Kabul, and Auckland who have come to rely on Nasemi for support—not actual nephews and nieces, but rather the children of cousins, which is still a close connection in Afghanistan.

The representative said his company employs two thousand translators across Afghanistan. Most are American citizens like Nasemi. He attends several such events at Dover each year.

At times throughout the day the thought kept recurring as these scenes unfolded, especially on the tarmac—this is what I have been anticipating for some time or at least was prepared to accept when I signed on for Afghanistan. But in my imagination it wasn't me being a witness to such events, it was rather myself as the object of them, my own extended family having gathered on this somber day as participants and witnesses in this sad drama marking my final trip home.

The day ended at dinner with Anne's family at the hotel where we are staying. These two hours were a combination of tears and laughter, especially focusing on Anne's final months in Afghanistan.

Anne's father is a highly successful lawyer in Chicago and her mother has raised several children well. The family has strong ties to their church and community, bedrocks of this country and a foundation that I hope will never slip away.

Dover/Washington, DC, 9 April

Up at 4:30 a.m. on account of jet lag—not much sleep. Talked to Jesse Alvarado by phone to discuss latest Kabul close-out discussions. We both agree—despite the events on Saturday, we can't immediately run away; there was a purpose in our drawdown and there is still work to do, however difficult and even onerous the task ahead.

Breakfast with Anne's family. I wish so much I could turn back the clock, that the trip to Zabul had never happened.

Drove to Washington and met with people at Afghan desk—Jim DeHart and Tim Wilder who served for a year in Uruzgan. Tim mentioned continuing reports of disagreements within the Taliban but said peace talks are getting nowhere.

After so many people had urged it, talked to Susan Welsby from the State medical unit. Mostly I wanted to tell the story of what happened on Saturday without being "there" for anyone else, simply as an ugly narrative that I witnessed and can never forget. Again I have this overwhelming desire to rewind the tape and stop it from going forward.

Met my parents for dinner hosted by Steve and Zeba Rasmussen, friends of many years, going back to our shared childhood in Pakistan; much later, Steve was best man at my Scottish wedding. My parents flew up from Atlanta along with my sister Nancy. Richard Adams, another long-time friend and former

FSO, also joined us along with his wife Sadia. He said he has suffered from PTSD for years and is concerned I may become a candidate for it.

I keep reliving what happened, longing for a different outcome—what is happening here is beyond my wildest nightmares. And yet I can't say everything that happened during these past months in Afghanistan is entirely bad.

I recall the feeling when I was lying in the shallow concrete ditch, wondering what might happen next. I didn't have a sense of fear or terror; rather it was this strange feeling of peace and acceptance of whatever might come my way, a recognition that this might be my appointed time to die.

Washington, DC, 10 April

Met Andrew Wilder at U.S. Institute for Peace, an attractive building with lots of glass across the street from State. The view toward the cherry blossoms out the huge front window is beautiful, presenting a wonderful scene so different from what I feel right now.

I think how very different this scene is from the one I was part of three days ago. Andrew is simultaneously appalled and sympathetic, having himself spent many years in Afghanistan.

Proceeded to State Department for longer conversation with Jim DeHart, covering again what happened on Saturday. Phil Russell accompanied me, signaling in advance possible responses to the inevitable question, "Is it worth it?"

Just prior to this meeting I ran into Special Representative for Afghanistan and Pakistan David Pierce. We talked briefly about the same things.

Met Phil again for lunch—he is in Washington on vacation but is vitally interested in what is happening now. He mentioned that Zabul had been too quiet in recent weeks, in some sense anticipating in advance concerns about what might happen there.

The narratives about 6 April are about to become more complicated. Already the McClatchy media company, which has a news correspondent in Kabul, has posted an article based on conversations with the two Afghan journalists who were with us, stating that our group was "lost." One journalist "saw" a white sheet placed over Anne—yet I know for sure she was still alive when she was flown to Apache on a helicopter. One critical blogger asked the question, "Was this the day that we almost lost another ambassador?"

Washington, DC, 11 April

Early-morning conversation with David Donahue about whether I should stay for Anne's funeral in Chicago or return to Kandahar as planned—in the end the argument for Kandahar carried the day.

Meeting at Reagan Building with Administrator Rajiv Shah and Alex Thier, head of USAID programs in Pakistan and Afghanistan. I also met for a few seconds with USAID deputy administrator Don Steinberg, who apologized that he was too busy to linger.

It felt strange to be back at USAID after being away for so long. From a distance I saw a few people I know—like ghosts almost, considering that we are all aging fast. My years at USAID seem a long time ago; the world has changed dramatically from the one I was part of when I first joined the agency in March 1984. A lot of water has since flowed down the Indus; everything is different.

Walked back to State for noon brown bag with Afghan Affairs organized by Tim Wilder, Andrew's brother who works for the State Department. Like me, both of them grew up in Pakistan and went to school at MCS. This meeting wasn't about recent events—rather, it focused on trends in Kandahar. In reality my perspective is limited—I know something but not a lot. No one knows for sure what will happen even a year from now or what will follow next spring's elections.

Mary Franjakis walked with David and me to the seventh floor to meet Deputy Secretary Bill Burns, my ambassador when I served in Jordan so many years ago. He was calm and authoritative. Mostly he wanted to express appreciation for our service in accompanying Anne's remains home.

Now on a crowded United flight from Dulles to Dubai, I have thirteen hours to think about everything, to recall as many moments as I can from last Saturday.

Did we actually take a wrong turn or was it more complicated than that? Did our military escort walk and clear the route beforehand? What happened at the gate at the agricultural office that we knocked on first and what else could we have done at the time?

While meeting in the *shura* room beforehand Tim Bashor said the initial plan was to have the event at the school for girls rather than the school for boys, but in the end the PRT determined that the school for boys would be the better site. Was there miscommunication in the planning process? Was everyone informed about the change?

At one point, while we waited inside the PRT, I did say—Let's talk about today's program. Where are we going and what will we see? But that was largely in a programmatic context, not a security one.

Desperately trying to remember every detail of what happened, I keep thinking that there were places where I might have changed the universe and made a difference, if only I had known what would happen next.

Dubai, 12 April

Arrived in Dubai at around 3:30 p.m. and then made my way to Holiday Inn Express for a few hours of rest. I am exhausted, even before I return to Kandahar.

Kandahar, 13 April

Up early for Fly Dubai flight to Kandahar via Bastion—it was only half full, the fewest number of passengers I've seen thus far. I struck up a conversation with several Pakistani support staff as we prepared to depart. They were surprised to hear a foreigner speak Urdu.

Dived straight into work on arrival, attending four successive meetings in four different places. At the end of the day looked through material from the Zabul bombings, including a selection of photos taken afterward that make me want to throw up.

The initial bomb hidden near the PRT wall weighed five pounds. The second was a hundred pounds in two parts, fifty pounds placed on each side of the vehicle. This bomb went off ten seconds after the first one, too soon to decimate a rescue squad. It makes me literally sick to my stomach.

More than ever I think this was a matter of being in the wrong place at the wrong time. I hate the fact that five people died. If I had arrived five seconds and fifteen yards earlier, I might well have been numbered among them.

Kandahar, 14 April

Early-morning video conference with embassy followed by video meeting with Tina Kaidanow, David Donahue, and head of security in Kabul, as well as all four SCRs. Tina asked about morale and then set out new security procedures—including embassy approval for any foot movements and any events advertised ahead of time.

The RSO said the embassy makes two thousand movements each month and almost all of them are successful. Tina came across as concerned and engaged. I still have this overwhelming sense that we were in the wrong place at the wrong time, with catastrophic results.

Attended weekly stand-up meeting with RC-South staff. I am exhausted and tired yet I want to do the right thing. I do my best anyway, working my way through an impossible situation on issues I have never dealt with before. It is hard, very hard.

More meetings throughout the day concluding with commander's barbeque for incoming Fourth Infantry Division here for their orientation.

Talked with incoming Australian brigadier who mentioned he served twenty years in the British Army before migrating to Australia six years ago and joining the Australian army. He was part of the first invasion of Iraq, serving in the British Army at the time. Their arrival was celebrated for the first couple of months—then they faced hostility.

Finally got a chance to talk to General Abrams about last week. He said the Army investigation is still under way but will likely state that the patrol got at least a couple of things wrong—they didn't look for IEDs first, they didn't use sniffer dogs, and they didn't close off the street ahead of time. How utterly gut-wrenching that it comes down to that. But maybe not. It is hard to separate fact from fiction after events like this and I'm still not sure I believe any of it.

One senior officer thinks someone close to Governor Naseri might have done the dirty work. He had either fired someone or had words with them. The theory is that in revenge the person fired notified the Taliban and told them about the event and the opportunity it would present.

There is also a suggestion that the first bomb, placed on the wall, was set for ISAF while the second bomb, delivered in a car, was meant for Naseri. As for the civilians at Kandahar Air Field, all future movements have to be cleared by the brigade commander first—and then, in my case as SCR, by the commanding general.

Kabul, 15 April

I am now flying over the Hindu Kush en route to Kabul where I'm not sure what to expect. The clouds gather as they always have and the higher mountains remain covered in snow. This could be a normal flight, like others I have taken before. But at this point I don't know what "normal" means—nothing can ever be the same again.

Catriona is making her final decisions on college and I'm not there with her. Probably it will be University of Victoria on Vancouver Island—a beautiful place to live. Fiona is holding things together in Ulaanbaatar with Iain and Cameron far away.

Extraordinarily busy day at the U.S. Embassy in Kabul, starting with a meeting with Ambassador Cunningham and his deputy Tina Kaidanow, herself a former ambassador. This was a good discussion. I appreciate their sympathy and welcome their commitment to continuing with our mission in Afghanistan.

At Ambassador Cunningham's suggestion, talked to the embassy RSO with experience in Iraq and Afghanistan. He wasn't very forthcoming, basically saying that I am a potential witness at a criminal trial and therefore shouldn't be "tainted."

He said some early information on the attack is simply "wrong." There wasn't necessarily an IED implanted on or near the wall after all—but one might have been contained in a box, satchel, or bag that was thrown on the ground by a passing vehicle. While acknowledging many what-ifs, he thinks the right security protocols were followed and what happened is part of the risk of doing business in Afghanistan.

Met Michael Younce, the embassy social worker who has already visited Kandahar several times to deal with the stress faced by those of us who live there. He is sympathetic and concerned—he says simply talking about the event of 6 April and its aftermath can be helpful.

Also met an embassy colleague from IPA. We agree that it is time to leave Afghanistan—but want to do it properly. We were disappointed to read newspaper accounts of critical comments made by a senior Afghan official at a recent ceremony marking the closing of KPRT. Yet we recognize a certain kind of logic in such public statements, especially as Afghans assume control and don't want to be beholden to the past.

Met Ambassador Hugo Llorens, previously ambassador to Honduras; he mentioned that he will be the next consul general in Sydney. He is sympathetic and supportive and I appreciate that a lot. At the end of our conversation, he said, "This is a commitment for life. If you ever need anything, if you ever need support, I will be happy to provide it."

Met Ken Yamashita ("Zen Ken"). Our conversation largely covered more personal issues related to Zabul. He is staying a second year in Afghanistan and I admire him for that.

Dinner (Mongolian barbeque from the DFAC) with David Snepp and Masha Hamilton in Masha's apartment. There were tears at this meeting—it is still hard to believe what happened hardly one week ago.

She wanted to thank David and me for our long trip back to Dover. I mentioned my Mongolia book. My thought was to cancel the launch scheduled for 22 May in Hong Kong at the Foreign Correspondents' Club. However, both Masha and David think that it *should* go forward.

While at Masha's squeezed in a phone conversation with Fiona—a shorter conversation than usual but at least we are finally in touch.

In other news, two shipwrecked Afghans whose Iranian boat sank in the Indian Ocean were repatriated home to Farah via Kandahar Air Field. They were rescued by the American Navy and were taken aboard the aircraft carrier USS *Eisenhower.*

Arrangements were made to hand them over to Governor Wesa at Kandahar Airport—he plans to buy them new clothes and send them on their way.

An amazing story, in every respect—probably they were illegal migrants to Iran; probably they were on a smuggling expedition in a dhow; and, amazingly enough, they were returned to their home in landlocked Afghanistan, courtesy of the ships and airplanes of the U.S. Navy.

Kabul, 16 April

Breakfast with Zabul PRT team, now about to break up permanently—Tim Bashor, Steve Overman, Maura Connelly, and Wesley Nguyen.

Talked to border coordination unit at embassy—they are looking toward drawdown and their plans look fine.

Talked briefly at regular staffing review, presenting our drawdown in RC-South: from fourteen locations when I arrived in late August 2012 to four by June 2013; from a hundred and thirty people when I arrived to fifty-one by this June and twenty-seven by the end of the year.

Embassy motor pool to airport. Stopped by ANSF at final gate for not having correct pass. Feeling vulnerable and with a sense of déjà vu, turned back and retraced our steps, reaching terminal one via terminal two instead.

Also contacted RSO in Kandahar who in turn got RSO in Kabul involved. Realistically, volunteering for Afghanistan means putting myself in harm's way—not only on account of insurgent action but also when there are mistakes and confusion on our side. These next four months are going to be long, hard, and sometimes nerve-wracking.

Bonnie was waiting when I arrived at Kandahar Air Field. I then went to two meetings in quick succession: a review of plans for the summer and fall, and another discussion on upcoming key leader engagements.

I thought it might be easy to return to a routine—but in truth I have a sense of foreboding about these engagements, or at least the movements to and from them. It is like when flares shot off our airplane as a precaution against missile attacks as we landed earlier this afternoon; my first instinct was to be alarmed at the noise and the flash of light around me.

Of course we live in a world where such things can happen anywhere, as witnessed by the Boston Marathon bombing earlier today. Perhaps as a country we will have to get used to violence of the type that already persists in places like Israel and Afghanistan.

Talked to General Abrams late in the day, concerned about Tim's comment earlier that videotape from the PRT had somehow been erased. He said video cameras on the walls of the FOB had been taken down some time ago. As for aerial footage, he watched it, but the angle was such he couldn't make out what was happening on the street. Again, it is striking and more than a little disconcerting how quickly rumors start, how incorrect information so quickly gets a life of its own.

The flight from Kabul on a clear day was at least beautiful, endless mountains covered in white snow and, as we approached Kandahar, a carpet of green in front of us.

FOB Apache (Zabul), 18 April

Morning Black Hawk flight to Apache to attend memorial service for the three soldiers killed in Zabul on 6 April—Sergeant Christopher Ward, Sergeant Delfin Santos, and Corporal Wilbel Robles-Santa. The oldest, Sergeant Ward, was twenty-five, the same age as Anne Smedinghoff. Sergeant Santos from California was the youngest of seventeen children. Corporal Robles-Santa from Puerto Rico leaves a wife and two young children behind.

The order of service brings it all back. I wish I could rewind the tape and start this day all over again, in a different way and with a different outcome.

The program included Psalm 23 as well as "Fiddler's Green" and "Garryowen," given that this was a cavalry troop. A lone bagpiper played Scottish laments. I talked briefly with Colonel Jim Crider, the Zabul PRT commander, expressing my sadness and concern.

Walking toward the chapel, we passed the emergency medical facility where Anne died and Kelly received emergency treatment, having been taken there by helicopter from the Zabul PRT. When I had heard that Anne reached Apache, I really thought that she would make it, that she would somehow survive.

I wanted that to happen so badly, I wanted her to make it from there to Kandahar Air Field and then Germany and finally Walter Reed, even if it meant many months in recovery. If only I could change the balance of the universe, if only there had been a different ending.

Kandahar, 19 April

Relatively quiet day, much of it spent in office. I realize that my movements will be limited for the rest of my time in Afghanistan—State wants outreach but is also very risk averse.

Late night talk with General Abrams. He knows I want more details about what happened in Zabul. He thinks the VBIED in Zabul on 6 April was meant for Governor Naseri. But he also expressed concern about my safety, suggesting that my next meeting with the governor of Uruzgan should be within the PRT, not at the governor's office.

Kandahar Airport, 20 April

Morning meetings at Kandahar Airport, first with Faizi and then with Wesa. Faizi has a hard job and complained vociferously about the way certain high officials interfere with the operation of the airport. In contrast Wesa was relatively quiet and even subdued.

Mostly we talked about operational matters related to USAID. I asked for more support in Panjwai with its growing opportunities for an expanded civilian presence. I expressed concern about the harsh comments made at the KPRT closing—Wesa claimed that the media had distorted what was said at that event.

Wrote long condolence note to the Smedinghoff family. This is a kind of guilt that will never go away—Why did I live? Why did others have to die? It is those few seconds in each direction that make things so difficult right now. Always and at odd times the endless what-ifs and if-onlys keep coming back.

Probably that is the feeling in Boston right now also. At least the two brothers from Chechnya that caused the carnage are finally off the scene, one dead and the other in custody.

Kandahar, 21 April

Afternoon phone call from David Donahue at IPA to deliver news that our staff in Uruzgan, Zaray, and Spin Boldak will have to conclude their assignments and go home by June.

Attended evening barbeque with general officers for General Terry, now on his farewell tour of RC-South. He remembers when he first arrived in southern Afghanistan in 2006 and it was the British, Canadians, and Australians who were most heavily involved. He described views at that time as "naïve." He also characterized David McKeirnan as the best general of his generation. He thinks the expanded Afghan army is a formidable security force but worries that it won't receive the support it needs from its civilian counterparts.

Kandahar, 22 April

Heavy morning rain. Worked on evaluations and award nominations. Said farewell to one member of the Zaray DST. Made sure the embassy in Kabul notified the Australians about our decision to depart Uruzgan.

Looked up Fiona's photographs posted on Facebook of Catriona coming home—the International School of Ulaanbaatar won both the boys' and girls' side of the soccer tournament in China; I only wish that I had been there to see it.

Each night I wake up thinking about the events of Zabul on 6 April. Each night I go to sleep thinking about them as well—this is something that won't ever go away.

I also keep reflecting on our efforts over the past ten years in Afghanistan. Realistically we swing between extremes far too easily—throughout one decade, we completely ignored Afghanistan; throughout the next one, we become much more heavily engaged than we ever should have been. We seem to be either "all in" or "all out." When it comes to foreign policy, balance isn't something we do well.

Kandahar, 23 April

Planned trip to Shah Wali Kot cancelled because of bad weather—including a storm with hailstones half the size of golf balls that damaged several helicopters. Now there is mud and water everywhere.

Talked to Fiona, and also Catriona about her China tournament. She scored four of her school's twelve goals, including one off a curved corner kick and another from a header. How great is that, that each of our kids won a soccer championship during their final year of high school?

Late in the evening General Chris Hughes dropped by to ask about me. There is a lot of sympathy and people recognize this is something I won't ever forget, casting a dark shadow over the rest of this assignment and very possibly the rest of my life.

But I appreciate Chris' comments. On the eve of the Gulf War a sergeant Akhbar ran through his camp in Kuwait, killing two soldiers and injuring eighteen others. Chris saw a lot that day that he too wishes he could forget.

Tarin Kot (Uruzgan), 24 April

Morning Embassy Air flight to Uruzgan—this time in a small Beechcraft. Met on arrival by Rob Sipe who accepts that the PRT is closing down. Lewis Gitter is on this trip along with Rohan Titus—the Australian diplomat, originally from Sri Lanka, who is based in Kandahar.

The Australian monitoring and evaluation group briefed us first. They noted that 30 percent of the residents of Uruzgan have access to power, mainly through solar panels or private diesel generators. The number one issue is the economy, more important even than security. Most locals are pleased with recent developments in health and education.

Early afternoon meeting with Akhundzada. He smiles a lot but it is hard to get anything out of him. Looking back on his first year in office, he expressed pride in convincing Kabul to increase Uruzgan's development budget. He presented a highly positive perspective, describing security as much better than it used to be. He says he has visited all six districts multiple times.

Also met Dr. Abdul Ghafar Stanikzai, head of the Afghan Independent Human Rights Commission. He reflects a different kind of Afghanistan, one that casts a critical eye in every direction yet somehow manages to promote a common humanity.

Stanikzai says Governor Akhundzada and provincial police chief Matullah Khan are open to his questions. He also said the Taliban ask him to investigate certain cases, most involving prisoners—but aren't pleased when he looks into allegations of human rights abuse against women.

Dinner with General Morrison, Australian army chief of staff; Senator David Feeney who heads the Senate Armed Forces Committee in Canberra was also present. I expressed regret we weren't able to keep American civilians in Uruzgan through the end of the year as previously planned. They expressed regret at recent events in Zabul and seem amazed I am still here to talk about it.

Shared CHU with Lewis Gitter—very spartan with two bunk beds and not much else. This base will close by the end of the year and every time I visit more has been taken down. Now there are many hollowed-out places. By July the gym will be gone.

Tarin Kot (Uruzgan), 25 April

Up at 4:00 a.m. for ANZAC commemoration in front of the Tarin Kot war memorial. Almost the entire Australian contingent—more than 1,500 soldiers—attended.

A lone piper on a parapet started the ceremony with "Dark Island" and concluded with "Flowers of the Forest." In between, two Australian soldiers sang "Abide with Me." The padre gave explicitly Christian prayers and remarks.

General Morrison also spoke, starting with a sad letter written by an Australian soldier on the western front in World War I shortly before the battle that killed him—seven thousand died on this particular front in the space of a week.

Morning briefing for General Abrams and senior Australian visitors. According to Combined Force Uruzgan, "The insurgency is most viable at the periphery."

Reassuringly most senior Afghan officers are Pushtuns, contrary to views expressed by international journalists in Kabul who think they are mostly Tajik or Uzbek. General Kandahari, a former mujahideen commander, gets high marks.

The civilian PRT leadership provided a mostly positive perspective, noting a 40 percent increase in Uruzgan's development budget over the past year. But they also said that no project is too small for graft and corruption.

Met line director for health in PRT *shura* room. He presented a positive perspective on changes over the past decade, starting with his arrival as a doctor from Jalalabad when the entire province had only two health centers and twenty medical staff. Now there are dozens of clinics served by more than two hundred health professionals. All the national figures point to improvements in health and education—and it is heartening that this is happening even in Uruzgan, one of Afghanistan's poorest, least developed and most isolated provinces.

Enjoyed another spectacular meal at Uruzgan, this one featuring smoked salmon—dinners at Gecko aside, this is surely the best DFAC food in southern Afghanistan.

Talked with PRT commander who recalled Commander Price's suicide just before Christmas and how hard it was for everyone to bear. He thinks it was related to the deployment, not issues back home. He had been in place only two months and already four of his soldiers had been killed.

Waited on flight line for General Abrams and his two Black Hawks. They eventually arrived and we took several detours, flying low over Taliban country east of Shah Wali Kot and extending into the knot of mountains that form Mya Neshin, following the river with its narrow valleys, tiny green threads of cultivation, and walled compounds guarded with towers that look like they might have been constructed in the Middle Ages. At one point we passed an unlikely caravan of seven vehicles—perhaps a wedding, perhaps a funeral, perhaps a Taliban military convoy of one kind or another.

It was dusty much of the way and by the time we reached Dahla Dam there was rain and lightning as well, forcing us to stop at Frontenac, a nearby FOB that will be among the last in southern Afghanistan to close.

We ended up staying there for a couple of hours, exhausted, trying to sleep on hard plywood benches. Everything is gray right now—the clouds, the mountains, the gravel, the concrete walls of the FOB. Eventually the sky cleared enough for us to make our way back to Kandahar Air Field and all the e-mails, meetings, and work that awaited me there.

Called Cameron as well as Mom and Dad—Fiona, Catriona, and Iain were not by their phones. The good news from Fiona via e-mail is that Catriona is ranked at the top of her class—as far as I know, the first Addleton to ever be valedictorian anywhere.

My thoughts are increasingly on Ulaanbaatar, her graduation—and the year of her life I mostly missed. When I look back I'm not sure I could have ordered my life any differently. But I am all too aware of the sacrifices involved, the many occasions I should have been with family but wasn't.

Kandahar, 26 April

Lunch with Generals Abrams, White, Hughes, and Brewer. We each offered our comments in turn. I said I felt I was in the thirteenth round of a boxing match, hit repeatedly in the face but somehow managing to stay on my feet. Nothing is settled, everything changes on a moment's notice. What is clear is that the era of PRTs and DSTs is over. From now on almost all our work will be conducted out of Kandahar Air Field.

Kandahar, 27 April

Phil Russell returned from leave, having visited Kelly Hunt at Walter Reed. She is still unconscious and faces an uncertain prognosis.

Evening dinner at Luxembourg DFAC to remember Nasemi. About twenty-five civilians attended, along with a few people in uniform, including Sergeant Rasool and Colonel Chris Valhola who will depart for the United States later tonight.

I started and finished the evening with reflections; others also recalled Nasemi's contributions since he arrived at Kandahar Air Field in December—his interest in chess, his workouts, his weight lifting, his life in the United States where he enjoyed dancing and planned to write a book. Lewis Gitter's reflections are especially moving, including his references to the empty chair where Nasemi once sat.

Everyone remembers Nasemi's quiet dignity, commitment, smile, and calm approach. Several photographs were placed in the room including one from our recent trip to Arghandab where we met the governor, talked to religious leaders, and admired the view.

I recalled Nasemi's comment that he once sold music cassettes from a sidewalk in Islamabad during the 1980s, a popular way for young refugees to earn a few rupees at the time. He would have been a teenager then; I had recently arrived in Pakistan to start my Foreign Service career. We used to joke that very possibly our paths first crossed on a sidewalk in Islamabad all those years ago in Pakistan. It reminds me yet again that Nasemi was a refugee for most of his life yet managed to support extended family while also building a life of promise and integrity that was cut short all too soon.

Walking home after dinner, it is sobering to see the flags at Kandahar Air Field at half-mast—this time for four airmen killed earlier today in a plane crash at Shah Joy in Zabul, not far from the border with Ghazni.

There was another rocket attack on Kandahar Air Field just as we started our dinner to remember Nasemi—an announcement by the Taliban, perhaps, that their spring offensive is about to begin.

Spin Boldak, 28 April

Morning Black Hawk flight to Spin Boldak for another remembrance service for Nasemi, this one involving several translators with whom he once worked. Again it was touching to hear the reflections. Translators never get enough credit or recognition for their work—without them, there would be no connection to Afghans at all.

Flying back I was struck by the colors in what otherwise seems like a bleak and hostile landscape—the blue sky above, the red sand of the Registan Desert, the dull brown of the Kandahar flood plain, the foreboding black of the mountains, and the occasional green field flung across the desert, vaguely suggesting that spring has finally arrived.

The road to the border is heavily trafficked, a narrow and precarious ribbon of tarmac connecting Afghanistan with Quetta, Karachi, and the rest of the world.

Spent rest of day in meetings—they never end. In my weekly with the RSO I mentioned that for me the most dangerous place in Afghanistan is the road between the embassy and Kabul Airport.

Kandahar, 29 April

Morning context brief with Max Boot and visiting delegation from Council on Foreign Relations in New York. Most were first-time visitors to Afghanistan, high flyers in finance or law, with degrees from Princeton and Harvard. The questions were reasonable enough, focusing on corruption, the Taliban, and the ethnic make-up of the Afghan National Army. Boot has been visiting Kandahar since 2008. He is surprised at the relative quiet in Arghandab as well as in Zaray, Panjwai, and Maiwand. He is also surprised at the extent to which Afghans really are in the lead.

FOB Davis (Zabul), 30 April

Early-morning rocket attack on Kandahar Air Field—four 107-mm rockets in all, one of which fell close to the NATO barracks, so close one soldier could feel the air blow across his face as the rocket passed him.

Woke up to news that Dr. Norval Christy, eye surgeon and long-time medical missionary at the Christian Hospital at Taxila in Pakistan, has passed away.

As chairman of the MCS school board, he signed my high school diploma. If Protestants had saints, he would be numbered among them.

Embassy Air flight to FOB Davis, a few hundred yards from Apache. The shooter tested his machine gun at one point, making an unexpected noise that almost made me jump.

Listening to the two throbbing helicopter rotors as we made our way through the dust, I thought of what happened in Qalat just over three weeks ago. That day started like this one, under the early-morning sun on the tarmac at Kandahar Air Field, waiting for helicopters to arrive.

I thought about it again on the return flight in the afternoon, when we passed over Alexander's Castle, FOB Smart, and the school we walked toward but never reached. The distances seem very small, especially from the air.

Spent most of day with team from Jordan that included two imams. The Jordanians believe their status as Arabs gives them special insights into religious aspects of this struggle and they are probably right. They are appalled at what they perceive as the ignorance of Afghans on religious matters. One described a near green-on-blue incident a couple of weeks ago: an armed NDS officer approached a Jordanian soldier and said they together should take out the unbelievers.

Breaking for lunch, we shared *mansaaf,* the traditional Jordanian Bedouin feast featuring rice, nuts, and mutton that I enjoyed on several occasions during the four years that we lived in Amman. The head of the goat that gave his life for us was placed on top of a mountain of rice, looking balefully in our direction. Memories of Wadi Rum, Wadi Dana, and Petra came flooding back— that was twelve years ago, but it seems as if it happened in another lifetime, as if it was something experienced by somebody else.

Commander Al Dozier, the Afghan hand from Alabama who I first met at the Zabul PRT, was also there. We talked briefly about the events of 6 April; he had been walking out of the PRT just before the bomb exploded—he was holding out his hand in front of the car but fortunately for him the bombs were in both doors and went off in another direction. He thinks a spotter was in a truck ahead and he thinks the bomb was meant for me.

I'm not so sure, but under any scenario it was a matter of seconds and yards. He keeps thinking about this day and has no interest in putting himself in harm's way again if he can help it. He has five years left in the military and expects to retire as soon as he is eligible. We embraced as we departed, sharing a common seconds-from-death experience that will connect us forever.

10

━◆━

MAY

Kandahar, 1 May 2013

Saw sickening Internet footage of 747 that went down at Bagram yesterday, killing seven crew members. The initial assessment is that the loadmaster made a mistake, that as the plane took off a vehicle strapped down in the body of the aircraft broke loose and started rolling, unbalancing the load and precipitating a stall and then a freefall. When the plane hit the ground it immediately turned into a fireball.

Kabul, 2 May

Up at 5:00 a.m. for early-morning C-130 flight to Kabul for change-of-command ceremony at IJC—General Allen giving way to General Milley. Deputy Governor Patyal and several Afghan military officers travelled with us. This is a beautiful day—the sky is blue and the endless ridges of snow-covered peaks in central Afghanistan seem to go on forever.

The ceremony was held in a large hangar. The small 101st Airborne Division band provided music. Milley's comments seemed ambitious, considering this is a year in which the ISAF presence will be severely diminished. He promised, "The Taliban will be defeated. They will never win." One of the American soldiers standing at attention fainted and had to be helped off.

Spoke at length with Asim Hafiz, imam to Her Majesty's Forces in Afghanistan. He has worked in Helmand and Kandahar as well as Kabul. He knows General Terry and they embraced, evoking several references to God. He said he was born in England but his family came from India. He launched the change-of-command ceremony with a reading from the Koran.

According to Hafiz, footage of the 747 crash at Bagram yesterday will be viewed by Afghans as the hand of God at work, like mujahideen narratives in which the soldiers of Allah attacked Soviet tanks with rocks—the rocks immediately turned into rockets once they hit the tanks, destroying them.

Also talked with two fellow SCRs, Karen Decker from RC-East and Paul O'Friel from RC-Southwest. We share the same frustrations as well as the same view that a transition is needed, but one that involves a longer time frame.

Talked with Deputy Governor Patyal while waiting for our plane to leave. He was born and raised in Kandahar. His sisters live abroad as refugees, one in the U.S., a second in England, a third in Sweden, and a fourth in Germany.

Patyal has three sons, the oldest not yet five. He is upbeat about Afghanistan, pointing to new schools, health centers, media outlets, and cell phones. His family grows pomegranates in Arghandab. He is a poet and said his first book, published in Peshawar, was well received in Pushto literary circles in Pakistan, Afghanistan, Dubai, and Canada.

On arrival at Kandahar Air Field informed by a colleague that General White had cancelled our dinner with Shah Wali Karzai. Partly this is because of lingering concerns that the Taliban may launch an attack in Aino Mina, partly because someone in our host's household might have talked about our prospective visit on an open phone line.

Watched State Department remembrance ceremony for Anne Smedinghoff via Internet. What happened on 6 April in Zabul keeps flooding back. There were many tributes. The recollections by Anne's father Tom were very moving. Mention was made to Kelly, still in the hospital. Steve Overman was in the audience. The three soldiers killed were cited by name, as was Nasemi.

Kandahar, 3 May

Morning context briefing for visiting Democratic senators and congressional representatives—John Donnelly (Indiana), Heidi Heitkamp (North Dakota), Tammy Baldwin (Wisconsin), Peter Welch (Vermont), and Christopher Murray (Connecticut). All of them are glad our part of the war in Afghanistan is finally almost over—they hope for some semblance of continued support after 2014 but think it will be difficult to justify it to their constituencies.

I repeated the line I have been using lately: In the 1990s we were "all out" in Afghanistan; in the 2000s we were "all in." Looking beyond 2014, we need to find a better balance between the two extremes, one that has us engaged in Afghanistan—but not overly engaged.

Afternoon context brief for Under Secretary of Defense for Policy James Miller. He was joined by David Samuel Sedney, deputy assistant secretary for

Afghanistan, Pakistan, and Central Asia. We met again for dinner—both were surprised when I told them I was in the attack on Zabul exactly four weeks ago.

Weekly commander's lunch, mostly revolving around impressions of yesterday's change-of-command ceremony in Kabul. General Milley seems different from General Allen—more aggressive, less circumspect; more ambitious, less measured. He strongly believes ANSF can still win this war.

The senior officers passed on something of Milley's thinking as he takes on his new assignment. For example, he said he respected the enemy and acknowledged Taliban planning skills. He added the Taliban want to control Kandahar while the Haqqani network seeks to place Kabul under siege—though there have been only seven significant attacks in Kabul since the start of the year. According to IJC, 10 percent of Afghans support the Taliban; even if that figure rises to 30 percent, the ANSF can still claim victory.

Other of the more interesting Milley statements included the following: "Disagreement is not the same thing as disloyalty." "I empower you to disobey orders from everyone but me." "Don't let any ISAF facility get overrun." "Avoid civilian casualties." "Don't tolerate war crimes." "Don't let the ANSF suffer either tactical or strategic defeat." "When I travel, it is not as a VIP or as a tourist—it is as a commander." "Don't give the Afghans any reason to fear abandonment." "Above all, work on building the confidence of the ANSF."

Early evening deep dive. Colonels Adgie and Getchell attended, blunt battlefield commanders accustomed to working outdoors. Staff officers have their roles to play in any military campaign—but they typically look more like office workers than soldiers in the field.

Kandahar, 4 May

Flags at half-mast—five soldiers were killed in an IED explosion while on patrol in Maiwand earlier today. I hate to hear such news. Combined with two ISAF soldiers killed in Helmand earlier today, this has been an awful few hours.

Romanian Chapel, Orthodox Easter, 5 May

Attended midnight Orthodox Easter service at Romanian Orthodox chapel, a wooden structure that would fit nicely in a forest setting somewhere in the hills of Transylvania. It was built in 2006 and took six weeks to construct. About sixty people attended, mostly Romanian soldiers. But the chaplain was an American Marine—I talked to him later and he said he grew up as an Anglican in Philadelphia.

Inside, the church is lined with icons of all shapes and sizes. One Romanian officer told me that when their soldiers arrive in Afghanistan they often carry an icon from their local monastery and then place it in the church in Kandahar. On one wall I noticed photographs of forty Romanian soldiers, all killed serving in Afghanistan.

Afterward talked to two American soldiers with Greek last names who attended. One is a helicopter pilot, the other a soldier stationed in Arghandab. Both were graduates of West Point, class of 2009. The pilot said he was at Zabul on 6 April and helped return some of the casualties to Kandahar Air Field.

Joined Bonnie Weaver and RSO Diane Latham for 1:00 a.m. ramp ceremony at Kandahar Air Field—seven soldiers, five killed in Maiwand and two others killed in a green-on-blue incident in western Afghanistan. The familiar part includes the flag-draped silver boxes, Psalm 23, and a slow version of "Amazing Grace."

Describing what happened in Maiwand, General Hughes said a five-hundred-pound IED had detonated at exactly the right place, destroying the Stryker. The wire used to detonate it stretched more than a mile. It was the fourth vehicle in the convoy. The youngest soldier killed was nineteen years old.

While waiting on the tarmac I talked briefly with Diane. She was the first one to meet me when I returned to Kandahar Air Field on the helicopter from Zabul on 6 April, standing just ahead of Bonnie on the flight line. She said this was her second career; her first involved movies and she had helped organize helicopters for *Black Hawk Down*. Many of the extras had served in Somalia. She said she saw director Ridley Scott nearly every day during the nine months of filming in Morocco.

Kandahar, 6 May

Attended long briefing involving General Milley. He raised several military analogies, mostly to World War II and the Civil War. He also referred to William Wallace and the medieval Scottish clans. He thinks ISAF can still win this war—while acknowledging they might just as easily lose it.

Tarin Kot (Uruzgan), 7 May

Late-night flight to Tarin Kot in C-130 piloted by a young ROTC graduate from the University of South Dakota. Talked briefly with another passenger, a Special Forces officer from Virginia Beach who had heard of Bach Christian Hospital in northern Pakistan, graduated from Columbia International University in South Carolina, and served for a time as a missionary in Europe. Always, I am amazed at the personal stories of those around me, both Afghan and American.

Tarin Kot (Uruzgan), 8 May

All day in Uruzgan with Ambassador Llorens from the U.S. and Ambassador Philp from Australia. About fifteen others from the U.S. Embassy flew down with this group, wanting to see the PRT before the last of our civilians depart.

Outside meetings included one with Governor Akhundzada and another with Mr. Noorzai, head of local independent elections commission. I've always described Akhundzada as the "leprechaun from Uruzgan." The PRT commander also appreciates his style, calling him a "lovable rogue." He is charming, despite the allegations of corruption that surround almost every politician across Afghanistan. He is quite young and it will be interesting to see what he does in the years ahead.

Joined others in attending ceremony to affirm U.S.-Australian partnership and mark the imminent departure of our last three civilians—Rob Sipe, Bob Mullen, and Steve St. Clair. I drafted remarks for Ambassador Llorens. Someone in Public Affairs in Kabul deleted my brief reference to the sacrifices that the Australians made at Gallipoli.

Returned to Kandahar Air Field in another C-130, this time sitting in back with a couple dozen sleeping soldiers. On arrival made small dent in the hundred-plus e-mails waiting for me. One e-mail was from the USAID employee evaluation committee in Washington, advising that my evaluation for this year should delete all references to what happened on 6 April in Zabul—the rating period ends on 31 March and anything occurring after that is considered inadmissible. Another e-mail was from USAID, my home agency, announcing a new slogan: "One team, one mission, one family" as part of an effort to turn USAID into a caring organization.

Kabul, 11 May

Afternoon flight to Kabul on a small Beechcraft. Several flares went off with a loud bang as we landed. Arrived in Kabul at about same time as visiting congressional delegation consisting of six members of Congress; one was Tammy Duckworth from Illinois, a former Black Hawk pilot who lost her legs when her helicopter was shot down in Iraq several years ago.

Dinner with Karen Decker, Ken Yamashita, and John Dunlap. I talked to Karen—she is SCR in RC-East and shares many of my concerns. John Dunlap stayed behind after Ken and Karen left, recalling when he was on patrol in Iraq in 2008 and attacked by a suicide bomber. Three American soldiers were killed in front of him. His emotional roller-coaster in many ways mirrors my own.

Kabul, 12 May

Morning meeting with Deputy Secretary Bill Burns—all the SCRs attended along with Tina Kaidanow, currently serving as chargé d'affaires, and assorted others from the embassy.

My reflections are consistent with those of Karen Decker (RC-East) and Paul O'Friel (RC-Southwest): the ANSF is doing a credible job, but our civilian drawdown needs to be synced with the military and take into account Afghan realities.

Spent rest of morning at IPA, starting with a briefing on upcoming SIGAR audits and continuing through my unusually passionate plea to somehow break loose the logjam of reporting cables that are languishing in Kabul.

One of our draft cables on the views of a prominent tribal leader toward the Karzai family dates back nearly two months—it has never seen the light of day and probably never will. Another draft report on tensions within the extended Karzai family in Kandahar is now definitively dead.

Now I am flying in a half-filled Embassy Air Dash 8 toward Kandahar. Outside the terrain looks forbidding—cliffs, mountains, valleys, winding roads, rushing streams, and countless small settlements clinging precariously to ridges. The snow pack, thick near Kabul, is beginning to disappear.

Closer to Kandahar I see the *kutchi* camps, possibly involved in gun-running for the Taliban. There is also the occasional ISAF military infrastructure, now in its dismantling phase, about to be bulldozed back into the earth.

Reflecting on this past decade and the centuries that preceded it, the phrase "graveyard of empires" does seem apt. Everything else may disappear—but the dirt, dust, and rocks of southern Afghanistan will endure forever.

Kandahar, 13 May

Walked to Asian DFAC for dinner, noticing the crescent moon overhead, as thin as a fingernail. Two more lunar months and it will be Eid al-Fitr.

Saw BBC headline about IED in Arghistan that killed fifteen civilians, most of them women and children. Elsewhere an ANSF soldier died attempting to disarm a bomb. The Taliban say they want to reduce civilian casualties—but, on the ground, that isn't happening.

The Taliban offensive this year—the so-called Khalid Ibn al-Walid campaign, as they have trumpeted it to their fellow Afghans—hasn't yet begun in earnest, though some in ISAF think it is about to start. Or perhaps the various rumors and media reports are right that internal arguments are causing problems in Quetta, in turn affecting coordination in the field.

Exchanged e-mails with Alex Thier at USAID in Washington. He says my potential Washington assignment is still in play, possibly ending our plans of living in Almaty in the fall. I'm not sure what to think. Perhaps it is time to finally return to the U.S., perhaps it is time to finally live closer to home.

Kandahar, 14 May

Morning context brief for Deputy Defense Secretary Ashton Carter. He already knows Afghanistan well. With General Abrams away and General Hughes sick with a stomach bug, General White led the discussion.

A dismal few hours on the war front. Yesterday three soldiers from the country of Georgia in the Caucasus were killed in a suicide attack in Helmand. Today at least three Americans were killed and many others injured in two IED explosions in Panjwai. Another American soldier is missing and rumors are already flying—one says he was walked away in civilian clothes, having been abducted by the Taliban.

Kandahar, 15 May

Met visiting management team from Kabul. We are about to reach closure on a compound built by a departing contractor—at $850,000 it is a bargain even if we have to leave Kandahar Air Field eighteen months from now. Previous plans for a consulate at Gecko cost tens of millions of dollars. Yet one visitor was skeptical about our new plan, proposing still other options.

Attended morning Purple Heart ceremony for those wounded following IED explosions in Panjwai yesterday. One was still unconscious and looked awful, but the other two should fully recover. General Hughes did the honors—his remarks were softer and quieter than those of General Abrams yet still heart-felt and sincere.

Attended late-night ramp ceremony for four soldiers, three of them killed in Panjwai yesterday. The fourth, a military policeman, drowned in a canal outside Kandahar Air Field. He was thirty-three and leaves a wife and three children behind. It was a hot day. He walked into the canal with his body armor on—and was immediately swept away.

Details on the Panjwai IED explosions are disturbing. The first explosion resulted in several wounded but no KIAs. It was only after the medevac was under way that there were two other explosions, killing three soldiers. A fourth is said to be "missing": he stepped on the IED and almost nothing is retrievable.

The ramp ceremony, by now very familiar, started with the slow-moving MRAPs flashing their yellow lights in the dark. Hundreds of soldiers lined up from all over Kandahar Air Field. Many EOD experts attended, their distinctive shoulder patches identifying them.

General Milley flew down from Kabul to join other generals from Romania and France. Several airmen from the plane that will carry the flag-draped remains home stood at attention throughout the ceremony.

Kandahar, 16 May

Full day of calls and meetings—including conference call with Kabul on our continued draw-down, a phone conversation with Masha Hamilton suggesting we will lose our last public affairs officer by August, and opening remarks at a meeting that Sergio Guzman organized involving all his USAID staff.

Dropped by Kandahar Air Field hospital to thank Dr. Zinder who is leaving shortly. He called Kelly's father late on 6 April and then again the next morning as she was medevaced to Germany. He has just been promoted to admiral—there can't be many Navy doctors who reach that rank.

Met five Belgian nurses, a mix of men and women, first at the hospital and then at the Asian DFAC. They just arrived in Afghanistan and will be here for two months. They said 80 percent of this latest Belgian medical contingent is Flemish-speaking.

Missed today's Purple Heart ceremony—it happened quickly and unexpectedly while I was out of the office. The medals were for five soldiers wounded in Zaray this morning—one lost both legs when he stepped on an IED.

What a hell hole—the first group that went in a couple of days ago had several wounded, three were killed in the second group, and now five more have been injured trying to pick up the pieces of the soldier whose remains were scattered everywhere. He is still listed as "missing" until the DNA matches are finalized.

Kandahar, 17 May

Attended context brief for Dr. Catherine Dale, a visiting military analyst who has written extensively about the war; also met with her afterward. I was diplomatic but passed on some of my work-related frustrations. She said she had heard it all before, having followed Afghanistan closely for most of the past decade.

Attended evening briefing with General Chris Hughes and Colonel "Doc" Holliday. At one point, someone passed Chris a brief note: a VBIED in Aino Mina just exploded, killing at least five people and injuring dozens of others. We have been waiting for an attack like this: it is why my last meeting to meet with Shah Wali Karzai in Aino Mina was cancelled.

Kandahar, 18 May

Morning flight to Apache cancelled due to another dust storm. I was scheduled to provide remarks at a ceremony marking the close of the Zabul PRT but Colonel Crider read my prepared remarks instead.

Meeting with Colonel King on why the Zabul Teacher Training College in Qalat will never be built. As he acknowledged, it is a sorry tale of inept contracting, incompetent construction companies, and a tendency to postpone problems rather than work them through, one at a time. This falls into the broken promises category—a succession of ambassadors visited Zabul promising this project and in the end it won't happen.

FOB Walton, 19 May

Morning video conference with embassy—Ambassador Cunningham is away so his deputy Tina Kaidanow chaired it. Eighteen names of the fallen were read out at the start of it—a lot by any measure, even if it covers two weeks. Most were soldiers killed in Kandahar.

First weekly all-hands meeting involving Afghan staff at Kandahar Air Field. Later I took five of them to lunch at Echoes; Brian Bachman and Sergio Guzman joined us. All five previously worked at KPRT and speak English well. Most have high school educations. All are wary of Pakistan. They were especially appalled at the recent bombing in Aino Mina that killed and wounded children.

I asked about cricket. One said Afghans are proud of their team, but it was initially seen as a largely Pushtun sport. I asked if anyone in the military is seen as a national hero—one mentioned the soldier killed in a skirmish on the Pakistan border last week and said everyone in Afghanistan knew his name.

We touched briefly on elections. One Afghan said he spent the day in Panjwai observing the 2009 elections. Everyone he talked to said they voted for Abdullah Abdullah—yet Karzai was shown as having won overwhelmingly. While critical of Karzai, several said any list of the most eloquent Afghan politicians would have to include both Karzai and Najibullah, the leader left in place when the Soviets departed. "Karzai makes people think he knows and loves Afghanistan."

Farewell meetings with civilians Tim Pfeiffer and Mike Sullivan. Both are departing soon—Tim to Florida, Mike to Massachusetts. We are being gutted and will soon have very few people left standing. Some of our dwindling number will find work at the embassy in Kabul, even as Kandahar becomes an afterthought.

Boarded Black Hawk for short journey to FOB Walton to attend memorial service for Sergeant Trenton Rhea from Missouri, age thirty-three. He was an MP assigned to Ready First, Combined Task Force Chesapeake. He leaves a wife Leah and three daughters—Joanna, Abigail, and Autumn. He was described as a strong Christian who loved his family and his country. One comrade recalled that when other soldiers criticized Afghans he stood up and defended them.

The circumstances of his death are very sad. He left his dark glasses on the other side of the canal—and, rather than walk a hundred extra yards in the blazing sun to cross a bridge and retrieve them, plunged into the water and was swept away. What happened next was caught on camera from an observation balloon. One soldier took off his own body armor and tried to save Rhea—but just couldn't hold on.

It took a long time to retrieve the body. Divers were looking nearly two miles downstream without success. An Afghan interpreter mentioned a place where several Afghans had previously drowned—and it was there where his remains were eventually found.

Local Afghans assisted in the search and were genuinely sad that he had drowned. Somehow I keep thinking of an Afghan proverb: "A Pushtun will always take a shortcut, even if it kills him."

The service was as melancholy as ever and included the national anthem and remarks by the battalion and company commanders as well as two fellow soldiers; it also included a reflection by Chaplain Hopkins. The last roll call and the volley of shots that followed were especially heart-wrenching. The service ended with "Amazing Grace" on the pipes.

More than a few deaths in Afghanistan seem avoidable—yet such things happen when we place ourselves in harm's way. Even momentary lapses in judgement may prove fatal and bad things happen even when the enemy is not involved.

The return flight to Kandahar Air Field was more enjoyable than usual, partly because it was sunset and partly because the glass windows on the helicopter had been removed, leaving the wind to blow freely through the cabin where General Brewer and I were sitting, Mark tightly holding his Australian-style military hat decorated with emu feathers to make sure it didn't blow away.

The fields near Kandahar Air Field are as green as they will ever get. We flew over the canal where Sergeant Rhea drowned. Arriving at Kandahar Air Field I noticed two Black Hawks marked with large red crosses taking off as we landed, perhaps heading off on yet another medevac flight somewhere in southern Afghanistan.

Dubai, 20 May

Departed Kandahar Air Field for Dubai just after noon. Six weeks ago I took this same flight in the other direction. I have never felt more exhausted or emotionally drained.

We flew west briefly before heading south across the Registan Desert toward Iran. I saw the distinctive outline of the Horn of Panjwai, the place of so much fighting and so many IED deaths over the past ten years. From the air it does look like one end of the horns of an ox.

The flight seemed briefer than usual—just over two hours but a world away from Kandahar. I mostly listened to music—Andrea Bocelli ("Passione"), Dire Straits ("Brothers in Arms"), and Emmylou Harris ("Old Yellow Moon"). Now I'm in Dubai, looking for ways to occupy time until the early-morning flight to Hong Kong.

Met Zane Barnes—formerly lead public affairs officer for RC-South, he now heads the Public Affairs section at the Iran office in our consulate in Dubai. He previously worked with Anne and Kelly and arrived in Dubai on 4 April, two days before our ill-fated trip to Zabul. We had dinner at a Thai restaurant. After six years in the Foreign Service, Zane seems tired and ready to move on.

Hong Kong, 21 May

Left Dubai at 4:00 a.m. on Emirates Airlines for Hong Kong. It was overcast when we arrived for my two-night stay at the YWCA.

Hong Kong, 22 May

Slept badly, waking up several times thinking I was in my small CHU in Kandahar rather than on the fifteenth floor of the YWCA Garden View overlooking the bright lights of Hong Kong. At other times images of what happened in Zabul crossed my mind repeatedly, like an endless spiral. The weather outside added to the strangeness—occasional flashes of lightning accompanied by the sound of loud thunder, as if someone was rolling metal barrels across the sky.

Attended official launch of my Mongolia book at Hong Kong Foreign Correspondents' Club. Keith Bradsher from the *New York Times* provided introductions—he is the son of Henry Bradsher, long-time AP reporter, now retired.

Met embassy press spokesperson Scott Robinson at the American consulate—he had arranged several meetings including with Consul General Stephen Young and a group of first- and second-tour officers. I opened up more than

I expected with the junior officers, detailing personal aspects of my life that I don't usually share—including recent events in Zabul as well as something that by this time seems almost like ancient news, the long-ago bouts of childhood rheumatic fever that initially kept me out of the Foreign Service and eventually required a new heart valve.

Ulaanbaatar, 23 May

Up early for noon flight to Ulaanbaatar where Fiona was waiting for me. This is the last of my allotted three trips outside Afghanistan.

Ulaanbaatar, 26 May

Spent part of evening sorting through old books as we prepare to dismantle our apartment in Mongolia. Read haunting reflection from a Scottish Covenanter just before his execution during the 1660s, one of several versions that so poignantly captures the last moments of his life on earth: "Farewell moon and stars, farewell world and time, farewell weak and frail body. Welcome eternity, welcome angels and saints, welcome savior of the world, welcome God, the judge of all."

Ulaanbaatar, 27 May

Walked to State Department store to look for gifts for friends in Kandahar.

Ulaanbaatar, 29 May

Official book launch for *Mongolia and the United States: A Diplomatic History*. This one was at the Internom Bookstore and was sponsored by the Jack Weatherford Foundation.

Ulaanbaatar, 30 May

Attended Catriona's graduation from the International School of Ulaanbaatar. Her class numbered eighteen—nine boys and nine girls. Countries represented included Mongolia, South Korea, Japan, Mozambique, Canada, and the United States. Several students cried as they gave their remarks, thanking parents, teachers, and fellow students for their success. I too became emotional, realizing yet again how close I came to missing this event.

11

—◇—

JUNE

Gun Galuut, 1 June

Drove to Gun Galuut with Frank Donovan, almost certainly the last USAID mission director in Mongolia. The road from Ulaanbaatar to the Genghis Khan monument is worse than I remember; there are also far too many plastic bags, bottles, and other litter. But Gun Galuut is the same as always—a wonderful place, far removed from Ulaanbaatar, even if it is hardly two hours away.

Spent most of afternoon walking along the Kherlen River taking in views while Fiona went in search of Argali sheep. I sat for a long time on a cut log beside the water, trying to figure out why I am alive and Anne and Nasemi are not. I don't know why I have been given the opportunity to once again hear the sound of moving water, feel the wind, smell the sweat from galloping horses, and see spacious landscapes such as this.

Hong Kong, 6 June

Said final goodbye to Fiona at 4:00 a.m. and then drove to the airport—on this occasion, I am also saying farewell to Mongolia and all that it has meant for us, possibly for the last time.

Dropped in to see Catriona in her mostly empty bedroom as I departed, thinking I could pass on my final goodbye as she slept. But she woke up, gave me a tight hug and said, "Thank you for everything you did for me during the first eighteen years of my life."

Dubai/Kandahar, 7 June

Landed in Dubai at midnight. Made my way to Terminal Two, finding space on the floor to sleep before the early-morning check-in for Kandahar. The Fly Dubai flight to Kandahar via Bastion was two-thirds full.

Most passengers got off at Bastion—most of them civilian contractors, tired and tanned and often covered with tattoos; some retired military, most in their final months in Afghanistan. The number of civilians assigned to the larger bases and even some of the smaller ones is strangely emblematic of the way that we now fight our wars—or, at least, this particular conflict, which relies almost entirely on the private sector to feed soldiers, clean toilets, maintain bases, and repair aircraft.

Bonnie Weaver was waiting for me at Kandahar Air Field. General Abrams has also returned—he will depart in early July, more than a month ahead of schedule.

Kandahar is always dusty during the dry season—but now the heat is also here in all its oppressive force. It will be like living in an oven for the rest of my time in Afghanistan.

Evening deep dive. General Abrams remains upbeat about ANSF. He thinks the Taliban are facing unexpected resistance in Panjwai and elsewhere. Their fighters seem younger and less experienced. Recently sixteen were seen laying IEDs—provoking an immediate and lethal response.

Travelled in darkened Black Hawk to Gecko for the usual briefings. Uncertainty as to whether Mullah Omar is alive or dead continues—no one seems to know for sure but the speculation continues.

Returned to Kandahar Air Field later than usual. Even at this hour the noise from the boardwalk is especially loud. Operation HOT is at Kandahar Air Field for a few days to Honor Our Troops. The music is from L.A.vation, a U2 tribute band based in Los Angeles.

I saw several parts of the program, one of a number of occasional such activities organized to build morale and entertain the troops. It started at 5:30 when former Notre Dame football coach Lou Holtz gave his inspirational talk through a noisy microphone to the large number of soldiers who had gathered around the boardwalk. The program also included a comedian and a hypnotist and is mostly organized by celebrity chefs. Earlier today they cooked up a New Orleans gumbo—for five thousand people.

Kandahar, 8 June

Spent much of day sorting through e-mails—more than eight hundred on the unclassified system alone, not to mention those on three separate classified accounts.

Met Mohammad Yahya Faqiri, my new translator. He left Afghanistan as a teenager in the late 1980s as the Soviet occupation was drawing to a close. He grew up speaking Pushto and Dari. He spent a year in Karachi before making his way to the U.S. to join relatives. He now lives in Florida. His wife is from Kenya and he has two young children.

Yahya knew about Nasemi but said he looks forward to working with me and is "happy to go wherever you want to go." He is used to tough assignments, having already completed several rotations as an ISAF translator.

Jack Weatherford—retired anthropology professor, author of the best-selling *Genghis Khan and the Making of the Modern World,* and a friend from our years in Mongolia—sent an e-mail from Charleston telling me that his wife Walker had passed away. It was sad to see her long decline—and inspiring to see his love and devotion as she slowly withered away. She looked beautiful in the photos from her youth that he attached, making me wish we had met her long before she became incapacitated.

Kandahar, 9 June

Farewell dinner for Brian Bachman. He leaves later this week for a new assignment in Washington. I bought a take-away meal from the nearby Indian restaurant, and then joined several others at a row of wooden tables set up outside another restaurant on the boardwalk.

Called Kelly Hunt before going to bed, speaking to her for the first time since the explosion in Zabul on 6 April. She was told it was the second explosion that caused her most-severe wounds. She is now recovering at a hospital in Ohio.

I am surprised at how far Kelly has come, at least from the sound of her voice—she seems as lively and animated as ever but is still coming to grips with what happened. She is reliving what she has been told but doesn't remember any of it. She faces further surgery, including placement of a titanium plate in her skull.

Kandahar, 10 June

Woke up to news that the Taliban have attacked Kabul Airport. Heard later about another attack in Zabul. Both events left thirteen Taliban dead—but there were no other Afghan fatalities, civilian or military. Perhaps ANSF is emerging as a stronger force than the Quetta *shura* anticipated.

General White showed me photos from the Georgian base in Helmand attacked a few days ago. It was a small base with fewer than thirty soldiers, each of whom would have grown up on either the Black Sea or the mountains of the Caucasus—the suicide bomber destroyed almost the entire base, bringing down reinforced concrete walls on those inside. In other news, the Taliban reportedly beheaded two young boys in Kandahar, one ten and the other sixteen years old.

Met visiting medical technician from the embassy in Kabul, here to provide pre-departure briefings. My blood pressure is far too high. He spent much of his career in Alaska and likes being in the field. He is unimpressed with many of the cases and concerns he must deal with in Kabul, presumably because he finds life there softer and less adventuresome. By contrast, he thinks highly of civilians he meets in places like Helmand and Kandahar, suggesting that they have a better sense for the realities of war.

Kandahar, 11 June

Provided remarks at start of day-long conference focused on female engagement teams. Also joined participants for dinner. It has been a frustrating yet interesting experience for most of them, especially those who spend time with Afghan women and children in the countryside.

Many of these female soldiers have learned at least rudimentary Pushto. One of them, Ashley from California, is only twenty and attractive in every way—she promised to sing a Pushto song about Mujnoon and Leila, the doomed pair of would-be lovers that figures prominently in the folklore of Pakistan and Afghanistan.

She said she joined the Army following a family dispute that has since been patched up. I was told later she is still struggling with the death of a soldier friend with whom she served in Zaray, killed a few weeks ago following several IED explosions. Since then she says she has "done her work" while also developing a "strong dislike for Afghans."

Kandahar, 12 June

Discussed two helicopter crashes yesterday at the regular 8:00 a.m. morning meeting with the generals. One involved a Black Hawk, the other a Kiowa; both helicopters, heavily damaged, were extracted without incident. According to General Abrams, the Kiowa pilot got carried away and was too aggressive in going after a Taliban on a motorcycle—he wheeled around and hit his target, destroying a $500 motorcycle but at the cost of an aircraft worth several million.

Afternoon video conference with civilian trainees at Muscatatuck in Indiana, preparing to depart for Afghanistan. All that seems like a long time ago. Only three from this group are coming to Kandahar—a year ago, it would have been a dozen at least. Two are auditors and the third is a security officer.

Farewell to Maggie Boehly who is headed for Kabul. She is a superstar, someone who arrived in Afghanistan without much relevant experience yet quickly made herself invaluable. Even General Abrams made a point of saying he wanted to personally wish her goodbye.

Kandahar, 14 June

Regular Friday lunch with Generals Abrams, White, and Hughes. General Brewer also attended, having just returned from his break in Australia. Australian soldiers, like American civilians, get three vacations during their year in Afghanistan—much to the chagrin and even annoyance of American soldiers who only get one.

After the discussion on work I asked about departure dates—early July for Abrams, late July for White and Hughes, and August for Brewer. The Third Infantry Division is giving way to the Fourth Infantry Division one month ahead of schedule. Even the generals are tired and ready to go home.

Unusually, we talked less about business and more about the personal. General Abrams was happy to be back in Hinesville for his son Robert's high school graduation. He arrived on the day of the Georgia state soccer championships on St. Simon's Island, surprising his son at the start of the game. Robert will attend University of Kentucky in the fall. He wants to be a medical doctor and is thinking about joining ROTC.

Attended 238th anniversary celebrations of U.S. Army, a Third Infantry Division event that attracted representatives from the many other nations at Kandahar Air Field. After the celebrations I had dinner with three enlisted soldiers, two of them women. All three talked about their prior careers as truck drivers.

Attended monthly Poet's Night for the soldiers. All the poets and almost everyone in the audience were African American. Every poem addressed at least one of the three great themes—love, sex, and God. As each poet was introduced, a murmur of appreciation swelled up from the audience in unison: "Speak, poet, speak." I can't forget a recurring refrain in one poem recited by a youthful soldier named Ebony: "Why do you always have to do me like that?"

Tomorrow I head for Kabul, once again playing the Afghan version of Russian roulette when taking the lightly armored motor pool vehicle between the airport and the embassy. I'm always pensive before such journeys. I hate to see the pictures of vehicles rammed by a suicide bomber and reduced to a twisted heap of burning metal. Afghan civilians are often killed in such attacks.

Kabul, 15 June

Departed for Kabul on Embassy Air for final SCR *shura,* at least for me. The summits of the higher mountains and the serrated ridges below them still have scattered traces of snow. By now the snow pack of central Afghanistan has mostly melted.

I wonder if this will be my last trip to Kabul Airport. Everyone in our embassy vehicle was quiet during most of the ten-minute drive to the embassy on a busy road that took us by a garish wedding palace and then Masood Circle. I noticed for the first time the network of observation cameras affixed to telephone poles that track our every move.

Evening reception to launch SCR conference, held at the fire pit near the old embassy. One of the long-standing traditions among FSOs who serve here is to warm themselves around the hot coals during the winter months. Kabul is much cooler than Kandahar. I talked with the new SCR replacing Keith Mines in Mazar. He knows he has big challenges ahead. Also talked with Paul Brand from RC-Southwest, recalling the events of Zabul on 6 April. Everyone is sympathetic but some are uncertain about raising the subject, perhaps concerned about my reaction.

Kabul, 16 June

Breakfast with Masha Hamilton at 8:00 a.m. She thinks the public affairs officer assigned to Kandahar is underemployed and wants to transfer him to Kabul. I'm skeptical—once again, we are disengaging from southern Afghanistan sooner than we need to.

Attended weekly country team, this time in person. I mentioned the atmospherics from the woman in Kandahar who expressed disappointment that she wasn't able to register to vote. According to the report, the men consoled her by saying, "Don't worry. We may be able to vote but it is the government and the Americans that will decide the results of the elections anyway."

Shura meetings continued throughout the day, starting with reflections from Ambassador Cunningham. No one really knows what will happen in Afghanistan after 2014. It is hard not to be pessimistic—yet somehow the Afghans might manage this transition better than we imagine. Even Najibullah lasted longer after the Soviets left than anyone thought possible.

Early evening meeting at Masha's apartment with several journalists, including Yaroslav Trofimov and Nathan Hodge from the *Wall Street Journal.* Yaroslav is interested in machinations within the Karzai family, including the apparent animosity between Shah Wali Karzai and his half-brother Mahmood in Kandahar.

Attended reception hosted by Ambassador Cunningham to say farewell to Llorens and McFarland, two of the several former ambassadors who serve in senior positions at the U.S. Embassy in Kabul. It was a pleasant evening with a nice sunset against the Hindu Kush, the tops of nearby mountains still covered in snow. I met several people including the head of the Afghan Independent Human Rights Commission, one of the bravest and most courageous women in Afghanistan.

Talked briefly with several Afghan generals as well as the head of the Afghan Bar Association. Met Amirzai Sangin, Afghanistan's minister of communications for the past nine years. He was the catalyst for this country's cell phone revolution. Educated in England, he spent several years in Sweden. Also met Nicholas "Fink" Haysom, number two at UNAMA. Originally from South Africa, he was for years Nelson Mandela's chief legal counsel.

Unexpectedly ran into Carter Malkasian when I dropped by the west side DFAC for a drink. He is now adviser to General Dunford. He previously spent several years in Afghanistan, first in Kunar and then in Helmand. His recent book—*War Comes to Garmser: Thirty Years of Conflict on the Afghan Frontier*—is said to be remarkable.

Kabul, 17 June

Second day of SCR *shura*. Early-morning sessions focused on civilian/military relations while in the afternoon we talked about business development. In between, Ambassador Llorens led a discussion on engaging with religious leaders and Ambassador Kaidanow provided definitive word that we can no longer leave Afghanistan directly from Kandahar.

The decision on mandatory departures from Kabul will be very demoralizing to people at Kandahar Air Field. Many see this as a security issue, dreading that last drive on open highway to the airport. Others fear a Taliban attack while they stand in the check-in line for their final flight home.

Met a second time with Yaroslav Trofimov from the *Wall Street Journal*. We talked about infighting within the Karzai family and political developments in Kandahar. At one point we also touched on recent elections in Pakistan. Partway through our conversation, Zalmay Khalilzad—the controversial former American ambassador to Kabul and possible future presidential candidate—walked by purposefully, presumably on his way to a meeting with Ambassador Cunningham in his residence.

Attended IPA farewell by the fire pit. The Afghan food was nice. I talked with David Donahue and others who are about to return to the U.S. Life in Kabul is much different from life in Kandahar. People look forward to the end of their Afghan assignments and are ready to go home.

Kabul, 18 June

Spent morning doing chores at embassy. This included picking up civilian awards for military colleagues and a drop by to see Khaililullah Wardak at USAID. We were together at Zabul on 6 April. He is taking it hard but happy to now be with his family in Kabul.

Also checked on Afghan visa renewal. Already my departure from Kabul rather than Kandahar is filling me with dread—I fully expect a last-minute screw-up on passports and visas and I do not believe I will ever leave Afghanistan on time.

Returned to hooch to pack bag and head for airport. It is a beautiful day in Kabul with blue skies, a few clouds, and nice views of the mountains. Walking across the embassy compound, I heard the cooing of birds and then a small dove—or perhaps it was a pigeon—taking a couple of small steps before flying away from the sidewalk in front of me.

Boarded small Beechcraft to cross the mountains of central Afghanistan en route to Kandahar Air Field. We flew lower than usual, providing nice views of scattered valleys framing the landscape, some very narrow and a few quite broad. It is much greener in the north than it is in Kandahar.

Returned to full e-mail box and several small management fires to put out. Realistically some of these fires will burn for the duration of my time at Kandahar Air Field—and maybe even beyond. Goodbye dinner on boardwalk for Susana Batelle and Ellen de Guzman, both headed to Kabul. The rest of my summer will be dominated by farewells.

Kandahar, 19 June

Attended change-of-command ceremony at Kandahar Air Field—Colonel Reed giving way to Colonel Shinners in a training assignment focused on Afghan security forces.

As per a request from Bill Fitzhugh from the Smithsonian Institution in Washington, wrote the foreword for the latest edition of *Genghis Khan and the Mongol Empire,* edited by William Fitzhugh, Morris Rossabi, and William Honeychurch. This reprint will be published in Hong Kong.

Tarin Kot (Uruzgan), 20 June

C-130 to Uruzgan for PRT change-of-command ceremony—Commander Ron Piret giving way to Commander Steve Matthews. The flight up was bumpier than usual. Several flares went off when the plane hit turbulence, making for a nauscous and nail-biting journey.

Piret and Matthews are Navy officers and the ceremony included a ship's bell and boatswain's pipe. Colonel Doug Cardinale and Australian PRT director

David Windsor also spoke. I usually leave Uruzgan with a good feeling—the human dimension somehow works better in Uruzgan than anywhere else in RC-South.

Returned to Kandahar Air Field for lunch with Kandahar mayor Omer, recently returned from three-week study trip to the U.S. The schedule included Washington, Albany, Tucson, and Pensacola. This was his first visit to the U.S. and he enjoyed it immensely. It was heartening to hear him express confidence in the ANSF and optimism about the future.

Mayor Omer estimates Kandahar's population at 1.5–1.8 million, a three-fold increase since 2001. He thinks 18,000 Pakistanis live in Kandahar as well as a much smaller number of Indians and Iranians. In his words, "Pakistanis built Aino Mina."

Gecko, 21 June

Noon commander's huddle with Generals Abrams, White, Hughes, and Brewer. The commanding general talked about his recent visit to see Afghan soldiers recovering in hospital. One was Sergeant Red Hat, an exceptionally effective IED locator who stepped on one at the end of a long day. He lost both legs and faces a very difficult future. As General Abrams noted, "You can see why some would rather die than lose limbs. At that point, they just become a burden on their families."

That launched a wider discussion on Afghanistan's wounded warriors. According to a story related to the general by his translator, one double amputee went home for a few months until his family sent him away. He returned to his army base in Panjwai where he stayed for a while, looked after by former comrades. Probably he will end up living on the streets.

There is interest in forming a charity for wounded Afghan soldiers, similar to the Wounded Warriors Project. General McChrystal has volunteered to head it and lead fund-raising efforts for it in the United States.

Read two interesting items from this week's unclassified local reporting from across southern Afghanistan:

- Villagers alleged a conspiracy by Americans to install NDS head Asadullah Khalid as president in 2014. The villagers agree he would make an excellent president and are glad that America intends to install him.
- A training session went bad when a suicide vest exploded, killing all those present. Taliban fighters were trying to demonstrate to a young boy how to deploy a suicide vest. According to these men, many Taliban were disappointed by the outcome of the training session.

Colonel Bagwell dropped by to talk about my complaint on the DynCorp security guards who treated two members of our Afghan staff abysmally. It is a war zone, but they still shouldn't behave like this. Bagwell talked briefly about his work and his engagements with ICRC on the laws of war. A few weeks ago an Afghan mine clearer employed indirectly by UNAMA was apparently laying mines in his off hours and he was later targeted for it.

Met with the generals in the evening, hearing some of their skepticism about the strength of the civilian governance in Afghanistan. They have a continued concern that the sacrifices made by ANSF are not being sufficiently honored and respected, making it difficult to sufficiently sustain and motivate Afghanistan's military during the difficult days ahead.

I have been thinking a lot about my upcoming trip to Governor Wesa's office, not to mention other trips I will take during these remaining weeks— and all the things that can go wrong. Having survived one attack, I'm not optimistic about living through another one. Flying back to Kandahar Air Field through the dark, I realize more than ever how much I put myself in harm's way when I volunteered to serve in Afghanistan.

Yet no matter what happens I have lived life more intensely here than in most places, taking in fully everything that happens within those brief moments of time that have been allotted to me. Everything is more vivid here—the warmth of hot air as I sat in the Black Hawk this evening, waiting for General Abrams to arrive; the last glimpse of fading light as the sun slips behind the line of dark ridges above Kandahar; the small fires lighting up the *kutchi* encampments we passed over as we departed Kandahar Air Field for Gecko; and the nearly full moon illuminating the night sky when we returned.

Life is beautiful even with its disappointments; life is wonderful even with its pain. In spite of everything, I somehow manage to retain this enormous sense of gratitude for the fleeting moments on this earth that have been given to me. I've never doubted its fragility—but perhaps that makes me appreciate it all the more.

Tonight I signed my short e-mail to Fiona, Iain, Cameron, and Catriona with the words "Love always," a signal of sorts about what ultimately endures, a feeble attempt at voicing what in the end matters most of all.

Governor's Palace, 22 June

Black Hawk flight to Walton followed by MRAPs to governor's palace to meet Wesa. We were a fairly large group this time around—Sergio, David Sias, Lewis, Erin, and Yahya, my interpreter. Sergeant Wassman led the escort and serves as guardian angel—two such soldiers have been assigned to each of us for the duration of this trip.

Governor Wesa recently returned from a trip to Washington along with several other governors and Minister Osmani, the man who holds Afghanistan's "poppy portfolio." Wesa was pleased about his trip but otherwise in an unhappy mood, possibly because U.S. soldiers no longer guard his compound.

Wesa wasn't very forthcoming and remained quiet for most of the meeting—sometimes I wonder if these key leader engagements are worth it. He did say Khakrezwal and Noorzai now at least talk to each other despite opposing each other on the provincial council. He is disappointed about Sarhadi's removal from his governorship in Zaray. His criticism of USG development programs is relentless; it never ends.

Walked through governor's garden and then rejoined our six-vehicle MRAP convoy. The lead vehicle is a minesweeper. Kandahar looks normal from inside my MRAP—it is those looking in our direction that must think us strange. It will be a long time before there is scope for normal embassy outreach in southern Afghanistan; if there are any American civilians left, the Taliban will target them.

Our Black Hawks arrived a few minutes after we reached Walton, blowing up tremendous gusts of dust along with torrid blasts of hot air. Some weeks ago an American soldier was killed when an arriving helicopter blew a loose door on top of him. Putting our backs to the rotor and feeling the force of the wind, it is easy to understand how this happened—anything not tied down is sent flying.

Kandahar, 23 June

Hosted Ambassador Tina Kaidanow for most of day—this included a private meeting, a discussion with senior staff, a meeting with FSOs and team leaders, and a tour of the prospective new embassy compound, purchased in the end from a departing contractor for $700,000.

This was largely a farewell visit. It also provided an opportunity to deliver at first-hand a strong message on the uncertain yet all too predictable path ahead. Washington has no appetite for serious engagement outside Kabul though it may in the end accept a small presence involving as few as two civilian officers at Kandahar Air Field.

Meanwhile peace talks with the Taliban in Qatar got off to a terrible start, the Taliban having hoisted their flag on the premises, to the outrage of President Karzai. Many Afghans are also disappointed. The pictures of smiling and well-fed senior Taliban officials in Qatar showing off with their chubby cheeks, oiled hair, fashionable turbans, and impeccable white suits are being met with skepticism and even disdain in some parts of Afghanistan, including among some of our Afghan staff at Kandahar Air Field. Corruption and profiting from poppy is reportedly rife among some elements of the Taliban, just as it is endemic elsewhere in Afghanistan.

Occasional reporting on atmospherics from across the region also continues to fascinate:

- A mullah in Arghandab said that during the time of the prophet Muslims had dignity. But today Muslims do not have a good name among other peoples of the world. During the Russian jihad when mujahideen were entering houses they would not hesitate to leave when women and children were present. Now the Taliban do not care and they emplace IEDs, killing innocent women and children. For this reason, people do not like beards and burkas anymore as the "Taliban have given us Muslims a bad name. Oh God, please give us shelter and save us from the enemies of Afghanistan."

- Another mullah, this time in Tarnek Wa Jaldak, said that suicide bombers are chosen by Allah and should be respected by all as they give their lives for Islam. Only those with fortitude and piety can become suicide bombers.

Stayed late to write Thomas Jefferson Star and Certificate of Valor nominations for Kelly Hunt, Abbas Kamwand, and Steve Overman, all injured in Zabul on 6 April. I should have done this weeks ago.

Kandahar, 24 June

All-day meeting on energy—USAID and Corps of Engineering staff from Kabul and Helmand attended. The plan is to prepare for the upcoming power *shura* at Kandahar Air Field in early July. The Afghans are supposed to take over and manage all the power plants in Kandahar by the end of the year.

Thirteen ANSF soldiers had been killed in two separate IED attacks in Uruzgan over the past twenty-four hours. It is painful to see Afghans suffer such heavy casualties even as they inflict pain on the Taliban.

Dinner at Asia DFAC with Philip Dayal, my translator Yahya, and a second Afghan American translator I have just met for the first time. He left his country for the first time as a refugee in 1978, after Amin murdered Taraki. He talked about his grandfather who was minister of defense in Kabul nearly a century ago. He claimed that two leaders were especially calamitous for Afghanistan—King Amanullah for accepting the Durand Line and Mohammad Daud for overthrowing King Zahir Shah, thereby turning the country over to the Soviets.

Camp Hero, 25 June

Attended farewell dinner for General Abrams and other senior officers from Third Infantry Division at Camp Hero. It was hosted by General Hamid at the 205th Heroes Division headquarters. Generals Habibi, Sherzai, and many others also attended.

Two cannon had been placed outside one of the Afghan military buildings, painted green like those decorating one of the main traffic circles in Kandahar. It looked like they might have been at the Battle of Maiwand more than 130 years ago.

We travelled by Black Hawk despite the short distance. We first walked to a sitting area, enjoying green tea, raisins, almonds, and pistachios in a vaguely Victorian setting. There was a picture of President Karzai on one wall—and, just below him, a picture of Masood dating to the days of the mujahideen.

I looked through an old Afghan army magazine featuring several prominent martyrs, including former president Mohammad Daud. The commanding general's translator wasn't impressed, saying vehemently that most of those pictured were corrupt traitors who destroyed Afghanistan.

We then walked to a nearby dining room, sitting at a long table laden with naan, kebabs, rice, roast chicken, curried okra, and mangoes. Generals Hamid and Abrams gave speeches, the former emphasizing appreciation for partnership, the latter noting the extraordinary hospitality of Afghans. General Abrams recalled visiting the sergeant who was badly injured a couple of days ago—and how desperately he wanted to return to his unit in Panjwai to once again search for mines and protect his brothers.

It was a heart-felt evening—somehow there is a soldier's code that transcends nationality, religion, and ideology. Afghans now bear the brunt of this war and are dying in the dozens. The Taliban say they want to avoid civilian casualties—yet today ten school children were blown up in Paktika Province and eight women were killed in an IED explosion in Kandahar.

The meal concluded with gift-giving. I didn't expect to be recognized— but I too received a certificate of appreciation from General Hamid as well as a *chapan* of the sort worn by President Karzai.

Kandahar, 26 June

General Abrams walked into my office at the beginning of the day—and dropped off the thick Army report on the 6 April attack in Zabul. It makes grim reading, bringing back in vivid and horrific detail everything that happened. It also leaves me deeply depressed.

The suicide bomber is identified as an x-ray technician named Sajadullah, son of Lal Mohammad. ID cards are included, some with his photograph. He must have been in his twenties. He had a slight beard. The report says the engine block landed close to where I was walking. The injuries of those around me are described in detail. I can't begin to fathom how I was left unscathed.

The draft cover letter mentions the civilian staff at the PRT. It also states that not all the civilians were wearing protective gear. Parts of the report are at odds with what I saw—or what I thought I saw. I'm sure all the civilians were wearing protective gear though not necessarily blast-proof glasses. Surprisingly, the military investigators did not interview any of the civilians present when preparing their report.

One thing did work: the bomb-laden Toyota was turned away by soldiers and not allowed to park just outside the PRT gate. I was stepping out of the gate when this happened. I don't know why the driver didn't choose that moment to detonate his bomb.

All the what-ifs keep flooding back. The consensus among the command staff here in Kandahar is that an attack in some form was inevitable that morning—the driver did in fact return and set off his explosion. If he had returned a minute or two later, several first responders might have been killed. If we had initially turned right rather than left the car might have been driven in our direction anyway.

The report answers a few questions—but not all of them. I wish to God I had never let us leave the PRT—either that, or a dust storm had blown in and we had never left Kandahar at all. It seems clear we were the target, and not the provincial governor.

Tried to put on a cheerful face while eating curry and rice in the Asian DFAC where I met Yahya and another translator. They were sitting next to an older American woman from Pennsylvania named Christina who asked me to join them. She said her late husband was originally a Muslim from Pakistan. They had four kids, all with Pakistani first names—but all of them raised Catholic. In fact, one of them has the name "Mohammad" on his birth certificate but now goes by "Joe." One of her children is marrying a Jewish man, giving her family a close connection with all the revealed religions.

Kandahar, 27 June

Fifty-six years old today—a quiet but mostly miserable day; I can't get beyond this recurring feeling that I'm spending time that more properly belongs to someone else.

Kandahar, 28 June

Another supposedly quiet day that turned into a very busy one. Phil Russell returned from his week in Dubai.

I reread parts of the Zabul report. There is nothing derogatory about my part in what happened. That said, I'm prepared to accept any blame the embassy or Washington may send in my direction. I'm very tired at this point—thoughts of a career or personal ambition seem far away and even meaningless.

The regular Friday lunch with the generals focused on final gifts for Afghan counterparts. The generals are deeply disappointed in the performance of provincial governors. There is also a feeling that the Afghan military is improving much faster than their civilian counterparts.

Attended Friday evening deep dive. More Fourth Infantry Division officers are becoming involved. Ten months into my tour, I am finally becoming familiar with the military culture as well as the Afghan tribal landscape that surrounds me.

Kandahar, 29 June

More fallout from the draft Zabul report. It is now with ISAF in Kabul. The embassy wants my copy ASAP—but I don't have it anymore. The Third Infantry Division staff retrieved it, stating that ISAF in Kabul wants to officially deliver the final version to the embassy. Help! Or maybe this is a good thing—it can't be considered complete until civilian witnesses are also interviewed.

The regular morning briefing included speculation on what might have happened in Zabul. Possibly, the Taliban had informants in Qalat, alerting them to our pending visit.

Met Deputy Governor Patyal at our *shura* room on Kandahar Air Field. I enjoy these meetings—our conversation is both interesting and entertaining. He thinks President Karzai really will step down at the end of his term.

Patyal considers the infighting reported among the Karzai family in southern Afghanistan as normal for any Afghan family in power: "Our royal families always fought among themselves," he said. He forecasts a lot of Afghan interest in the April 2014 elections. He thinks a new generation is ready to enter politics, pushing the older one aside.

Kandahar, 30 June

Country team with embassy in Kabul via video followed by all-hands meeting at Kandahar Air Field. As usual, met with our Afghan staff afterward—one of my favorite occasions of the week. For their sake, I hope Afghanistan's future somehow turns out better than seems possible right now.

Attended traditional Protestant service at Fraise Chapel for first time in many months. About fifty people attended, most of them soldiers. The chaplain mentioned a Christian cleaner from Pakistan named Khalil who talked to him last week, proffering several Bibles he had uncovered in a trashcan—and asking the chaplain to ensure that his Holy Book would be handled in a more respectful fashion in the future.

Met Deputy Secretary General Jan Eliasson of the UN, along with a large team from Kandahar, Kabul, and New York. Formerly a Swedish navy commander, Eliasson also served as Swedish foreign minister, state secretary, and ambassador to the United States.

The meeting got off to a bad start when Eliasson described one leading politician in southern Afghanistan as a "good man" and another as "interesting and informative." The senior staff here in Kandahar is much less enthusiastic, criticizing one of those mentioned for his limited accomplishments and describing the other one as an illiterate opium addict.

The senior military staff presented a fairly upbeat perspective on security. Someone else at the table reported hearing from one Afghan source that reports of a lack of security may be only a ruse employed by Karzai supporters to either postpone elections or encourage Karzai to run for a third term.

Evening partner dinner hosted by Third Infantry Division. Mostly this was a formal farewell for several Afghan officers including General Hamid. I sat next to Colonel Hadi, operations officer for the 205th Corps. He is from Kabul and has never left Afghanistan, regardless of those in power—Soviets, Taliban, ISAF, and now Karzai.

Hadi has four sons and two daughters—the oldest son is in the military and the second son is a computer science student who wants to study overseas. He said his children are optimistic about Afghanistan's future. Colonel Chris Boyle was seated to my right—it was nice to finally have a chance to talk about his family and past career. He leaves with General Abrams next week to return to Fort Stewart, Georgia.

At the end of the day General Abrams dropped by my office to say the Zabul investigation had searched further for Anne's medical records, missing from the original report—and found them. At both the Zabul PRT and Apache where she arrived by helicopter less than an hour after the attack, heroic efforts were made to save her life. Once again I am reliving everything, including the memory of her broken body as she was carried away on a stretcher, her hand I held as she was taken first to the PRT first aid post and then to the waiting helicopter, and my fervent hopes that she might somehow survive.

Read further unclassified reporting before going to bed. June 2013 has been the deadliest month for ISAF since September 2012 when I started my assignment at Kandahar Air Field: twenty-seven soldiers killed across Afghanistan so far, seventeen of them American.

12

—◇—

JULY

Kandahar Airport, 1 July

Attended morning power *shura* at Kandahar Airport. Governor Wesa and General White launched the event; unexpectedly, I was asked to talk briefly. The discussion went around in circles. We want to get out of power and end direct diesel subsidies. The Afghans want subsidies to continue for as long as possible.

Sat next to Wesa at lunch. He extended an open invitation to have Catriona meet his daughter in Vancouver. Also saw airport director Faizi, the chief operating officer for the Afghan power company visiting from Kabul, and the head of the Kandahar Chamber of Commerce, among many others. I hope Afghans figure out a way to keep the lights on after ISAF leaves.

Talked to my two guardian angels, both coming and going to the airport. One is from near the Everglades in Florida, the other grew up in New Mexico. Both soldiers look forward to the end of this deployment. Passed on Mongolian coin to Lieutenant Cohn who headed the command group's security detail throughout much of my time in Kandahar.

Attended evening promotion ceremony for Chris Willis, now a full colonel. His family watched via video from Fort Benning. The room was full of fellow soldiers. General Abrams spoke about service and commitment. Moments like this make my assignment in Afghanistan worth it after all.

Met General Paul LaCamera, commanding general for the Fourth Infantry Division out of Fort Carson, Colorado—he is quieter and more introverted than General Abrams.

The *Wall Street Journal* article on conflicts among the Karzai family in Kandahar is finally out. Lewis Gitter covered much of this material weeks and even months ago though much of our reporting never got beyond Kabul.

Kandahar, 2 July

Relatively calm day. Bonnie left for Kabul for a few days. Attended evening briefings with Generals Abrams and LaCamera. My time in Afghanistan will finish in less than eight weeks. That hardly seems possible—at times it seemed that this assignment would never end.

Kandahar Airport/FOB Apache (Zabul), 3 July

Met all three members of the Pakistan consulate for lunch at Kandahar Airport, diplomatic counterparts who at some level have also become acquaintances and even friends, given shared experiences in a place of hardship. I brought dates from Dubai—but they outdid me with gifts of their own, including a small leather wallet and two boxes of mangoes.

These are useful and even informative meetings, but I sometimes wonder about what is left unsaid. Referring to the recent statement by the head of the Afghan army that Pakistan could end this war in weeks, the deputy consul general stated, "ISAF hasn't been able to end this war in more than ten years. How do people think we can end it in a few weeks?"

They mentioned the many sacrifices made by Pakistan in the long war on terrorism. They think Nawaz Sharif offers hope, both in addressing Pakistan's power crisis and in dealing with terrorism. Only this week blasts left dozens dead in Quetta and Peshawar.

Black Hawk to Apache with General White to meet Governor Naseri. The governor is depressed that the PRT has shut down and even more depressed to hear that the Zabul Teacher Training College will probably not be built.

I'm also disappointed—but the contractor from Kandahar didn't perform. I told Naseri the Afghan government has convinced donors to focus on government programs managed out of Kabul—and his efforts are rightly being directed there rather than toward the U.S. military.

Our meeting dragged on for a long time. The governor did most of the talking. Eventually we pulled ourselves away, crossing a desolate landscape for the thirty-minute flight back to Kandahar Air Field.

We flew alongside Highway One for most of the journey, observing in places the bases and guard posts built over the past ten years. I noticed a lot of traffic heading in both directions.

Tarin Kot (Uruzgan), Independence Day, 4 July

Morning Fourth of July celebrations in Marne Garden, just outside command headquarters. It was short and simple, but the remarks by General Abrams were drowned out twice by loudspeakers announcing a controlled detonation at Kandahar Air Field.

Somehow things couldn't be coordinated to have the explosions postponed even a couple of hours. It is another hot day in Kandahar, hot enough so that one of the standing soldiers fainted and had to be taken away for medical attention.

Attended ceremony for newly minted Sergeant Williams who works with Bonnie and assists with computers. Afterward gave my parting gift to General White—a likeness of Genghis Khan on a horse.

Afternoon trip to Uruzgan with General White in Black Hawks— Lewis and Yahya accompanied us. We drove directly from the flight line to the governor's compound in a convoy consisting of seven Bushmasters. The Australian security contingent is very professional. Our route was different from the usual one, providing opportunities to see the bazaar and suburbs at the edge of town.

The governor's compound is more substantial than ever. The front garden is impressive with roses, sunflowers, and lots of green grass. Large portraits of historical Afghan figures were painted on several sections of the compound wall.

Governor Akhundzada greeted us warmly despite our bulky protective gear. His office includes new furniture, cupboards, and carpets. We covered a lot of ground in only an hour. Akhundzada is my favorite governor, hands down. He is more traditional than other governors such as Wesa with his Canadian passport and Naseri with his history as a school teacher in refugee camps in Pakistan. Whatever happens, I can't imagine Akhundzada in any place other than Afghanistan. Politics is a game for him—one he is very good at.

He recently spent a week in Istanbul for medical treatment and was impressed with what he saw: "They had mosques and they had clubs, they are Muslims but they also spend time at the beach."

The governor would be happy if Afghanistan were to somehow move in a similar direction. I didn't plan to bring up the recent talks in Doha but he went there on his own: "I was in Turkey when the Taliban opened their office in Qatar," he said. "I cried when I saw the Taliban flag being raised. It meant that all our efforts over the past ten years have been wasted."

We talked about the governor's conference in Kabul. He spoke three times and hopes that the provinces will be given more authority and a larger budget.

The meeting finished with gifts—a box with a logo from the Third Infantry Division from General White, a State Department medal mounted on a plaster T-wall from me. The difference is that military budget covers their gifts while I personally pay for mine.

I love the view from Akhundzada's office toward the fields and mountains of Uruzgan. I also appreciate the hospitality—green tea, pistachios, raisins, apricots, and mangoes. The apricots come from Khas Uruzgan, a heavily contested area. The mangoes come from Pakistan. Akhundzada said he likes mangoes—but didn't touch these because, he said, "I don't like Pakistan."

After the meeting we walked through the garden to the waiting Australian Bushmasters and then took a different route to Camp Holland. Our two Black Hawks were already waiting for us on the flight line.

Left Tarin Kot at 5:30 p.m. Already the sun was falling lower in the sky, improving the lighting and casting shadows off the mountains. More than ever I see southern Afghanistan as an ocean of brown only occasionally filled by small green islands and archipelagoes marking the few places where cultivation is somehow possible. I'm tired and ready to go home. But I also realize there are things about this place that I will miss, memories that I will carry with me for as long as I live.

The Taliban are also celebrating Fourth of July—just before midnight a rocket was lobbed in our direction. The base radar picked it up, momentarily sending everyone to their bunkers.

Kandahar, 5 July

Flags at half-mast, never a good sign. This one is for a fallen hero en route from RC-West to Dover via Kandahar Air Field. He was killed by an IED in a firefight, a rare occurrence in that part of the country.

Noon lunch with the generals, this time involving General LaCamera for the first time. We talked about Gizab in Daikundi Province. Unusually there has been conflict there in recent weeks. This was largely a local event among the Achakzai, one faction wanting Gizab to be part of Daikundi and the other pressing for it to be annexed by Uruzgan.

Afternoon ramp ceremony amidst intense heat. Dozens—perhaps hundreds—of soldiers from many nations turned up, several collapsing because of the conditions. It was largely conducted in silence—other than the sound of several airplanes taking off: a 747 first and then two F-16s in quick succession.

The hot wind warmed our faces; toward the mountain ridge in the distance I saw occasional swirls of dust. The scripture ("Come unto me all ye that are weary and heavy-laden and I will give you rest") was followed by the Third Infantry Division brass band playing "Amazing Grace."

Private Errol Maillard was from Brooklyn. He belonged to a sapper company and served as a combat engineer. He was born in 1994, the same year as Catriona—and, like her, was only eighteen years old.

Farewell dinner for General Abrams involving many gifts and tributes. His next assignment will be in Washington, though it is uncertain exactly where. Satirical Australian commentary included the suggestion that he would end up as commanding general for PowerPoint, which he hates.

Colonels Adgie, Getchell, Stuart, and Pepin all gave parting remarks. It is hard to believe that the senior officers will soon be going their separate ways, breaking apart what I have come to think of as an impressive command structure. My contributions seem very modest by comparison.

General Abrams offered his extended reflections, thanking everyone and acknowledging that he had sometimes been tough on people. Several speakers commented on the commanding general's stare, and he wanted to set the record straight: he stares partly because he is somewhat deaf and has to read people's lips, and partly because he is thinking even as he tries to hear others speak.

Other quotes from General Abrams included the following lines: "I like being a soldier." "I know what is at stake." "I want to serve my country." "It is intensely personal for me." "We've seen some horrific stuff." "I always ask, am I meeting my responsibility?" "It is not about me. It is about our mission." "I always ask, is it worth sending twenty-one people outside the wire on this mission?" "That is a responsibility I want." "I believe in our soldiers. I believe in our families." "I am a soldier. We go where we are told, when we are told." "It isn't about the mission you want: it is about the mission you're given."

Kandahar, 6 July

Spent much of day with former ambassador to Afghanistan Ron Neumann. He was accompanied by Carter Malkasian, a fluent Pushto speaker now serving as political adviser to General Dunford in Kabul. Phil Russell and I met with them for an hour; in between, they attended one of our weekly meetings and then talked over dinner with all ten FSOs, both USAID and State, serving in Kandahar.

Ambassador Neumann first visited Afghanistan in 1967 when his father was ambassador. Nearly four decades later he assumed the same position. Reflecting on recent years, he thinks Afghanistan has advanced tremendously—but would be in a much better place if it did not have to simultaneously fight an insurgency. He thinks the Afghan army is stronger than ever but is surprised at how little we know of the careers and aspirations of the emerging officer corps.

He saw Hamid Karzai in Kabul recently. Karzai was convinced the U.S. wants bases in Afghanistan and will accept almost anything to get them. He likened Afghanistan to a house, noting that the owners of the house might decide to rent an upstairs room to a paying guest such as the Americans. Afghans might not like the cooking, smells, or noises coming from that upstairs room—but they would somehow figure out a way to get along.

Carter described Zabul as a mess, placing Ghazni, Wardak, and Sangin in upper Helmand in that same category. He said that Khost, accessible only by high mountain passes, is vulnerable and at some point could fall to the Taliban. The study he is working on focuses on the Afghan local police, which he says works reasonably well in most of southern Afghanistan but is less successful in the northern and the western parts of the country.

Kansas City Star published the article on Marilyn McBee, the ten-year-old girl from Kansas who died of polio in Kandahar in 1954. The small cemetery where she is buried is now completely overgrown. One of our Afghan staff told me he was advised to not visit the cemetery for fear he might step on a land mine.

Kandahar, 7 July

Attended contemporary Protestant service in Fraise Chapel, taking communion for the first time in several months.

General Abrams came to my office in the evening with a parting gift—a signed color print depicting the Third Infantry Division at the Battle of the Marne during World War I. This was also the general's last CUA—and the last time that I will ever have occasion to sing "Dog Face Soldiers" or say "Rock of the Marne."

Kandahar, 8 July

Attended early-morning awards presentation for General Abrams—General Milley came down from Kabul to do the honors. Abrams received a bronze star and Legion of Merit, along with compliments and applause. Talking about the campaign, Milley this time referenced Gettysburg and Vicksburg, suggesting that future historians might look back on the summer of 2013 in Kandahar as one of the decisive moments of the Afghan campaign.

Met Ambassador Cunningham on flight line at 9:00 a.m. and then drove to change-of-command ceremony at the Fest Tent. Ten months ago I was at a similar event—only then it was General Abrams assuming command. Like last year, the event started with the NATO hymn and the Afghan and American national anthems. Then Mullah Rahmatullah from the 205th Corps and

Chaplain Walker from the Third Infantry Division gave separate invocations, followed by the casing and uncasing of the colors

The generals spoke in turn—Milley, Hamid, Abrams, and LaCamera. I hope the optimism expressed is warranted. Fifty-four soldiers were killed and nearly four hundred wounded during the Third Infantry Division's deployment in southern Afghanistan.

Talked with several Afghans at the beginning of the ceremony or in the reception that followed. This included General Habibi, NDS chief Esa Mohammad, police chief General Razziq, and Panjwai district governor Haji Faisal Mohammad. Neither Governor Naseri nor Governor Akhundzada were able to fly down, a dust storm having kept the helicopters away.

General Habibi attributed almost all Afghan casualties to IEDs rather than firefights. He said the Taliban were afraid, implanting IEDs so quickly they sometimes blow themselves up.

Ambassador Cunningham kept his distance from General Razziq. I am amazed at Razziq's recovery since the bomb blast that almost killed him one year ago. I'm surprised at how young and enthusiastic he looks, almost like a high school student. As for Haji Faisal Mohammad, he failed his recent governor's test in Kabul but still seems resilient.

Ambassador Cunningham met privately with Governor Wesa who seemed relaxed. I've attended so many such meetings it is hard to learn anything new. Wesa is skeptical about the provincial council but optimistic about the next elections.

Ambassador Cunningham addressed all the civilians on the platform, including our Afghan staff. He talked a lot about Doha and the failure of the Taliban to live up to their promises. He said he had heard from across Afghanistan that Taliban officials looked ridiculous on television, preening in their nice clothes and oiled hair but far removed from the realities of a drastically changed Afghanistan.

He ended the meeting by handing out awards, recognizing several people including Akemi Tinder who accompanied Kelly Hunt on her medical evacuation flight to Germany in early April. I also thanked David Donahue, the IPA director visiting from Kabul—he departs at the end of the week, having completed his year in Afghanistan.

We left the Kabul party on the flight line. We then drove to a different ramp, hoping to say a final farewell to General Abrams and his team. We were too late—he had already departed Kandahar, leaving me with an empty feeling. The past six weeks will not be the same without him—I wish that I somehow could have left first.

Attended evening CUA. All the insignia has been changed, confirming that the Fourth Infantry Division is now in charge. The blue-and-white stripes signifying the Third Infantry Division have been replaced by the green four-leaf clovers of the Fourth. The slogan is also different—rather than Rock of the Marne we now say Steadfast and Faithful.

Kandahar, 9 July

Met Captain Keith Kosik from 141st Military History Detachment. His calling card included this memorable line: "Life is short; history is forever." He said the records that he gathers will be kept at Fort Myer outside Washington, DC. It may take years—but they will eventually provide raw material for a history of the Afghan campaign.

Spent afternoon in office following Kandahar Air Field–wide alarm announcing a ground attack. We have yet to hear the definitive story, but this may have been a green-on-blue incident. Several Slovak soldiers were fired on from a guard tower at the far end of the base. One Slovak soldier was killed and six others injured, a sad loss on the eve of Ramadan.

Kandahar, 10 July

Morning briefing included comparison of last year's fighting season with this one. ISAF casualties are down, ANSF casualties are up. Civilian casualties have increased markedly, the overwhelming majority inflicted by the Taliban. Just yesterday seventeen civilians, mostly women and children, were killed in an IED explosion on a road outside Herat.

Attended ramp ceremony for Slovak soldier killed yesterday at Kandahar Air Field—the first Slovak soldier to die while deployed in Afghanistan. The Slovak prime minister and minister of defense flew in from Bratislava to accompany the remains home. Hundreds of soldiers gathered on the tarmac to pay their last respects. The Slovak chaplain wore a long black cassock over his combat uniform and dusty boots. The entire chaplain corps, most of them American, wore dark glasses. Despite the sun no one wore a hat.

A clutch of Slovakian reporters gathered in the shade underneath their prime minister's plane to film the event. The Fourth Infantry Division brass band again played a slow, dirge-like version of "Amazing Grace" as the coffin was carried to the cargo hold.

The Afghan who killed the Slovak soldier recently returned from Nangahar, home province to nearly half of all green-on-blue attackers. He served in the Afghan army for five years. Two other Slovak soldiers were badly injured in the attack.

Flight-line farewell for Rick Gregory, our RSO who is leaving after one year at Kandahar Air Field. Diane Latham and Steve May arrived to wish Rick well as he heads for Helsinki with his family.

Kandahar, First Day of Ramadan, 11 July

First day of Ramadan. We hope for a quiet month—but have been told insurgents believe any mujahideen killed will obtain special rewards. Unclassified reporting from around southern Afghanistan has included words of thanks for the "honorable mujahideen" for fulfilling their "great religious obligation" in advancing a struggle that is "genuine and holy."

Attended Purple Heart ceremony with General LaCamera. The ceremony was for a soldier wounded in a firefight in Maiwand, shot in the thigh but emerging with only a broken femur. He is from West Virginia and his wife is expecting their first child in early August. LaCamera's style for pinning Purple Hearts is different from Abrams'—quicker, quieter, more streamlined. This was a good night because no limbs are missing and this soldier should recover.

Promotion ceremony in Marne Garden for newly minted Sergeant Shoemaker from Ohio. He asked me to exchange his specialist cap for a sergeant's one and I felt very honored to do it. He hopes to become an Army aviator and fly helicopters.

Fiona and Catriona are back in Georgia and I've had long talks by phone with both of them. I have just over six weeks left in Kandahar—that seems like a short time but a lot can happen, and I live in dread that something awful will hit us. Not me—I can accept that—but someone else who is part of this civilian team and for whom I am responsible.

Kandahar, 12 July

Received touching note from David Donahue on his departure from Kabul. It has been a difficult year for all of us—our relations with IPA have sometimes been rocky and at times I have been tempted to expunge references to these disagreements from this daily chronicle. Yet that was part of this year, also—the inevitable disagreements between Kabul and the field, some of them very deep.

Commander's lunch at noon, our first with General LaCamera. It was less structured and more free-wheeling than with General Abrams. As our military pulls back he sees the need for more diplomacy—something that will be difficult when we are risk averse on the civilian side and our numbers continue to decline.

Walked along boardwalk in the afternoon, ordering Indian chai at one stall and frozen yogurt at another one. Took fleeting look at several boardwalk war memorials, all of which will disappear when ISAF leaves. One recognizes war dogs killed in the line of duty, sniffing out IEDs. Another remembers Canadian soldiers killed, yet another those involved in Special Forces operations. There is also a small plaque for those killed on 9/11, the event that started the blood-letting. Even twelve years on more Americans were killed on that single day in New York and Washington, DC, than have died in the entire Afghan campaign.

Talked with Jesse Alvarado on the responsibilities he will take on as chief of staff. A former Marine, he will bring a lot to the job—most importantly he has the confidence of the Fourth Infantry Division leadership who are happy about the continuity at a time when most FSOs are moving on.

The new SCR for Kandahar has also been announced—Ned Alford, U.S. ambassador to Gambia. Approaching age sixty-five, he served three years in the Army and had previous FSO assignments in Pakistan and Iraq. He won't arrive until late September.

Weekly deep dive covered several issues including Taliban financing. Both in these meetings and in the media the view is sometimes expressed that ISAF contracts and various community development programs also help fund the insurgency, prolonging the conflict. Senior officers are also annoyed that some Taliban sympathizers reportedly operate shops on the boardwalk, making money that is then used to lob rockets back on Kandahar Air Field. The rockets supposedly originate from Pakistan, Iran, and China. Speculation abounds on what might happen if surface-to-air missiles are ever introduced.

Regular reporting collected from across the region continues to fascinate:

- One man feels ISAF could have defeated the Taliban but the British prevented them because the Afghans defeated the British in their quest to colonize Afghanistan years ago.
- Lots of discussion about elections—whether Karzai will run for a third term, whether there will even be elections at all. If either scenario unfolds, international support for Afghanistan will plummet even farther.
- More indications about the new commanding general's leadership style. Yesterday he talked about sexual harassment, wondering out loud "why we can't provide the same care and respect to people when they are alive that we give them when they are dead."
- LaCamera can't stand pink pillows or soft toys hanging out of backpacks. He holds officers to a higher standard: "If you walk by and see a problem, it is your job to fix it."

Kandahar, 13 July

Handed commanding general background cables on several pending visits—Vice President Joe Biden to India, Senator Corker to Pakistan, and CENTCOM commanding general to Kazakhstan. In each case there is at least one paragraph referring to Afghanistan. The Afghans want to be at the center of attention; already they think the planet revolves entirely around them.

More insights from today's reporting, gathered from around the region:

- A couple of men from District Six are disappointed at the lack of professionalism displayed at Kandahar University. They think the teachers are biased and their dialects and accents make it difficult for Pushtuns to learn.
- Two men voice their anger toward the Taliban for their destruction of schools. They say they dislike the Taliban for their policy of attacking anything that represents progress for the country.
- Two men in Baba Sahed praise the Qatar peace talks. They are displeased with Karzai, though, for impeding the process. They say his behavior toward ISAF and America has been odd lately.

Morning meeting with visitors from Joint Border Task Force in Kabul. Their hoped-for visit to Spin Boldak was turned off at the last minute—just yesterday there was a suicide bomber attack on the Wesh-Chaman crossing, the second in a week.

Evening farewell for departing Chief of Staff Phil Russell at Mama Mia's on the boardwalk. He leaves Kandahar in ten days after nearly thirty months in Afghanistan. Despite different management styles, I could not have made it through this year without him; indeed, in several important ways we complemented each other.

Kandahar, 14 July

More atmospherics, this time focused on Friday sermons:

- One mullah, to his congregation: "Suicide bombers are giving Islam a bad name. They are killing innocent Muslim men, women and children. They should not label it jihad and throw Islam's name in the dirt."
- Another mullah, also to his congregation: "Muslim brothers, you should look and listen to what I have to say. I heard that during this holy month of Ramadan a member of parliament from Kandahar, Abdul Rahim, held a party. At his Ramadan party he had little boys dancing for his pleasure. He and his friends were drinking alcohol and abusing little boys; this is what we can expect from the leadership of our government. Even the infidels would not have little boys dance for them."

Earlier today the Afghan who killed the Slovak soldier at Kandahar Air Field walked out of his confinement. He was accompanied and no doubt aided and abetted by Master Sergeant Ehsanullah Mohrai from Teyzan village near Kabul who also disappeared. I don't know how these things happen—the Slovaks will be furious. Far too many green-on-blue attackers get away with it.

Kandahar, 16 July

Another quiet day—it is difficult to arrange trips outside Kandahar Air Field during these early days of Ramadan. I gave coins and certificates of appreciation to several departing soldiers, including members of the former commanding general's security detail. They risked their lives to make our meetings with Afghans possible.

Heard second-hand that the Afghan who killed the Slovak soldier is now in Pakistan. He told his uncle that he wished he had been killed in the attack and now wanted to become a suicide bomber. I still can't believe the Afghan army let him escape, a breach of faith that is almost unforgivable. Supposedly, he was held in a cell controlled by ANSF at Kandahar Air Field.

Evening intel briefing, the second involving the new commanding general with his tag line Iron Horse Six. He asks good questions—but I am struck by his very different style. He doesn't give much away and it is not always easy to know what he is thinking.

Musam Ghar, 17 July

Early-morning Black Hawk flight with General LaCamera to Musam Ghar in eastern Panjwai. We stopped briefly at Camp Hero en route to pick up General Hamid and his bodyguards. On arrival we met the acting deputy governor. He has a black beard, large belly, Sindhi hat, and limp right arm, possibly signifying an old war injury. He presented a bleak account of the state of affairs in Panjwai.

Afterward an interpreter commented that our visitor was playing to the gallery—he dreads the day when ISAF leaves because ISAF contracts have been so lucrative. It is in his interests that the new ISAF commander should think the security situation is really, really bad.

I asked the acting district governor about one of his relatives, another prominent tribal leader from the same area. In keeping with the Afghan tradition of often having stormy relations with cousins, he quickly commented that this particular cousin would "spread a wonderful table for you but wouldn't give even ten afs [afghanis] to a beggar." He added that his now prominent and very wealthy cousin with whom he had a strained relationship once had "hardly enough money for a motorcycle." Yet now he is so wealthy he owes someone in Kabul "eight million dollars." Finally, he stated that every Afghan knows you can't be wealthy in Afghanistan "unless you are corrupt or commit a crime."

Asked about Doha, the acting deputy governor said, "People believe in the Taliban" but the television broadcast from their shiny new office convinced Afghans "they are not fighting for a holy cause, only for power." As for GIRoA, "Afghans want to love their government but are left upset and disappointed by it." Looking ahead, "People think bloodshed will only increase once ISAF leaves."

He asked for better equipment and technology for ANSF. General LaCamera wasn't impressed: "I would trade all my blimps for your knowledge of the district."

According to the acting deputy governor, the Taliban mostly stay in mosques though "everything they do is against our religion." He added, "Afghans are so religious they won't even scratch their beards in a mosque, for fear a hair will fall out" and desecrate the place. However, "The Taliban commit suicide attacks in mosques and shed blood."

He also told LaCamera, "Your company commanders stay with your soldiers but our company commanders stay in their offices." He added, "Both sides kick down doors—the government during the day, the Taliban during the night." He also said ANSF soldiers spend their time at checkpoints or bases without patrolling. During Ramadan, "They sleep all day and play cards all night."

He mentioned a recent ANSF offense involving 1,800 Afghan soldiers that resulted in the capture of a single Taliban fighter. He mentioned that district governor Haji Faisal Mohammad had been shot seven times as a mujahideen ("from head to toe"). He is fifty-five years old but with his white beard and wrinkled face looks more like seventy. As for the acting deputy governor, he has lost two brothers in the fight against the Taliban.

The Panjwai uprising had limited results and entails two separate movements, each involving a particular family and tribe. The first uprising led by Wadood Agha, an Achakzai, was well supported by the government—so well supported that those involved were soon driving three-wheeled off-road vehicles, to the envy of everyone else.

When a second family led by Haji Habibullah revolted, they hardly received anything: "It was the Achakzais who were getting all the support." Haji Habibullah is a Gilzai and "doesn't even have a government permit to carry a pistol."

The acting deputy governor took a dim view of Afghan politicians, stating that no one wants to face elections: "They benefit from the chairs they are sitting on and don't want to lose them." He mentioned the Kandahar Provincial Council chairman, hand-picked by Karzai. Previously this man repaired truck tires. Now he has enough money to "construct buildings." Yet most politicians are so uneducated they "don't know how to speak in front of a camera."

Asked if he might enter politics, he acknowledged, "Maybe if I get into the chair, I will also become corrupt."

We then boarded battery-powered mules, similar to small golf carts, riding up a steep dirt road to the top of a nearby hill. The views toward Zaray to the north, Sperwan Ghar and the Registan Desert to the south were especially nice, a mix of green fields and brown mountains, enveloped by the blue sky above us.

Our view also embraced a network of barbed wire, like something out of *Beau Geste*. When I look at such scenes I wonder yet again how the U.S. became so entangled in Afghanistan, to the extent of having to set up armed camps in such remote and desolate places as this.

Returned to flight line only to be told one of our helicopters had hydraulic problems. It took another hour for two replacement helicopters to arrive. We then headed to the Mosum Ghar DFAC for lunch. I expected expeditionary food but it turned out to be much better—tuna fish in pita bread, chips, and the best fresh peaches I have eaten since arriving in Afghanistan.

Our two helicopters eventually arrived in a swirl of dust to take us back to Kandahar Air Field. The doors were left completely open. Once in the air there was nothing between me and the ground hundreds of feet below. At one point I thought my helmet might fly out the open door.

Returned to Kandahar Air Field for video conference with students at Muscatatuck, Indiana. Four of them will soon depart for Kandahar.

Walked with Bonnie to Asian DFAC for dinner. Looking back, the sky toward the north was by turns orange, red, and purple, the colors deepened by dust blowing in from the desert to the south.

Tarin Kot (Uruzgan), 18 July

Fairly busy day starting with 8:00 a.m. stand-up and continuing through video conference with other SCRs. I also distributed certificates of appreciation and various awards to our Australian, Romanian, and British military colleagues— including a small Genghis Khan statue to General Brewer and an engraved Mongolian hip flask to Colonel King.

Late afternoon Black Hawk to Tarin Kot for *iftar* dinner organized by the Australians. It was a wonderful event—everyone was relaxed, the discussion all the more productive because of it. Governor Akhundzada embraced me on arrival and his expressions and manner reminded me yet again that he is the most agreeable Afghan of all the governors.

Akhundzada mentioned that he has four young sons in Kabul, all of whom enjoy computers and are learning English. He spoke disparagingly about the security situation in Helmand, perhaps hoping he might eventually be sent back to his home province to fix it. He wonders if he should attend the regional conference Wesa is organizing in Kandahar.

Several local dignitaries attended the *iftar*, including Tarin Kot mayor Najib-ur-Rahman who is an engineer and speaks English, Uruzgan IEC director Osmani, and Uruzgan Human Rights Commission director Abdul Ghafar Stanikzai. By December everyone from ISAF, including the Australians, will be gone.

Returned to Kandahar Air Field on 9:30 p.m. C-130 flight. It waited for us for ninety minutes and was packed with soldiers flying down from Kabul including the commanding general's new chief of staff, Colonel Antonio. I felt like a ghost walking across the tarmac to board the plane. Everything was quiet when we boarded and almost everything was dark other than the yellow moon overhead and the blue-colored runway lights.

Ed Birsner and I sat in the flight deck where it was also dark, save only for the green glow of the instrument panel and occasional lights from isolated villages shining out of the darkness below. Meanwhile David Sias and Yahya sat in the main cabin with everyone else.

This was one of my better days in Kandahar. I like the *shura* room at Camp Holland and have had some of my best conversations there. Built by the Dutch, it is furnished in a more traditional Afghan style with marble vases, plastic flowers, and cushions on the floor. We broke fast with dates and our meal included rice, naan, curried okra, lamb *karai,* salad, sweet melons, and green tea.

Gecko, 19 July

A relatively quiet Friday. At the noon commander's lunch, we focused on broader issues. One senior officer present commented that the ISAF detention policy would have been much clearer "if we had just said everyone captured on the battlefield is a POW."

Once again, I find the reporting from across the region both interesting and informative:

- A group of fifteen men in Qalat comment very positively about the call to prayer broadcast from FOB Apache. One man says the broadcast is loud and clear and as many as fifteen villages in the area can hear it. Another man calls the speaker's voice "soothing and wonderful." A third man says many hope the broadcasts will continue after Ramadan.

- Several men in the Qalat bazaar discuss the call to prayer broadcast over loud speakers from FOB Apache. One man says most people are happy about the American call to prayer, saying the speakers in Qalat city don't always work or aren't loud enough.
- A couple of men from District Six are shocked and puzzled by President Obama's statements regarding the departure of American soldiers in 2014. They believe ANSF requires additional training and assistance because they are incapable of solely maintaining security.
- According to two men from District One, an Afghan man intends to travel to Mecca by bicycle. They state that he intends to prove to the world that Afghans are educated and civil, contrary to negative media perceptions. They are happy because it is representing Afghanistan proudly and positively.
- Villagers in Pashmul praise the suicide bombing in Pakistan recently that killed and wounded dozens of Pakistanis. They say Pakistanis deserve such attacks for sending suicide bombers and insurgents into Afghanistan.
- Villagers in Pasab lament the harassment of people in Howz-e-Madad seen eating during Ramadan. They say the government should not interfere in personal choices about religion.
- A shopkeeper complains of being forced to sell beer to ANA [Afghan National Army] at gunpoint. His friend understands the backlash against religious rule but feels ANSF should respect Islamic regulations.
- Several men in the Qalat bazaar discuss ISAF leaving at the end of 2014 and they all seem to believe that Afghanistan will fall into chaos. According to one man in the bazaar, the Taliban and GIRoA will start fighting and the Taliban will win.

Passed on parting gifts to Colonel "Doc" Holliday and Sergeant Major Watson, both of whom will be leaving Kandahar Air Field in the next few days. After a year of living intensely and even dangerously, each of us are about to go our separate ways, almost certainly never to meet again.

Also took what will probably be one of my final night flights in a Black Hawk. Riding with the new commanding general means flying with open doors. He asked me if I wanted to sit on the outside—I said no thanks; I'm not scared of heights but I don't much like the idea of sitting at the edge of eternity with nothing but darkness below.

We flew close to the ground, a hot wind rushing through the cabin, the fires from the *kutchi* camps faintly flickering in the distance. Returning to Kandahar Air Field at 10:00 p.m., I suddenly heard the sound of two flares going off and saw a flash of orange on each side of us. We weren't being chased by a heat-seeking missile—but the equipment is sensitive and occasionally the flares are automatically let loose anyway.

Kandahar, 20 July

Dinner with Lewis Gitter at Luxembourg DFAC. He leaves in a couple of days, first for language training in Washington and then to Mozambique. He has been frustrated at some of the constraints on our reporting and at some aspects of the Third Infantry Division close embrace that he describes as occasionally smothering. We have never talked about it—but Lewis was on the initial manifest for the 6 April trip to Zabul, backing out at the last minute only when it became clear that a political officer from Kandahar was not necessary on this particular trip; others from the Zabul PRT could do the needful in his place. Thank God he did not come with us.

Kandahar, 21 July

Hosted *iftar* for fifteen members of Kandahar business community. It is hard to get inside Kandahar Air Field but they seemed happy to visit, if only out of curiosity. One businessman said he last saw inside the airport during Taliban times. He was impressed by the new buildings. He said because he has a beard he can't visit Korea and the United States though he had been to China and India.

We broke fast in our big *shura* room, having bought imported dates from the Kandahar bazaar. We gave our guests time to pray before driving them to the Independence DFAC. Some of the food must have seemed strange, including the salmon. But most guests returned for second and third helpings.

Conversation covered a lot of territory, including deep concern about the power sector. At times the discussion became quite animated. I was surprised at the industries represented—cotton, marble, ice, feed, paper recycling, beverages (Kool Kola), and steel, among others.

Kandahar, 23 July

A day for farewells: I saw Phil Russell off at the flight line; had separate close-out meetings with David Kraus, Lewis Gitter, and Charlie Wintermeyer; and attended a farewell dinner on the boardwalk for three departing civilians who served at the KPRT.

Late night rocket attack, keeping me in the office until well past midnight. I heard the boom first and then the alarm signaling a rocket attack; usually, it is the other way around.

Governor's Palace/Walton, 24 July

Morning Black Hawk flight to Camp Nathan Smith followed by MRAP convoy to governor's palace and Kandahar municipal offices for the regional *shura* convened by Governor Wesa. The governors of Helmand, Zabul, Daikundi, and Uruzgan attended, along with the ministers of finance, public works, local government, and rural development from Kabul. Other notables include Haji Dastageeri and several district governors and provincial council members.

The day focused on polio, local governance, and security. At times the discussion became quite noisy. There is a rift between Afghan civilians and the security forces, and there is a gulf between southern Afghanistan and Kabul. Sometimes people just need to shout at each other.

I enjoyed taking in the scene—the six Afghan flags lined up in front of the meeting hall, a large photograph of President Karzai on one wall, two paintings on another, one featuring Kandahar as a walled city with *kutchis* in the front, the other showing a bazaar scene. A third wall displayed a large photo from a century ago, suggesting things here haven't changed much—lots of beards and turbans, a big tandoor oven, a couple of Kashmiri shawls, and a sagging mud roof with a young man sitting on it. I wonder whatever became of him.

Wesa started the proceedings by commenting, "Kandahar has seen a lot of history but has never been defeated—it has always defended the honor of Afghanistan."

General Hamid said 363 Taliban have been killed in southern Afghanistan over the past 3 months; a further 37 were killed in Panjwai only a couple of days ago. The latter figure in particular seems inflated.

General Razziq attended, eager, engaged, and looking like a precocious adolescent. He said, "Soldiers are dying every day but the government just makes excuses." He blames lack of development on Kabul. He also said the inability to return dead soldiers to their home villages for burial has a corrosive effect on ANSF morale.

Returned in another MRAP convoy, this one to FOB Walton. Our security detail was led by an MP unit from Maryland. As with the helicopter gunner on the trip to Spin Boldak near the beginning of my time in southern Afghanistan nearly one year ago, the gunner for this MRAP was remarkably young, not much bigger than Catriona, and not much older either.

Ambassador Robinson from Kabul reached Walton a few minutes after we arrived. I offered my perspective on events in Kandahar over the past year. We were then joined by members of our religious engagement team including a twenty-year-old Army translator, an Armenian from Iran who spoke Farsi and at age fourteen had sought asylum in the United States.

Noorullah Aziz, line director for the Ministry of Hajj and Religious Affairs, arrived late. He said he served in the Taliban for seventeen years—but finally crossed over to the government's side and has been happy with his life ever since.

We then headed to the *shura* tent to break the fast, followed by an *iftar* dinner at the Marco Polo catered by a local Afghan restaurant. About ten local religious leaders eventually arrived, including the head of the provincial Peace Council.

Dinner was disorganized, partly because people arrived and left at different times. We nonetheless stumbled through the speeches and food, hearing interesting views on elections along the way. Afghans can be remarkably candid about defects in their own country and society though they don't like others to point them out. Corruption is seen as pervasive and there is widespread skepticism about next year's elections.

After hurried goodbyes we walked to the flight line for our late-night Black Hawk ride home. The wash from arriving helicopters covered us with a cascade of dust so thick it enveloped us.

Kandahar Airport, 25 July

Long day starting with breakfast at Lux with Ambassador Robinson and his party from Kabul including several security guards. We then moved to our little *shura* room for briefing on elections involving Sean Goad, Erin Tariot, Andrew Manhart, Ken Monahan, Nichole Malick, and others.

Drove short distance to Kandahar Airport to meet Governor Naseri from Zabul. There were four planes outside the civilian terminal when we arrived, the most I've ever seen—Kam Air and Ariana, along with planes from ICRC and the World Food Program.

Naseri is quite eloquent in making the case for his province—and quite vocal in expressing his anger and disappointment at the fate of several USG projects including SIKA, CCI, and Zabul Teacher Training College.

Also met with Governor Wesa at Kandahar Air Field. I've heard most of it before. Some parts of the presentation are upbeat, others darkly pessimistic, the contrasting views perhaps reflecting how conflicted Afghans are about their future.

Lunch at Echoes followed by quick tour of prospective new embassy compound. We then met with General LaCamera. Everyone thinks what happens next in Afghanistan will be determined by American domestic policy, not necessarily by facts on the ground in Afghanistan. According to General LaCamera, "The White House promised the American people that we will leave Afghanistan and they are going to deliver on that promise."

According to General LaCamera, the U.S. should have declared war on al-Qaeda in September 2001. Recalling conversations in Mongolia at the time, I remember thinking that 9/11 marked the beginning of a hundred years' war, given the depth of hatred among radical Islamists for all things American.

Saw Ambassador Robinson and his party off at Valdez. Despite inevitable hiccups, this was a successful visit. I'm happy it is behind us rather than ahead of us. The ambassador is a genuinely nice guy. He served much of his career in Latin America, including three years as ambassador to Guyana.

Kandahar, 26 July

Eleven months in Afghanistan—one month to go. I met several soldiers on the boardwalk, including Sergeant Carter getting ready to depart for Kuwait.

Drinking my guava smoothie I noticed a small brown dove pecking at the small bits of food in front of me. At that moment another soldier from the Third Infantry Division walked by, shook my hand, and told me to stay safe, adding how much he had appreciated working together these past many months.

Noon lunch with Generals LaCamera, Thompson, Rainey, and Kidd. Earlier, General White dropped by to say goodbye. With all the generals gone the Third Infantry Division has finally, definitively, and completely given way to the Fourth Infantry Division. At least one of those arriving recently described General Abrams as "an extrovert surrounded by introverts." Word is now out that General Abrams will take up his new position at the Pentagon as chief assistant to Secretary of Defense Chuck Hagel, perhaps a steppingstone to joining the chiefs of staff. This will be a difficult assignment for him—what he enjoys most is being in command.

It will be interesting to watch LaCamera find his way during my final three weeks at Kandahar Air Field. Some around him are concerned he will uproot everything, just to show that he is different. LaCamera does ask good questions, voicing things that others have a hard time talking about. The task ahead is very difficult, partly because the status of forces agreement remains elusive and partly because the election process remains murky—no one really knows how this story will end.

Talked briefly to several people at office just before they departed to board their final flight out of Afghanistan—Sergeants Watson, Carter, Williams, and Shoemaker. We have worked at close quarters for nearly a year and now, quite suddenly, it is time to say goodbye.

Kandahar, 27 July

Busy Saturday, partly because of report that a cleaner found a box of discarded books in a trash can at Camp Nathan Smith—one was an English translation of the Koran. That started a flurry of activity, all driven by fear about what might happen next. Apparently, an ill-informed lieutenant colonel at IJC in Kabul had called the director of the KMIC to inform him that a Koran had been burned when it had simply been handed over to an Afghan army officer for safekeeping.

Kandahar, 28 July

Read transcript of Taliban video from Al Amara Jihadi Studio on its latest champion, Numbar Khan from Jalalabad. He was the Afghan army turncoat who killed the Slovak soldier at Kandahar Air Field before escaping to Quetta.

The studio promised to show the reality and full picture of jihad in Afghanistan, though what it really provides is a litany of lies starting with the statement that he had attacked two truckloads of soldiers who "carried out night raids in Marjah" and killed several of them. He claims to have fired two hundred rounds and received two thousand bullets in reply:

> But Allah protected me. . . . I wanted to join the Afghan Special Forces so that I could kill more infidels. . . . I joined the Afghan Air Force. . . . Finally, the infidels showed up and I killed them. Then I tried to run away but my commander Raqiz Sherzai caught me alive and asked me, "Why did you do this?" I lied to him and said that these infidels shot at me first. . . . I'm telling you, safeguard your Koran and Islam and where you see Kandahar Air Fieldirs [*sic*], don't let them in Afghanistan. . . . Most of the Afghans have lost faith in Islam and are drinking alcohol. . . . I am not happy that I have become a *ghazi*. I would have been happier if I had been martyred. . . . Hey, brothers, wherever you are in the ANA [Afghan National Army], please kill infidels.

Lieutenant Ihsanullah who helped Numbar Khan escape also said his piece: "I didn't want this *ghazi* to be turned over to the Americans. . . . These infidels who have come to Afghanistan do not want shariah in our country. They want to spread their Christianity. . . . I myself was motivated by that barbaric incident of the infidels in Panjwai. . . . I will chant 'Allahu Akhbar' and 'jihad' until the last drop of blood in my body."

Spin Boldak, 29 July

Black Hawk to Spin Boldak for *iftar* organized around women's issue. Spent hour beforehand talking to Rogiya Achackzai, line director for women's affairs in Kandahar. She was accompanied by her husband, a traffic policeman. Her driver is also her son-in-law.

Rogiya recently returned from a U.S. study tour that included Washington, Minneapolis, Texas, and California. Her only previous foreign experience had been a brief trip to Iran. She said she was impressed by the politeness of Americans as well as the diversity of its population. She was *not* impressed by American family life, saying it revolved too much around young children rather than their grandparents. She was appalled to see adult children go for years without visiting their mothers and fathers.

Joined several others for dinner including representatives from new NGO run by Noorzais (Khalida, Bibigud, and Roziyah Noorzai) and a second run by Achakzais (Naziya Achackzai and Sedigah Razage). They were accompanied by a couple of male escorts, one of whom had several pictures taken beside an especially attractive young American soldier with blonde hair.

Our side included Stephanie Foster from the Public Affairs section in Kabul who became so dehydrated medics had to provide an IV; Nicole Malick, our RC-South gender specialist; and several female soldiers from FOB Spin Boldak, along with Lieutenant Colonel Henry McNeilly, the battalion commander.

We brought Lieutenant Colonel Ann Theriault and Parween Mohammad, a Kurdish cultural adviser from Kandahar Air Field—both were happy to finally see something of the real Afghanistan outside of Kandahar Air Field. My translator Yahya Faqiri and the FOB Spin Boldak female interpreter Zubi, both Afghan Americans, joined us.

The Afghan meal spread before us was excellent—dates, *kabuli pilau,* beef curry, lamb curry, eggplant, naan, and lots of fresh fruit. It is hard to get out and see people, yet the Afghans seem to also enjoy it when it finally happens.

I mentioned Malala of Maiwand and Malala of Swat. Rogiya wasn't impressed that Malala of Swat has become so famous, claiming, "There are hundreds of girls across Afghanistan who are just as brave, but they just aren't written about in the newspapers."

We gave each woman a box of chocolates as they departed. They filled their bags with leftover naan, dates, and grapes. A mosque in Denver provided a donation of pencils, notebooks, and toiletry items to the various NGOs represented.

The Black Hawks taking us to Kandahar Air Field were nearly an hour late due to faulty radios. We waited for them in a small airport terminal built of plywood. The sky for our late afternoon flight was filled with dust but by evening this had largely disappeared.

I took a last glance up at the stars in the night sky and then across the hills toward the lights of Chaman. From here the Pakistan border is less than three miles away. I am astonished that I am here at all.

Kandahar, 30 July

Morning meeting on Kandahar Air Field with head of Kandahar IEC. He is confident about elections but concerned about security. Voter registration offices have been set up across the province, including in remote places. The IEC is having a hard time recruiting women to provide needed support at the various polling stations. However, the director said in some cases respected elders are being hired to encourage women to register to vote.

The Fourth Infantry Division is introducing many schedule changes—tonight we had another deep dive followed by a 9:00 p.m. meeting with the commanding general and his generals. This will take the place of the 8:00 a.m. gathering that used to cover the same ground.

My planned trip to Zaray tomorrow will not happen after all—the district governor is in Kabul and the main point of this journey was to meet him.

Still not sure about my next assignment. Alex Thier said he is frustrated but would ask again if I am still being considered for Washington. Also received e-mail from Denise Rollins asking about my arrival date in Almaty. I am ambivalent at this stage—I would be happy with either assignment. That said, in my heart of hearts I would welcome the chance to once again look toward the snow-covered Tien Shan from my office window. The best cities in the world all have mountains in back of them.

Kandahar, 31 July

Relatively quiet day following cancellation of my trip to Zaray. I exercised at the platform and packed one more gorilla box to send to Macon. My office now looks empty.

Introduction meeting with Horacio Ureta, new head of our Pol/Econ office. He attended the Air Force Academy, became a pilot, and had a thirteen-year Air Force career followed by another eighteen years in the Foreign Service. He seems well-suited for Kandahar and is already talking about a second year elsewhere in Afghanistan.

Said farewell to Bob Schuknect, leaving after three years in Kandahar, most of it working on municipal issues. Now he can return to his Moldavan wife and stepdaughter in Sioux Falls, South Dakota. He will then look for another overseas assignment, possibly in South Sudan. He said he is leaving on a high and is very satisfied with his Afghanistan experience.

Read unsolicited letter from an Afghan government official in Kandahar, describing an attack after a soccer game in June in which he and his son were badly injured:

I can only say that those who kill innocent people don't know the great words of Islam; they are cruel and anti-human. . . . It was a dark street and we were followed by two gunmen on a motorbike. . . . While going to the hospital I only remember that someone told me, "Don't worry, you will be okay." . . . On the second day I opened my eyes in the hospital. My son Qudrat was on another bed. God blessed us and we were both alive. . . . I am sure that the enemy will not tolerate this failed action and they will keep trying their best to kill me and my family.

If the Taliban return to power surely the depth of fear and brutality that they inflict will be one of the main reasons why.

13

$\Longleftrightarrow$

AUGUST

Kandahar, 1 August

Briefing this morning mentioned issues associated with the RIAB program in Shah Wali Kot as well as a concern that the radios might have fallen into the wrong hands and been used to spread Taliban propaganda, something Kelly Hunt had been concerned about. According to one report, a local disc jockey has been detained.

Conference call with Kabul involving SCRs—this one included Ambassador Robinson and was mostly about political reporting, allowing some of us to vent our frustrations. One SCR stated that her staff is unhappy because they don't get credit for their work, and another recalled a cable never sent because it reflected Afghan feelings of abandonment, a view not everyone wants to hear. I also mentioned concerns over the fate of certain draft cables sent from Kandahar that never went any farther.

We touched briefly on worldwide security concerns on 4 August as a result of al-Qaeda threats—so much so no travel will be allowed on that day anywhere in Afghanistan. RC-South colleagues are especially unhappy that we have to transit Kabul when we depart. I hate the fact that these trips are called the airport shuttles—we are already vulnerable enough and the idea that we have to take a regularly scheduled shuttle for our final trip in Afghanistan is appalling.

Also attended a discussion on security issues later in the day. Talked briefly with one of the main briefers afterward. A Puerto Rican who lives in New York, he spent several weeks in Maiwand and loved his work despite the dangers. He mentioned rumors that the Taliban are gathering in Maiwand and predicts that it could be among the first districts taken after ISAF departs.

Met with headquarters staff in General Kidd's office at 8:00 p.m. to watch game three of the Ashes. Kidd had a career in the British Army before joining the Australian Army. His sympathies in this cricket match clearly lie with England, perhaps because it has endured so much humiliation in recent years. The Australians gave a brief lesson in cricket to the Americans. Australian food was on offer, including vegemite and margarine on crackers. I am surprised at how many senior Australian officers previously served in either the British or Canadian military. The Afghan generals are also surprised.

Kandahar, 2 August

Lunch at Lux with Generals LaCamera, Rainey, Thompson, and Kidd. I mentioned closures of American embassies across the Middle East in the wake of al-Qaeda threats. The military thinks the State Department is overly cautious. We also speculated about the April 2014 elections in Afghanistan. Under one scenario there will be a *loya jirga* in the fall to bless an Afghan consensus candidate—followed by national elections as a gesture to the foreign community.

Very hot and dusty for most of the day, causing helicopter flights to be cancelled. However, it became cooler toward evening. There is also a slight breeze, providing further relief.

More local reporting, providing a perspective that is always interesting:

- A couple of men from District Two in Kandahar are displeased with Americans because they believe they are dishonest and withholding information from Afghans.
- According to a couple of men from District One in Kandahar, the Taliban murdered more than a hundred innocent civilians in the Panjwai District via IED within the past five months. The people are angry because their deeds oppose Islam.
- A group of men are angered by the introduction of the Urdu language in some schools in Tarin Kot. They believe that if the practice is not stopped, Pakistan will wipe away the identity of the Afghans.
- The influence of Western music, the Internet, and other areas is having a negative impact on Afghan culture and society, especially on younger Afghans, according to these men in the Qalat City bazaar. Apparently, three young Afghan girls from Qalat ran away recently and the influence of Western culture is blamed for it.
- Two men disagreed with a scholar who suggested that it is lawful for Muslims to kill infidels.
- Three gentlemen in Panjwai feel the current presidential candidates are not worth voting for, and that the next Afghan leader will be determined by his power and wealth.

Kandahar, 3 August

Early-morning rocket attack. One rocket damaged a hangar and two Royal Air Force Tornadoes. Each time there is a rocket attack the Kandahar Air Field command closes down the boardwalk for at least two days.

Morning briefing included references to an incident in Spin Boldak that is making the rounds among the Afghans though no one knows for sure whether it is fact or fiction—apparently, seven Afghan border police were invited by two men to attend an *iftar* dinner. The food was laced with poison and five later died. I can't see how the ANSF can sustain the casualties they are taking right now. During July alone at least thirty-seven Afghan soldiers and policemen were killed.

Met David Brantley, civilian head of Australian PRT in Uruzgan. He just returned from three weeks in New York and Chicago with his partner. I still hope to visit Uruzgan at least a couple more times before I finally leave Afghanistan.

Late-night meeting with the four Fourth Infantry Division generals as well as Chief of Staff Antonia and the sergeant major. We gathered outside our hooches soon after General LaCamera returned from mass. It had rained briefly, and that plus a gentle breeze makes it cooler than usual tonight.

Returned to office at midnight to read e-mails, prepare for tomorrow's embassy country team—and call Kelly Hunt, recovering from her most recent surgery at Walter Reed. She now has a new metal plate in her head. Kelly is always enthusiastic but seems almost too cheerful, given the circumstances. She said she "thinks often of Afghanistan, perhaps too much."

Kandahar, 4 August

Cool morning following last night's brief rain—but by noon Kandahar was once again like a furnace.

Attended change-of-command ceremony, the 794th Medical Detachment from New England giving way to the 988th Medical Detachment out of Texas. I stayed for most of it because Captain Pratistha Bhandari had invited me. She migrated to the U.S. from Nepal in 2003. Her mother worked for the U.S. Embassy in Katmandu. A civilian in the New Hampshire National Guard, she worked in post-earthquake Haiti.

Video conference involving General Milley and field commanders from across Afghanistan. Reports are mostly positive, including from the Spanish general in the west and the German general in the north. Perhaps the optimism is about short-term tactical gains. Over the long term it is hard to imagine Afghanistan without the Taliban.

Lashkar Gah, 5 August

Departed at 6:00 p.m. on C-130 for Bastion/Leatherneck. Met on arrival by acting SCR Paul Berg. Following an initial briefing we flew to Lashkar Gah in a Sea Stallion that seemed to be leaking oil—the cabin of the aircraft was full of it. As the civilian presence draws down in the south, the SCR in Helmand will not be replaced. Instead, my successor will have Helmand included in his area of responsibility, along with Kandahar, Zabul, Uruzgan, and Daikundi. Kabul also thought it would be useful for me to visit before my own imminent departure.

Lashkar Gah is the capital of Helmand Province, and the British PRT there is the nicest and most well-appointed I've seen anywhere—it could easily be a small consulate. Outside there is a rose garden and green grass.

Briefed first by U.S. staff and then by Catriona Laing, the senior British officer who is about to depart for an ambassadorship somewhere in Africa. Her office includes a painting of a British soldier attacking the Taliban in Sangin, an incident for which he was awarded a Victoria Cross.

Catriona is a dominating personality and the Americans who met us implied the relationship is sometimes rocky. The British focus on governance while the Americans want development to play a bigger part. The PRT will be closed by the end of year, making it all academic now.

Returned to Bastion, this time on an Osprey that switched in the air from a helicopter to a plane. I rode in the cockpit. It is a strange sensation and the ride is different from that in other aircraft, the tall rotors beating the sky in a peculiar movement like a pelican flapping its wings. We waited in the flight line for forty-five minutes for a general who never showed up.

Bastion is flatter, more spread out, and possibly more organized than Kandahar Air Field. One British compound is called Brydon Lines, presumably named by someone with a mordant sense of humor after the sole survivor of the retreat from Kabul to Jalalabad during the later stages of the First Afghan War. There are a couple of restaurants, one run by Danes who along with the Americans and British have contributed heavily to the Helmand campaign.

Dinner with two soldiers from Special Forces, one Army and the other Marine. They have had multiple deployments to Afghanistan, some involving billets with small detachments in remote corners of the country. The two soldiers love their work though the Army captain did not expect to reenlist—he said the highlight of his career was sixteen months in Iraq leading an infantry platoon and he did not think it would ever get any better. I wonder if their stories will ever be written up. Once again, the length and depth of our engagement in Afghanistan astounds me.

Bastion, 6 August

Up early for breakfast. Met Sergeant Moody from Macon, Georgia—he heads the commanding general's security detail at Leatherneck; our parents know each other from church.

Read e-mails before driving to flight line for return trip to Kandahar Air Field. We travelled in an Embassy Air CH-46, completing our complement of four flights on four different aircraft in two days—C-130, Sea Stallion, Osprey, and CH-46. I leaned against the plastic window on the emergency exit when I first boarded the helicopter—and it immediately broke into several pieces.

We flew low across the Registan Desert, crossing several *kutchi* camps along the way. The landscape looks like Mars. Closer to Kandahar Air Field we followed the Arghandab River, a small brown string of mud separating the white dust to the north from the red dust to the south. On arrival at Kandahar Air Field one of the Embassy Air crewmen asked to see my camera, claiming that I had taken pictures on the flight line—which I hadn't. Yet another annoying incident involving a civilian flight—for trips like this I far prefer the military.

Dinner at the Niagara DFAC with Generals LaCamera, Thompson, Rainey, and Kidd. I am a short-timer now. It is as if the 365 grains of sand that were once in my Afghan hour glass have been to reduced twenty—and even these are disappearing fast.

Stayed up late looking through redacted reports based on interviews with Taliban detainees. It makes for fascinating reading. The rank and file are confident their cause will prevail. Pakistan is deeply unpopular. Kabul is seen as a notably un-Islamic corner of Afghanistan, a den of iniquity and sin. Many changes during the past decade are viewed as highly problematic and the recent Westernization of Afghan society is largely blamed on the infidels.

Tarin Kot (Uruzgan), 7 August

C 130 flight to Tarin Kot aborted at last minute—there was a sudden dust storm and we had to turn back just before landing, visibility having been reduced to a few hundred yards. That is very disappointing. I wanted a final chance to meet Governor Akhundzada and say my final farewells.

Lunch with Generals Odierno and Milley. Odierno was tired, leaving Milley to do most of the talking. I asked more questions than usual. Discussing Mullah Omar's statement on Eid al-Fitr, Milley agrees the Taliban are increasingly on the defensive about the growing number of civilian casualties. Recalling the post-Soviet Afghan army, he thinks it won most of its battles against the rising Taliban—but in the end imploded.

Made it to Tarin Kot on the second attempt, this time departing Kandahar Air Field in midafternoon. This trip was mostly about expressing appreciation to Colonel Ian Stuart for his nine months in Uruzgan. The C-130, based in Arkansas, was largely empty.

Hosted dinner at Lux DFAC for Faizi, director of Kandahar Airport. He is a Popalzai and has lived in Kandahar for most of his life. He was a school teacher during Taliban times. He grew a beard and wore a black turban—the day the Taliban fled was the day he shaved his beard. Despite the odds Faizi has done a good job managing Kandahar Airport. Someone leaving for Dubai was recently apprehended carrying 200,000 euros and $50,000 in a false bottom suitcase. When Faizi informed the governor, he did not seem very enthusiastic about the news.

Faizi said Mahmood Karzai left yesterday for Dubai to celebrate Eid al-Fitr—and passed on his personal greetings, perhaps realizing I won't be in Afghanistan much longer. Looking ahead Faizi said he is "pessimistic" about Afghanistan over the short term—but "optimistic" over the long term. He thinks Afghans working for ISAF as interpreters will soon have to go into business for themselves.

Kandahar, First Day of Eid al-Fitr, 8 August

Spent part of afternoon at Valdez flight line waiting to say goodbye to Bonnie Weaver. She has completed two years in Kandahar and is departing for Washington. We overlapped for nearly a year—she met me at the end of every helicopter journey and helped keep my life organized.

Read through various reports assessing Taliban organizational and budgetary issues. The costs of maintaining operations in a single district seem miniscule, at least considering what it costs ISAF to keep a single soldier in Afghanistan for a year. No wonder we call this asymmetrical warfare.

Most trends are worrisome. ANSF suffered more than four hundred KIAs across Afghanistan in July, a horrific toll. This translates into almost five thousand battlefield deaths annually. I can't see how Afghans will sustain these losses once ISAF departs.

Kandahar, Second Day of Eid al-Fitr, 9 August

Friday lunch with all four generals in Niagara DFAC. Some conversations go above me, especially in-house talk involving Army politics. But sometimes it is entertaining. General Kidd occasionally challenges the commanding general, throwing out comments that can be jarring. He is skeptical and even scathing about much of what has happened in both Iraq and Afghanistan. As for more recent events, everyone thinks Karzai will convene a *loya jirga* in early fall, providing cover to sign the BSA shortly after.

Spent part of the day reading reports offering various local perspectives:

- Two men from District Six in Kandahar mocked Mullah Omar's recent remarks regarding the American armed forces. They believe the people refuse to support the Taliban because they have lost their credibility.
- A small group of people voiced their frustration over delaying tactics at registration centers in Tarin Kot. One of the men feels he is being discriminated against because he is Hazara.
- Two residents in Nawa Kalay near Spin Boldak say that the Taliban are nothing more than animals; they are kidnapping young boys and forcing them to become suicide attackers.
- Two men at the Kandahar Stadium praised ANSF for providing security. They said that it was impossible for them to play soccer at night in the past because of security threats.
- A group of people praised ISAF for their dedication and professionalism when they go out on patrol. They criticized ANSF, however, for being unprofessional in their interactions.
- Senjaray villagers are happy that the ALP [Afghan local police] was able to prevail against the Taliban attack on their checkpoint in Zhari Dasht but would like to see the dead Taliban bodies removed from the street.
- Two men have different views on the tribe of their next president. One man feels that if he hails from the Hazara or Tajik tribe, it would affect the Pushtun people. The other believes that the tribal affiliation of the next president doesn't matter.
- According to two men visiting Mansurabad, villagers are furious with the ALP [Afghan local police] commander because he ordered them to feed his forty officers daily. Unfortunately, the villagers are poor and can hardly feed themselves.
- Zangabad residents express their displeasure toward the Taliban's arrogant attitude.
- Several angry and concerned men in Shah Joy discuss a recent incident: the Taliban went into a grade school and threatened students and teachers. The Taliban were apparently angered by the grade schoolers studying a book written in English and the fact that there were some young girls in the class. The Taliban threatened the children, saying if the children came back to school they would kill their parents.
- Two men from District Two in Kandahar are outraged with the ALP's misbehavior. According to them, officers are making inappropriate comments and staring at women.

- Kandahar residents are depressed and grieving over the loss of innocent people's lives due to Taliban attacks. They are upset because they continue to kill people during the month of Ramadan.

Kandahar, 10 August

Again, spent part of the day reading through various reporting from across southern Afghanistan, including news reports from local mosques:

- A mullah at a mosque in Dand District: "Ramadan is ending soon and the *eid* celebrations will begin. This is a peaceful and happy time. I urge everyone including the Taliban to be at peace and refrain from fighting."
- A mullah at a mosque in Kandahar: "*Eid* is a very joyous and happy time. Everyone, Taliban and Americans, should refrain from fighting. Muslims must not be angry, fight, or hurt anyone. The Taliban must not kill innocent people with explosives. This is a big sin and *eid* must remain a peaceful time."
- A mullah at a mosque in Tarin Kot: "People who carry out suicide bombings are not Muslims but paid agents of the Pakistani government."
- A mullah at a mosque in Keliwal spoke out against the Taliban. He did not call them out by name but by deed because there were Taliban fighters in attendance.
- A mullah at a mosque in Spin Boldak talked about the importance of charity and criticized the administration in Kandahar for conducting parties every night, drinking alcohol but refusing to help the poor during Ramadan.
- A mullah at another mosque in Spin Boldak talked about dreams. He said a good dream is from God while a bad dream is from Satan. A good person will always have nice dreams and a sinner will have bad dreams. He did not say much about politics but every Friday he ends the sermon by praying to God to destroy all non-Muslims from Afghanistan and for the Taliban to gain victory.
- A mullah at a third mosque in Spin Boldak: "To be a friend with Allah, a Muslim must not tease or hurt another Muslim. Any Muslim who kills another Muslim will stay in hell forever."
- A mullah at a fourth mosque in Spin Boldak: "GIRoA officials are corrupt, dishonest, and robbers. . . . Muslims have forgotten the commands of Allah."
- Another mullah at a mosque in Kandahar: "Muslims must have faith in Allah. People are too worried about foreigners leaving our country."
- Another Mullah at a mosque in Dand District: "We must help rid all polio cases from our village. Please allow the aid workers to give out vaccines to your children and anyone in need."

- A mullah in Arghandab: "I encourage every corrupt government official that has accepted bribes to clean their conscience immediately, and to perform good deeds and serve the Afghan people."

Kandahar Airport, 11 August

Met Haji Dastageeri at Kandahar Airport. The departure hall was deserted, the electricity was off, and it was very hot. Niceta Redd drove and Steve May accompanied as a shooter. I brought nuts and dates.

The tip of one of Dastageeri's fingers is missing, either shot or sliced off in an accident. On first appearance Dastageeri might be mistaken for a Talib and during the 1990s he no doubt made his peace with them. Some rumors also suggest that he assisted al-Qaeda in their escape from Afghanistan in the early 2000s. Yet he also projects a gentle and self-effacing style, perhaps to disguise the fact that on the inside he is as tough as nails. He became wealthy as a construction contractor and now wields power in Kandahar and especially in Panjwai. A member of the provincial council since 2004, he said his friends are encouraging him to run for a seat in the next parliament.

Dastageeri warmed especially to the theme of Taliban as slaves and puppets of Pakistan. He said that Pakistan and Iran are "thirsty for Afghan blood, thirsty for Afghan water and thirsty for Afghan land." He thinks some Taliban are tired of war and long to return home. Referring to Mullah Omar's *eid* speech, he described it as conciliatory.

Missed Purple Heart ceremony for soldier shot in the chest near Belambai in Panjwai. I was later told it might have been friendly fire. The soldier is flying to Germany with the bullet still in him. He is expected to fully recover.

Late night cigar smoking session outside our hooches with chief of staff, the sergeant major, and four generals. I'm the outsider at these events though some of the military conversations are interesting. It is a clear night, illuminated only by the occasional orange flares shot off by helicopters in the dark sky above us. In the background we can hear planes and helicopters leaving Kandahar Air Field.

According to the commanding general, Taliban fighters think the observation balloons tethered above ISAF bases are manned by troops; the reason they are occasionally brought down to earth is so the soldiers inside can eat and use the toilet. Other Taliban think the balloons are manned by little people.

One week left in Kandahar. Now I go slowly, taking everything in and trying to preserve it, looking at the scenes in front of me as if I am seeing them for the last time. Life in Kandahar will continue—but I will no longer be part of it.

Kandahar, 12 August

A relatively quiet day. Two planned trips—one to Daikundi, the other to the governor's palace in Kandahar—are now definitely off. Sorting through old papers I read again the report by explosive experts following the Zabul attack. The photos with debris strewn across the road outside FOB Smart sicken me. The bomb hidden behind a pallet on the PRT wall weighed five pounds. The two bombs placed on each side of the car weighed fifty pounds each. I must have walked through the killing zone twice, once coming and once going.

I also reread Commander Ralph Gall's medical report written soon after I returned to Kandahar Air Field, coming across it while I was packing and sorting. He describes my slight scratches as "battle related" and recommends "light duties" for the next seven days, as if that would ever have been possible at the time. In his words, "Patient appears acutely exhausted."

Another intel briefing, this one on IED networks in southern Afghanistan. Also had a side discussion on tribal aspects of the conflict. More disenfranchised tribes gravitate toward the Taliban for obvious reason. One Afghan military officer got it right when he said there will never be peace until there is justice between the tribes.

Kandahar, 14 August

Accompanied Kabul visitors to briefing at Kandahar Air Field on a wide range of issues associated with all aspects of Afghanistan. Reflections on the use of drones in warfare were especially sobering. Apparently, a small sonic boom can be heard two seconds before a missile arrives, giving the target just enough time to be conscious of what will happen next. Each missile costs several hundred thousand dollars.

Off-the-record interview with Margherita Stancatti from the *Wall Street Journal*. A young reporter from Italy, she arrived in Afghanistan recently, having previously reported from India. She is writing on the fate of women in Afghanistan and was interested to hear about Malala of Maiwand.

Kandahar, 15 August

Weekly commander's conference. It was quieter than anyone expected during Eid al-Fitr and in the days that followed. Perhaps that means something big is about to happen. My parting comment involved a Pushto proverb: "Listening to others quarrel is almost as much fun as *eid*."

Another round of atmospherics, some revealing, some amusing, some both:

- Locals in Deh Rawood complained about the decline in security. Residents prefer going to the Taliban for arbitration because they are always available and are not corrupt as compared with government officials.
- The Ashoqa villagers in Pasab are happy that the presidential elections are getting closer. They are looking forward to getting someone different than Karzai as their president. The villagers want ISAF to stay long enough to make sure they have elections.
- Two men in Shah Joy District say that the U.S. controls all things in Afghanistan, including next year's elections. The men say that only the people the U.S. wants to win will be elected. One man says that the U.S. should just appoint people and not bother with an election.
- Taliban violence has many in Qalat angry. The men say the Taliban are losing support. One man says, "The killing must stop."
- Two men from Kandahar are displeased with their governor's performance. The men state that their governor is foolish, rude, uneducated, and inefficient.
- The Siah Choy villagers in Pasab are happy to hear that the Taliban trying to emplace an IED near their village were blown up by their own explosive device.
- Several men in Qalat discuss next year's elections. The men are apparently all Pashtun and all seem to be saying that only a fellow Pashtun will get their votes. One man says it does not matter if the candidate is qualified or not: if he is Pashtun he will get their vote.
- Two men in Spin Boldak wish that the Taliban end up in hell, as they exploded a mine on a motorcycle in the sheep market, killing five innocent civilians and wounding several others.
- After a U.S. air strike killed twelve members of a household including children in Mya Neshin, one resident of Spin Boldak says that U.S. soldiers are cruel and must leave Afghanistan. However, another resident says that coalition forces have no desire to kill innocent people but have orders to attack the Taliban whenever they enter a village.

Shah Wali Karzai's Residence, 16 August

Morning meeting with Shah Wali Karzai at his residence in Aino Mina. General Thompson accompanied along with Horacio, Yahya, and our security detail. We flew first to Walton, meeting armored cars there for the short drive to Shah Wali Karzai's house. He was very welcoming—it has been a long time since we last met.

Our conversation focused first on elections and security. He thinks his brother is the only Pushtun who can lead Afghanistan. He strongly supports a bilateral strategic agreement and thinks most Afghans do as well. A *loya jirga* is being organized for the fall: "Even if President Karzai doesn't want it, the *loya jirga* will force him to support it."

He acknowledges that a *loya jirga* might open up other issues, including a third term for President Karzai. He thinks Sherzai lacks Pushtun support and Sayyaf lacks Tajik, Uzbek, and Hazara support. He views the foreign minister as a viable candidate. He doesn't think Afghanistan should be in a rush for democracy.

He described Mullah Omar's Eid al-Fitr message as conciliatory but wonders if he actually wrote it. He hopes Saudi Arabia clergy will denounce bombing, especially during the hajj. As always, Pakistan remains the root of all evil.

Shah Wali Karzai convinced us to stay for lunch—my last meal in his home. I enjoyed the *kabuli pilau* while our security detail loved the pumpkin.

On my departure I was given a magnificent large carpet—I accepted it on behalf of all the civilians in Kandahar. Perhaps it will find a more permanent home at the embassy in Kabul or even in Washington.

Very likely, this was my last Black Hawk flight in Afghanistan. Both side doors were left wide open and as we banked it seemed as if someone might fall out. I sat closest to the so-called bitch seat, the place where the wash from the rotors is at its most notoriously severe.

It is still a dusty day but the landscape below is lovely, especially the green grape orchards dotted by an occasional raisin-drying building constructed out of mud and straw. I'm ready to leave Kandahar—but I will miss some things about this place when I am gone.

Tracked down whereabouts of two American brothers, visiting Kandahar to pass on a donation to the families of those killed by Sergeant Bales during his rampage in Belambai last year. Representing a church in Utah, they arrived on a commercial flight from Kabul and are staying at a hotel just outside Kandahar Air Field. Now they want to take a taxi to Panjwai to do their good deed, seemingly unaware of the dangers they face. The hotel manager, realizing their folly, is making sure they don't leave the compound. He is also working to ensure they return to Kabul as quickly as possible.

Attended early-evening Purple Heart ceremony for several soldiers at Kandahar Air Field trauma center. Fourteen were wounded this morning, six in an MRAP turnover and eight more in a suicide attack when they arrived to tow the MRAP away.

The MRAP flipped when it swerved to avoid a motorcycle—one soldier lost a hand and another remains in critical condition. Those in the MRAP were not wounded in battle and are therefore ineligible for a Purple Heart. However, those in the vehicles that arrived to rescue them will receive medals.

The rescue group took a couple of hours to arrive. After securing a perimeter to hook up a tow rope they were approached by a young Afghan wearing a suicide vest. I talked to the soldier closest to the suicide bomber, wounded by a ball bearing that struck him in the cheek. He thought the bomber was perhaps fourteen years old and said he looked like death. The American soldier put up a hand to stop him but the Afghan detonated himself anyway. Another wounded soldier said he saw a flash of orange, felt the blast, and watched pieces of flesh flying by.

One British soldier was involved, a mechanic. He arrived in Kandahar four months ago, was raised in south London, and now lives in Salisbury in the south of England. All the soldiers realize how lucky they are to survive, and how fortunate it is that on this day there were no ISAF fatalities anywhere in southern Afghanistan.

Dinner at Mama Mia's on the boardwalk—a farewell for Erin Tariot who just finished her year in Kandahar and departs tomorrow. She became very emotional when talking about Brittany, the young intelligence officer stationed at Camp Nathan Smith who was killed in Maruuf last October. Erin is staying in Afghanistan for a second year, this time in Kabul. The next farewell dinner involving civilian staff will be for me.

It is past midnight—following a late-night rocket attack I am back in my room. Now it is the roar of F-16s, two at a time, keeping me awake.

Kandahar, 17 August

Attended Purple Heart ceremony for yesterday's wounded. Some are quite badly injured and will be flying to Germany. The only person killed in this particular attack was the suicide bomber.

Kandahar, 18 August

Regular weekly video conference with Kabul involving SCRs. This was my last such meeting yet no one mentioned it or even seemed to know that I am about to depart. This appears to be a common feeling among many of those serving in Afghanistan, including those assigned to Kabul. It is not unusual for officers to leave with a somehow empty feeling, trying to conjure up meaning and purpose when it is otherwise so hard to find.

Last all-hands meeting in Kandahar followed by the usual weekly discussion with our Afghan staff. This is the best part of my day—I admire them greatly for what they bring to us and for what they have to put up with from us. The Afghans must surely fear for their future though in their assessment this was the best Eid al-Fitr in Kandahar in a long time. There were no incidents of violence anywhere. Ghazi Park was crowded. Families ventured out in large numbers to have picnics and enjoy themselves.

Walked along boardwalk, ordering curry and chai from the Moghul Indian Restaurant. Briefly watched part of Hindi film called *Ek Zindagi Milegi, Dobara Nahin* [You only get one life, there is no second time around].

Paid $300 for Baluchi carpet made in Herat. I will mail it to Macon. This takes the place of the much larger Turkmen carpet that Shah Wali Karzai gave me a few days ago but that I couldn't keep.

Evening information effects briefing. General LaCamera invited me to the front of the room and then presented me with a large framed collage of my travels over the past year. He said nice things and then everyone filed past, shaking my hand. Several Australians attended. Now time is really speeding up and everything is in fast motion. Once the weeks stretched ahead interminably, as if they would never end. Now, suddenly, it is nearly time to leave.

The atmospherics are again interesting, providing a window on a world I can no longer enter. Tonight there was a reference to the Taliban swearing at ISAF helicopter pilots on their radios.

Another rocket attack at Kandahar Air Field. It hit just before leaving with Niceta for my farewell dinner at the Lux. The jambalaya prepared by Alice from North Carolina was very good. I spoke for too long, ending with the quote from Philo of Alexandria that I evoked in the all-hands meeting at Kandahar Air Field just after the Zabul attack, one that I will always remember: "Be kind to those you meet for they too are involved in a great struggle." Life in Kandahar is hard, harder than people want to admit. Perhaps the most commonly evoked final phrase is, "Stay safe."

My time here did not go quickly when I was living it. But now one year has come and gone and soon it will all seem like a dream. Two more spins of Russian roulette on the road between Kabul Airport and the embassy and then it really will be over.

Kabul, 19 August

Final early-morning briefing with the generals. The Taliban were hammered over the past twenty-four hours.

Atmospherics point to a creeping tiredness, with one commander imploring that he be allowed to return to Quetta for a rest. Another is quoted as saying, "Oh God, now they have Daud." Several fighters have been killed or captured in recent days. Yet the Taliban always come back.

I ate my final lunch at the Niagara DFAC, alone. I had spaghetti and tomato sauce with salad, olives, and vanilla ice cream.

Horacio and our new management officer, both recently arrived, dropped by briefly. My year is almost over while theirs is just beginning. It would be very hard if someone suddenly announced I had another twelve months to go. I can understand why the Taliban are tired—their war never ends.

Niceta drove me to Valdez for my Embassy Air flight to Kabul. Several people were waiting for me there: Jesse, just back from his day with farmers in Shah Wali Kot; Sergio who departs ten days from now; Diane the acting RSO who was the first person to meet me when I returned alone from Zabul on 6 April; Nichole who said that it was only during the last year that anyone seemed to care about her work with Afghan women; and David Sias from Texas, one of the last of our staff left on Kandahar Air Field with links to KPRT.

I checked in at the weighing station, assisted by the tall young lady with long blonde hair and silver braces. Within minutes my luggage was being taken to the plane—two suitcases, one Army knapsack, and my protective gear. I'll be happy to not ever have to wear body armor again.

Now I am on the afternoon Dash 8 flight to Kabul, looking through the clouds at the dusty landscape below. I am one of three passengers on this flight, the same number as were on the plane when I took that first flight from Kabul to Kandahar nearly one year ago. Then I was taking my first look at Kandahar Air Field—now I am having a last look at it from the sky.

We have been travelling in clouds for tens of minutes, not the final flight to Kabul that I hoped to have. I should be departing directly from Kandahar, not having to transit through Kabul at all.

We are out of the clouds again, flying over a rugged landscape, thin splashes of green marking the narrow valleys, gashes down the mountain where water runs off when the rain comes down in torrents.

We finally approach Kabul, a much broader valley, increasingly built up. On one side I see an oval cricket field, on the other a large prison. There are military installations below and many new housing developments. Kabul is expanding in every direction. The sky is mostly clear when we land, the temperature much cooler than in Kandahar.

Now I'm waiting for the embassy car to arrive. The Gurkha guards are talking among themselves, wondering why my vehicle is so late. One of them has just cut out the side of an old cardboard box, placing it on a cart for me to sit on. I'm happy enough to enjoy the sun, the breeze, the cool air, and the view toward distant mountains, much higher here than the more modest brown hills of Kandahar.

One Nepali guard named Sher (Lion) is talkative as he describes his days in the Indian Army. He spent several years in Kashmir, witnessing fighting on Siachin Glacier during the Kargil campaigns. Now he draws an army pension while doing international security work on contract in places like Afghanistan.

Eventually the embassy car arrived, taking me at dusk by crowded streets, a wedding palace, Masood Circle, and finally the embassy. I'm staying in Florida 69, a small but sufficient hooch that will be my home for the next six days.

Kabul, 20 August

Breakfast with Governor Wesa and USAID director Bill Hammink. Wesa is optimistic about Kandahar's future—and scathing about our aid efforts.

Afternoon meeting with Governor Naseri and Director Hammink, this time in USAID's Richard Holbrooke Conference Room. Naseri did most of the talking. He thinks Zabul should receive more aid from other donors as well as from the government of Afghanistan.

Kabul is very different from Kandahar, starting with the blue skies, cool days, and occasional breeze. It is jarring to see people walking by with tennis rackets and tank tops. Returned to my room to watch Afghanistan trounce Pakistan 3–0 in an international soccer friendly. The stadium looked full and the Kabul crowds loved every minute of it.

Dinner with Bill Hammink and other USAID colleagues. People seem horrified when I give even the short version of what happened in Zabul. Sarah Wines mentioned a young FSL named Greg Dempsey who killed himself in Michigan a few days ago, on the day after the first anniversary of the death of a fellow USAID officer in eastern Afghanistan at the hands of a suicide bomber. She attributed it to survivor's guilt or survivor's remorse—he would have been part of the group had he not been on leave at the time.

Kabul, 21 August

Morning meeting with Ambassador Kaidanow and Ambassador Robinson, members of the senior embassy management team, providing an opportunity for final reflections on the last year in Afghanistan. Mostly it went fine—at the end Tina thanked me for my service and said we could all draw pride in what we have been part of. Her emphasis is less on Afghanistan and more on internal management, especially the large drawdown in staff and locations over the past twelve months.

Also met the new head of IPA. He thinks his office will disappear during the first half of next year. He briefly touched on challenges in the field—including references to one SCR elsewhere in times past who occasionally fell asleep during meetings. He was also known to launch into critiques of Islam at odd moments during discussions with Afghans. Not surprisingly, relationships with the military were also at times problematic.

Turned in my cell phone and blackberry along with my helmet and other protective gear. That's one burden I am very happy to shed.

Read e-mails before joining Bill and his wife Marie Eve for dinner again, this time with Kevin Rushing from USAID. He leaves tomorrow after splitting a year between Mazar and Herat.

Kabul, 22 August

Numerous meetings including lunch with new Kandahar political officer named Bernie Link and coffee with INL country director Baxter Hunt.

Attended required hour-long medical briefing, touching first on malaria and TB and then on PTSD. If I think too much I may end up diagnosing myself as having PTSD.

Noticed several mynah birds hopping about outside my room. Somehow it is always mynahs, kingfishers, parrots, and hoopoe birds that evoke deep memories from my early years in Pakistan.

Joined Ambassador Robinson and Rob Sipe for meeting with Governor Akhundzada. Afterward Rob and I took Akhundzada and his chief of staff to embassy DFAC for dinner. Almost certainly this was my final key leader engagement in Afghanistan.

The governor is as jovial and voluble as ever, his eyes flashing with delight. At least for Kabul audiences, he is optimistic about the security situation in Uruzgan. He says the right things, repeatedly emphasizing the importance of working with the people rather than security forces as the key to progress in Afghanistan. He has two wives and five children. Toward the end of our conversation he told me, "The biggest mistake of my life was to marry twice."

Finished day at embassy's first Thursday night SpeakEasy at Muncy Hall. This was sponsored by the Community Liaison Office and provided a venue for attendees to tell stories. It was led by Zack Warren, an Asia Foundation employee who has a degree from Harvard Divinity School. Zack mentioned that he previously toured Afghanistan as part of a travelling circus, adding that he is an active member of Clowns Without Borders. I continue to be amazed at the people who end up in Afghanistan.

Kabul, 23 August

A quiet day. I spent part of it shopping, first at the ISAF Friday market and then at the embassy. I ended up buying a lot of gifts—jewelry and handbags mostly.

Going through old papers, read a few final atmospherics from southern Afghanistan:

- One of the mullahs in Spin Boldak talked about the prophet and his loving daughter Fatimah. He said Muslims should not torture their daughters. The mullah criticized the Pashtun tribe, which he believes is cruel toward women and sells daughters for cash.
- The preacher at a village mosque in Arghandab said, "People who embed mines on bridges and roads in order to hurt people are committing horrible sins. Allah will punish them on judgement day."
- Villagers in Arghandab want the government to establish vocational schools and provide jobs to the youth because young men are loitering and smoking hashish near the roads and shops.
- Villagers in Siah Choy are happy to hear that President Obama promised to continue to help the people of Afghanistan even after U.S. forces leave their country in 2014.
- Two men from Zaray criticized America for attempting to implement a democracy in Afghanistan. They doubt it will work because they do not have enough resources to fulfill the residents' needs. In addition, they stated that Islamic law has and will always be the best form of governance for Afghanistan.
- Two men from District One in Kandahar responded negatively to Mullah Omar's recent speech. They condemned his remarks and accused the Taliban of killing innocent people. Additionally, they said many people disbelieve what he said so they are ignoring his speech.

Kabul, 25 August

Final day in Afghanistan, again focused on administration. After four months there is still no movement on the Department of State travel voucher for the early April trip to Dover and Washington, DC, that was submitted weeks ago. I never did hear back from USAID on the job that I was asked to consider shortly after the Zabul attack, followed by a phone interview with the USAID administrator, at which time I was told that someone would let me know "soon," one way or another. In the bureaucratic circle of life, service in Afghanistan doesn't necessarily count for much.

For reasons I can't understand, I am more melancholic than I should be as I prepare to depart. Perhaps it is because I have mixed feelings on returning to USAID—these past twelve months in Kandahar have made me more cynical that I used to be. Perhaps I really have been changed forever. One good thing about the pending assignment in Almaty is that I will be as far away from Washington as possible.

Kabul, 26 August

Woke at 4:45 a.m. for final run to Kabul Airport. Checked e-mails—Cameron just had his twenty-first birthday party on Ben Hill Drive and Catriona is about to depart for Vancouver Island.

Eight of us are leaving from the embassy this morning, either for R&R or on completion of our assignments. Three of us are going out on Fly Dubai, the others on Safi Airlines; all of us are headed to Dubai.

I saw some traffic this early on the road to Masood Circle and the airport—but not a lot. I twice paid Afghans $2 each to help move my bags a short distance, mostly to help the local economy, not because I needed them.

President Karzai is leaving this morning for Islamabad but the airport scenes are calm enough. Afghanistan and Pakistan somehow need to get along. Check-in procedures went fine and for once I chose the right line.

Gradually the departure lounge is beginning to fill up. I don't recognize anyone. Prior to typing this I cleaned my computer screen with the sleeve of my shirt—a thick caking of dust from Kandahar, wiped off the face of the earth in seconds, as if it had never been.

AFTERWORD

It has been more than three years since I left Afghanistan. I still think about that country and my twelve months there almost every day. If I could, I would take back one twenty-four-hour period from that year, rearranging the sequence of events and rewriting an alternative outcome. If reliving every day of that year again and again for an eternity would make that possible, I would gladly do it. More than anything, I wish I could set the tape back on 6 April 2013, in Zabul, rewinding it to ensure a different ending.

The Afghans with whom I met on a regular basis have taken different paths. Some have left the country and others have been killed. The death of Deputy Governor Patyal is especially hard to take, partly because he was young and left a family with three young children behind, and partly because he was a gentle and reflective person with a literary frame of mind. He was also the face of a very different Afghanistan, someone who abhorred violence, loved poetry, and believed in negotiations with the Taliban.

Governor Wesa's chief of staff Pervez Najib was also killed, as was Matullah Khan, the police chief in Uruzgan, a hard man who helped keep the peace. He was feared by the Taliban, loathed by the international media, and appreciated by the Australian military with whom he worked. Abdul Stanikzai, head of the Afghan Independent Human Rights Commission in Uruzgan, migrated to Australia in the months after I departed. He is now raising his young family there, proud to be on the path to Australian citizenship while cheering the Afghan national cricket team whenever it tours Australia.

The future of Afghanistan still hangs in the balance, making it difficult to assess the impact of that year in Kandahar. We weren't a consulate, but at times we pretended to be one, attempting to take on many of the usual consulate functions including outreach and reporting on the political and economic situation across the region in which we lived and worked. We also attempted to help make the elections, scheduled for the following year, more viable and credible. And we sought to explain ourselves, our policies, and our future plans to local leaders, preparing them for the time when foreign military assistance and a broader international presence would largely disappear.

Perhaps a new version of WikiLeaks will one day reveal the substance of the cables that we wrote or contributed to from Kandahar. I am proud of almost all of them, though I wish that a few more of them had actually been transmitted to Washington in the form in which we originally wrote them. We covered most of the significant issues of the day—economic trends, electoral politics, views of the clergy, political controversies within the region. Most of our reporting was on target and will stand the test of time. Some of it might even have helped influence, inform, or shape views in Kabul and Washington in modest ways. A few of the holes that should have been more extensively covered but weren't include disputes within the Karzai family and the problematic Afghan security chiefs who helped keep a kind of peace during my time there and in the months that followed, a relative though perhaps temporary peace that might have surprised some, given southern Afghanistan's reputation as the most violent corner in an already violent country. Some of the substance of our reporting saw the light of day eventually, albeit in a different form. For example, our draft cables on personal conflicts within the Karzai family never got very far—but the *Wall Street Journal* eventually covered for a wide readership most of the issues that we had written up for a strictly internal audience several months earlier, given our front-row seats on what was actually happening on the ground.

Our outreach wasn't only about reporting. We also engaged with key leaders of various kinds, providing them with our view of the world, our reasons for engaging with Afghanistan, and our hopes for the future. Perhaps to a surprising extent to those critical of every aspect of ISAF's involvement in Afghanistan, our conversations with local leaders often suggested a broadly similar vision for the future. Certainly, many Afghans I talked to were tired of the decades of violence and uncertainty that had destroyed much of their country and desperately hoped for something different. They welcomed especially the establishment of schools and health centers in places where they had either been destroyed or had never existed at all. They also appreciated our joint efforts to improve agriculture and deliver electricity, even if efforts organized around the latter continue to flounder, partly because adding that elusive third turbine to Kajaki Dam seems so hard and partly because the Afghans now responsible for their own power sector have found it very difficult to continue to subsidize the expensive fuel required to run the American-built diesel power plant in Kandahar.

My most satisfying external conversations were with a wide range of religious figures, tribal leaders, entrepreneurs, activists, and local officials. I did not think that any of these encounters would significantly change our small corner of southern Afghanistan or dramatically alter the future course of events in Afghanistan. But I did go into these conversations with the aim of humanizing relationships, moving beyond the stereotypical views that we had of each other, and in at least a small way changing the nature of our encounters. In this we succeeded, at least to some extent. Certainly, I looked on those with whom we met as real people with unique hopes, dreams, and aspirations. And, reflecting on the nature of some of our conversations, I believe that many of those with whom we interacted also left with different views of the United States and the broader international effort in Afghanistan.

The military—largely American but also including many other nationalities, most especially Australians and Romanians—was by far the dominant foreign presence in southern Afghanistan during that year. As civilians, we were far overshadowed and at times even overwhelmed by this presence. We also depended on them for our transportation across southern Afghanistan as well as for our protection. The relations we forged were largely positive, at least in the development aspects of our shared world in which military officers and civilian staff worked together to increase the likelihood of Afghan success. Throughout the year, we emphasized that the foreign presence was diminishing and that Afghan local authorities should look to Kabul, not ISAF, for budgets and new development projects. Undoubtedly, by the end of that year our Afghan counterparts realized that foreign funds would continue to decrease while Afghan solutions would become more important than ever. At a more personal level, I left Kandahar with a deeper respect for the essential humanity of the soldiers, both Afghan and foreign, with whom I worked. I also left with respect for the personal sacrifices made across the region, sacrifices that were made more obvious at every Purple Heart ceremony, ramp ceremony, and memorial service that I attended.

This same respect extends to the many dozens of civilians with whom I served. At the time, all of us were subjected to stress and threats of violence at every turn. Everyone responded in different ways. Relational issues were inevitable and I had to inject myself into some of them. I hope I made life easier for my colleagues on at least some days. I also hope my leadership made for a more effective civilian presence. Regrettably, the poor living conditions that I witnessed when I first arrived in August 2012 were still largely in place when I left one year later, though a move to a new compound at Kandahar Air

Field vacated by a departing U.S. contractor was scheduled to take place not long afterward. That move was eventually made, though it involved far fewer people than we in Kandahar had initially expected as the drawdown in State Department civilians posted to southern Afghanistan continued unabated. This drawdown mirrored an equally steep drawdown in the military. As a result, the number of meetings outside the wire and anywhere other than at Kandahar Air Field eventually dwindled into almost nothing. Now there is no embassy presence in southern Afghanistan at all.

The suicide attack that killed five Americans including my translator Nasemi, fellow FSO Anne Smedinghoff, Sergeant Christopher Ward, Sergeant Delfin Santos, and Corporal Wilbel Robles-Santa in Zabul on 6 April 2013 continues to haunt me. One year after the attack, the *Chicago Tribune* published the main findings from the military report assessing the incident, highlighting in particular what was described in the headline as the poor planning involved. The article, published in April 2014, never received the wider media visibility accorded to the violence in Benghazi that resulted in the death of Ambassador Christopher Stephens and three others, largely because the circumstances were different. In Libya, the State Department was responsible for its own security; in Afghanistan, that responsibility was specifically delegated to the U.S. military. To this day I don't know why the civilians in our party were never interviewed by the military investigators in their after-action report. I also do not accept the assertion contained in the report that the civilians involved in that mission did not use the required safety equipment—in fact, all of us wore helmets and other protective gear on that awful day. Colleagues assigned to the Zabul PRT also indicate that the route first attempted and then closed off because of a locked door had been used previously on a number of other occasions.

In the end, it is hard to separate the personal aspects of what I witnessed during my twelve months in southern Afghanistan from the larger American civilian and military effort there. I acknowledge that I cannot be completely objective. I recognize a certain hubris in some aspects of what we tried to accomplish, an ambitious over-reaching in the goals that we set for ourselves. As for the Taliban, they were involved in a no-holds-barred existential struggle for the future of their country, fired by a particular religious vision rooted in a specific reading of their holy scriptures as well as the Afghan past. Many—probably most—of their fellow Afghans did not share in this vision, yet they recognized the Taliban as fellow citizens and fellow believers, albeit in their view misguided ones, exploited at every turn by the countries surrounding Afghanistan with which they shared historic enmities. International forces attempting to move Afghanistan to a different place could support local Afghan allies and perhaps even see themselves for a time as yet another tribe, working to change the balance of power in the south and move it in another direction. But for those of us from outside the country it was never a truly existential struggle and we never aspired to be a permanent part of the Afghan social and political landscape. We would be there for a time and then move on.

Impressed with the depth of the personal sacrifice that I saw around me every day, it is difficult to think that in the end all of our efforts might have been in vain. Was our presence mostly symbolic, whether involving meetings with key leaders or visits to local schools? Or did it result in some measure of lasting change? Again, I'm not sure I know—or perhaps it is still too early to tell. But there is one thing I know for sure: Afghans will now write their own history, as they have so often in the past and, as in past centuries, the large-scale American presence will become an ever-more distant chapter in that history, one that is part of a much larger and more complex story than any of us can ever fully imagine or ever fully understand.

ACKNOWLEDGMENTS

Many people made this book possible, including Glenn Griffith, Adam Nettina, and Gary Thompson at the Naval Institute Press in Annapolis who first saw this unsolicited manuscript and believed it might eventually emerge in published form. I thank them and their colleagues for their support—first in accepting the draft submission for eventual publication, and then in seeing it through to the end of a long production process. Alison Hope was extremely helpful as a copy editor, working to ensure consistency and sparing me in places from considerable embarrassment. Marlena Montagna also played a central role throughout the production process.

I must also thank Shawn Dorman at the *Foreign Service Journal* for publishing the stand-alone article "Dust of Kandahar" in October 2015. This article, which evoked a positive response from many readers, formed the basis for the introduction to this book by the same name, summarizing in a few pages what the rest of the book is about.

Cartographer Chris Robinson from Laurel, Maryland, prepared the two maps that are included; one depicts Afghanistan in the broader region of South and Central Asia and the other focuses largely on the areas of southern Afghanistan that I often visited. Jim Bever was the first USAID colleague to read the manuscript in its entirety. Larry Sampler was another early USAID reader whose comments, along with those of Jim Bever, turned this into a better document. Stephanie Bluma and Frank Walsh also offered important advice during the USAID clearance process. While appreciating their interest and support, I must note that this book does not purport to represent the views of USAID, the U.S. State Department, or any other part of the U.S. government. On the contrary—the views expressed are purely personal and any faults and mistakes that appear are mine alone.

My wife Fiona and our three children—Iain, Cameron, and Catriona—figure in the text on a number of occasions, mostly as distant loved ones whom I thought about often and from whom I drew strength and inspiration. Fiona and Catriona spent that year in Ulaanbaatar, Fiona travelling across more of the vastness of Mongolia even as Catriona finished her final year of high school there. Meanwhile, Cameron spent the year as a sophomore at Georgia

Tech in Atlanta while Iain joined the Air Force, spending part of those twelve months on training status in San Angelo, Texas. My immediate family has followed me to the ends of the earth—including on Foreign Service assignments in Pakistan, Yemen, South Africa, Kazakhstan, Jordan, Cambodia, Mongolia, and Belgium. It can't be said often enough: I will always be grateful for their love, forbearance, and support.

My extended family—including my parents Hubert and Bettie and my brother David and sister Nancy—have also been supportive over many decades. Never was that support more important than in the immediate aftermath of the bombing in Zabul on 6 April, when they offered their unconditional love.

Every name mentioned in this diary and referenced again in the index—Afghan and American, British and Australian, soldier and civilian—was part of the year I spent in southern Afghanistan. While not listing them individually again here, I want to express my sincere appreciation for their service and contributions. My embassy colleagues working in RC-South—whether representing State, USAID, Agriculture, Justice, Treasury, or other departments and agencies—were an essential part of my own twelve months in Kandahar. More than anybody, they shared in the experiences described and were a vital part of the common life that we together made in southern Afghanistan.

Beyond that, I want to thank my military colleagues and Afghan counterparts for their hospitality and for their continuous support in matters both large and small. Their names, too, are mentioned in the main body of this book, and some names are repeated often. It was a privilege to serve alongside ISAF colleagues for twelve months, providing memories that will stay with me always. As others have sometimes commented, the hospitality of the Afghan is also remarkable, even during a time of war. Much of this hospitality is described in the text, including feasts in locales in various parts of southern Afghanistan that often involved tea, mangoes, pomegranates, and *kabuli pilau*. The lessons I learned from these encounters are highlighted throughout a narrative that is necessarily focused on life as it is experienced amidst considerable stress and, at times, in the most extreme of circumstances.

Not everyone came home. More than anything, I want to acknowledge and affirm the service as well as the supreme sacrifice paid by the five colleagues who walked with me outside the Zabul PRT on 6 April 2013: my translator Nasemi, my fellow FSO Anne Smedinghoff, and our three guardian angels: Staff Sergeant Christopher Ward, Sergeant Delfin Santos, and Corporal Wilbel Robles-Santa. Second Samuel 18:33 says it best and in words that are difficult for me to improve upon, imagining as it does alternative endings and lamenting with deep sorrow what might have been. I too will always remember. I too can never forget.

ACRONYMS AND ABBREVIATIONS

ANSF	Afghan National Security Forces
ANZAC	Australia New Zealand Army Corps
AP	Associated Press
BSA	bilateral security agreement
CCI	Community Cohesion Initiative
CENTCOM	central command
CERP	Commander's Emergency Response Program
CHU	containerized housing unit
CUA	commander's update assessment
DCM	deputy chief of mission
DFAC	dining facility
DoD	U.S. Department of Defense
DST	district support team
EOD	explosive ordnance disposal
FAA	Federal Aviation Administration
FOB	forward operating base
FSL	Foreign Service Limited
FSO	Foreign Service Officer
GIRoA	Government of the Islamic Republic of Afghanistan
ICRC	International Committee for the Red Cross
ICU	intensive care unit
IEC	independent electoral commission
IED	improvised explosive device
IG	inspector general
IJC	International Joint Command
INL	Bureau of International Narcotics and Law Enforcement
IPA	Inter-Provincial Affairs
ISAF	International Security Assistance Force

ISI	Inter-Services Intelligence
KMIC	Kandahar Media Information Center
KPRT	Kandahar Provincial Reconstruction Team
MCS	Murree Christian School
MRAP	mine-resistant ambush proof
MRX	mission rehearsal exercise
NDS	National Directorate of Security
NFC	National Football Conference
OBO	Office of Buildings and Operations
PIA	Pakistan International Airlines
PRT	provincial reconstruction team
PTSD	post-traumatic stress disorder
R&R	rest and recreation
RAMP-UP	Regional Afghan Municipal Program for Urban Populations
RC-East	Regional Command East
RC-South	Regional Command South
RC-Southwest	Regional Command Southwest
RC-West	Regional Command West
RIAB	radio in a box
RPG	rocket-propelled grenade
RSO	regional security officer
SCR	senior civilian representative
SDO	senior development officer
SFAT	Security Force Assistance Team
SIGAR	Special Inspector General for Afghanistan Reconstruction
SIKA	stability in key areas
UNAMA	United Nations Assistance Mission in Afghanistan
USAID	United States Agency for International Development
USG	U.S. government
VBIED	vehicle-borne improvised explosive device

GLOSSARY

chapan	Afghan-style overcoat
chappati	South Asian flat bread
chappli kebab	a type of spiced minced meat kebab especially popular in Peshawar
dahl	lentils
Dosti Darvaza	Friendship Gate
eid	Islamic holiday
fatwa	religious legal opinion pertaining to Islamic law
ghazal	poetic form consisting of rhyming couplets and a refrain
ghazi	a Muslim warrior engaged in religious warfare
green-on-blue	an attack on ISAF by members of Afghan security forces
hajj	annual pilgrimage to Mecca
iftar	evening meal eaten to break the fast
imam	worship leader in a mosque
jirga	traditional assembly of Afghan tribal leaders
kabuli pilau	rice with nuts and raisins, Kabul style
kandak	battalion
karai	South Asian meal cooked in a cast iron saucepan
kareʐ	ancient underground irrigation system on which agriculture depends
kebab	common Afghan dish, usually involving meat cooked on a skewer over an open fire
kutchi	Afghan nomad
loya jirga	traditional gathering of Afghan leaders to resolve important matters of state
Loya Kandahar	Kandahar and the larger region of southern Afghanistan surrounding it

madrassah	religious school
malik	male leader or headman
mansaaf	Jordanian dish that includes spiced lamb
masala chai	Indian spiced tea with milk
maulvi	learned Islamic teacher
muhajir	refugee
mujahideen	holy warrior
mullah	religious scholar trained in Islamic traditions
mustafiat	government department responsible for fiscal and financial matters
naan	South Asian bread cooked in a clay oven
pilau	rice dish usually cooked with a mix of onions and spices
rat line	term used in Afghanistan to describe a mujahideen supply route
shura	Afghan tribal council
talib	religious student
tandoor	South Asian clay oven
ulema	learned religious scholars

INDEX

9/11 commemoration ceremony, 20

A

Abrams, Robert ("Abe"): on ANSF,
57, 58, 131, 174; awards ceremony
for, 194; farewell dinner for, 184–
85, 193; on Governor Wesa, 47;
on Kandahar Air Field hospital,
51; optimism of, 136; on Panjwai
uprising, 131–32; style of, 15, 19;
on the Taliban, 18; on U.S. military
presence, 12; on the Zabul attack,
150
Achackzai, Rogiya, 209–10
Afghan Independent Human Rights
Commission, 104, 110, 156
Afghan National Security Forces
(ANSF): casualties in, 6, 60, 96,
184, 195, 196, 215, 218; and civilian
government, 182; effectiveness
of, 201; independence of, 96;
international forces training, 3;
lack of reporting on, 234; as leaders
in the war, 53; optimism about,
125, 131–32, 163, 174; in Panjwai,
133; professionalism of, 219;
readiness of, 57, 58; strength of, 60
Afghan police. See police, Afghan
Afghan proverbs, 60
agriculture, 35, 40, 234
Ahmadi, Mohammed, 77
Aino Mina, 102–3, 168
Akhundzada, Amir Mohammad: at
the Australian *iftar* dinner, 202–3;

described, 45–46; on development,
20, 155–56; on Doha Peace talks,
191; optimism of, 229
Akhunzada, Masood, 5, 106, 109–10
alcohol, 17–18, 20
Alexander's Castle (Qalat, Zabul),
39–40, 59
Alford, Ned, 198
Alvarado, Jesse, 198
American presence, post-2014, 118,
119, 120
ANZAC (Australia New Zealand
Army Corps) commemoration,
156
Apache FOB, 203
Arghandab, 29–30, 54, 76–77
Army Corps of Engineers, 27–28
atmospherics. *See* regional reporting
Australian armed forces, 16–17,
44–45, 69
Aziz, Noorullah, 75, 76, 207

B

Babari Company, 126
Bagram, 161–62
Barakzai, Obaidullah, 62
Bari, Ahmed, 127
Barnes, Zane, 171
Bashor, Tim, 91–92, 137–38, 148
Bastion, 216
Belgian armed forces, 64
Belgian medical personnel, 168
Benghazi, Libya, attack, 20

bilateral security agreement (BSA), 64, 66–67, 87, 90

Black Hawk crash, March 12, 2013, 130

Blass, Steven, 132

Boot, Max, 158

Bradsher, Keith, 171

burkas, 133–34

business leaders, Afghan, 87, 126, 205

C

cables from the Southern Embassy: on Karzai family conflict, 123–24, 166; logjam of, 166, 213, 234; on outreach, 107, 113

call to prayer broadcasts, 203–4

Camp Holland, 203

Camp Nathan Smith, 58–59, 74–76, 78, 97

Camp Valdez, 22, 48

Canada, weir funded by, 29

Carter, Ashton, 167

casualties: American, 104; ANSF, 6, 60, 96, 184, 195, 196, 215, 218; civilian, 6, 66, 166, 185, 196, 214, 217; comparison in, by year, 196; geographic origins of, 4; from IEDs, 87, 166, 196, 214; ISAF, 188, 196; New Zealand, 121; Pakistani, 85; in Panjwai, 11; Third Infantry Division, 195; *ulema,* 106; in the Zabul attack, 139

cell phone theory of economics, 65

Chambers, David, 91

change-of-command ceremonies: at Camp Nathan Smith, 58–59; at IJC, 161; at Kandahar Air Field, 15, 69, 180; for medical detachments, 215; at Mosum Ghar, 65–66; at Tarin Kot, 44, 180–81; at Zabul PRT, 59

children: abuse of, 199; killed by Taliban, 166, 184, 185, 196; killed in airstrikes, 142, 223; in migration, 136; threatened by Taliban, 219

Christian chapels in the drawdown, 108

Christy, Norval, 159–60

civilians: in Afghan success, 235; in airstrikes, 142; and alcohol prohibition, 17–18; casualties, 6, 66, 166, 185, 196, 214, 217; concerns of, 74; drawdown of, 21, 156, 166, 236; in Kandahar, 176–77; killed by IEDs, 166; on military bases, 174; in Panjwai, 154, 214; personal sacrifices of, 235–36; Taliban targeting, 183

Civil-Military Strategic Framework for Afghanistan, 89

Cohn, Brad, 2, 113

commanders, Afghan, 42, 60, 156

congressional delegations, 89, 162, 165

corruption: allegations of, 23, 122; of governors, 116; in the Karzai family, 116; lack of concern about, 62; local complaints about, 223; of mullahs, 91; mullahs on, 221; and wealth, 201

Cunningham, James, 119, 131, 195

D

Dahla Dam, 37, 42

Dale, Catherine, 38

Dalrymple, William: *Return of a King,* 134

Dastageeri, Agha, 5, 39, 90, 108–10, 221

Davis, Jonathan, 119

development programs: American focus on, 216; media, 73–74; need for, 20; relations built in, 235; in Uruzgan, 155–56, 157. *See also* USAID (United States Agency for International Development)

district support teams (DSTs), 56, 67, 69, 71, 158

Dolan, John, 95, 96
Dozier, Al, 139, 160
drawdown: civilian, 21, 166, 236; human aspects of, 120; Panjwai campaign in, 88; pessimism about, 86; process of, 106–8, 152; as real mission, 101; speed of, 95
Drayal, Philip, 54
drones in warfare, 222
Dunlop, John, 165
Durani, Maryam, 72
DynCorp security guards, 181–82

E
Ebbert, Kevin, 68
education: in Kandahar, 30; *maliks* on, 39; in Nuristan, 68; in Uruzgan, 31, 157. *See also* schools
Eid al-Fitr, 218, 224, 226
elections: Afghan staff on, 169; message on, 120; national, 214; provincial, 113, 117; rumors about, 198; skepticism about, 112–13; tribal affiliation in, 219; villagers on, 223
Eliasson, Jan, 188
employees, Afghan, 74–75, 169
external conversations, 235

F
Faizi, Ahmadullah, 35, 59, 154, 189, 218
Faqiri, Mohammad Yahya, 175
Federal Aviation Administration (FAA), 59
Federal Bureau of Investigation (FBI), 142
female engagement teams, 69, 176
final days in Kabul, 227–31
Fish Mountain, 38
Foreign Relations, Council on (New York), 159
Fort Stewart, Georgia, 80–81

Fourth Infantry Division, 107, 177, 211
Fourth of July celebrations, 191
Fraise Chapel, Kabul, 27
fruit exports, 35

G
Gecko, 13, 73
General Order Number One, 17–18
Gitter, Lewis, 155, 158, 190, 205
Government of the Islamic Republic of Afghanistan (GIRoA): Afghan disappointment in, 201; agreement on rhetoric with Taliban, 102; confidence in, 204; mullahs on, 220; response of in Panjwai, 114; skepticism about, 182
Governor's Palace, Kandahar, 24–25
green-on-blue attacks: effect of on ISAF efforts, 22–23; in Helmand, 10; meeting on, 14–15; Slovak soldier killed in, 196; Taliban implants in, 58; in Zabul, 22, 28
Gun Galuut, Mongolia, 173

H
Hafiz, Asim, 161–62
Hamda, Yonas, 66
Hamid, Abdul, 70–71, 185
Hamilton, Masha, 10, 37, 151, 178
Hashim Agha, Mohammad, 61
Haysom, Nicholas, 179
helicopter crashes, 130, 133, 176
Helmand, 10, 22, 167, 175–76
Henderson, Bryan, 132
heroin smuggling in Spin Boldak, 1
Hodge, Nathan, 178
Holbrooke, Richard: *To End a War*, 121
Honor Our Troops (HOT), 174
hooch, all-metal, 9, 11
Huggins, James L., 15, 58–59, 74

Hughes, Chris, 132, 155, 184
human rights abuses: allegations of, 12, 122; against women, 104, 110, 156
human rights groups, 104, 110, 156
Hunt, Kelly, 136–39, 142, 158, 175, 215

I
IEDs (improvised explosive devices): casualties from, 87, 166, 196, 214; as leading cause of death, 71; locating, 104; in Maiwand, 163; networks of, 222; in Panjwai, 167; women killed by, 185; in the Zabul attack, 138, 149
iftar dinners, 202–3, 205, 207, 209–10, 215
immunity, 64, 66–67, 87, 90
India, contractors from, 95
Indian Consulate, Camp Nathan Smith, 74–76, 97
Indian Embassy, 21
insider threats. *See* green-on-blue attacks
intensity of life in Afghanistan, 182
International Security Assistance Force (ISAF): casualties, 121, 188, 196; detention policy of, 203; as dominant foreign presence, 235; on draft Zabul attack report, 187; fear of departure of, 111–12, 115; immunity for, 64, 66–67; limited, post-2014, 127; mandate of, 3; peace projected after departure of, 102; professionalism of, 219; Taliban killed by in Panjwai, 42; in Tarin Kot, Uruzgan, 44. *See also* green-on-blue attacks
Inter-Provincial Affairs (IPA), 154, 197, 228–29
irrigation, 23, 29, 63

J
Jehani, Abdul Bari, 50
Joint Border Coordination group, 100
Jordan, 160
journalists, 74, 120
justice: defined, 5; in lasting peace, 115, 222

K
Kabul: August meetings in, 9–10; final days in, 227–31; mandatory departures from, 179; un-Islamic image of, 217
Kabul Airport, Taliban attack on, 175
Kaidanow, Tina, 86, 119, 149, 183, 228
Kajaki Dam, 129–30
Kamwand, Abbas, 139
Kandahar: education in, 30; first days in, 15–19; landscape of, 10–11; population of, 181; Provincial Council elections, 113, 117; religious affairs in, 102, 108; U.S. Embassy in, 2
Kandahar Air Field: alcohol issues at, 20; change-of-command ceremony at, 15, 69, 180; described, 11; future of, 96; housing, 21; and KPRT, 17; living conditions at, 17, 21; population of, 22; trauma center, 51, 78; in U.S. enduring presence, 118
Kandahar Airport: FAA visiting, 59; improvements at, 127; official interference at, 154; security procedures avoided at, 24; smuggling arrest at, 218; viability of, 35
Kandahar Fresh Fruit Association, 35
Kandahar Provincial Council, 72
Kandahar Provincial Reconstruction Team (KPRT), 17, 25, 58–59, 96
Kandahar Ulema Council, 72–73
Kandahar University, 33–34, 37–38, 199

Kantor, Matthew, 58
karezes (irrigation systems), 23
Karzai, Hamid: on Australian raid in Uruzgan, 16–17; comparison of U.S. and Taliban by, 130, 131; on family and diplomats, 116; on U.S. bases, 194
Karzai, Mahmood, 102–3
Karzai, Wali: bilateral strategic agreement supported by, 224; first meeting with, 36–37; on India and the Taliban, 87–88; as major contact, 5; on national and provincial elections, 112–13; personality of, 57
Karzai family conflict: cables on, 123–24, 166; as normal, 187; reporting on, 190, 234; roots of, 116, 117
Kerry, John, 106–7
Khalid, Asadullah, 181
Khalid Ibn al-Walid campaign, 166
Khan, Matullah, 122, 125
Khan, Numbar, 199, 209
Kitchings, Brian, 65
KMIC (Kandahar Media Information Center), 37–38
Knutson, Sara, 132
Koran, 209
Kosik, Keith, 196
Kraft, Justin, 139
Kramer, Dale, 95, 124
Kunar attack, 9–10
kutchis (Afghan nomads), 93

L
LaCamera, Paul, 189, 197, 198
Lashkar Gah, 216
last roll call, 28, 132
living conditions: at Camp Valdez, 48; at Kandahar Air Field, 17, 21; for staff, 2, 11, 235–36
Llorens, Hugo, 151

local perspectives, 219
Lodin, Rahimullah, 40
loya jirga (gathering of leaders), 214, 219, 224
Loya Kandahar. *See* Kandahar

M
Macon, Georgia, 80–85
madrassahs, 106
Maillard, Errol, 192–93
Maiwand, 11, 23–24, 163, 164, 213
Malala of Maiwand, 41, 43, 210. *See also* "two Malalas" story
maliks (male leaders), 39, 55
Malkasian, Carter, 179
Mara, Al Jihadi Studio, 209
maulvi (learned Islamic teacher), 115
McBee, Marilyn, op-ed on, 124, 133, 194
McEarchern, Paul, 51
media development conference, 73–74
melancholy at departure, 230
Memon, Kashif, 49, 58
memorial services: described, 3–4; for Ebbert, Kevin, 68; for Nasemi, Amon, 158–59; for Rhea, Trenton, 170; for Smedinghoff, Anne, 162; for soldiers in Black Hat 14, 132; for Swindle, Jason, 31–32; at Tarin Kot, November 9, 2012, 58; for Zabul attack victims, 153
memorials to soldiers: ANZAC commemoration, 156; on the boardwalk, 197–98; in drawdown, 108; at Fort Stewart, 80–81; in Uruzgan, 30
Middle Eastern embassies, closure of, 214
military dogs, 31, 123
Milley, Mark A., 161, 163, 164
mine placement as sin, 230
missing people, 113–14, 167

Mitzell, Cydney, 113–14
Mohammad, Faisal, 38–39, 66
Mongolia and the United States
    (Addleton), 116, 151, 171, 172
morale, 174, 206
Mosum Ghar, 65–66
MRAPs (Mine-Resistant, Ambush
    Proof vehicles), 2, 224–25
Mullah Omar. *See* Omar, Mohammed
mullahs: corruption of, 91; on modern
    Muslims, 184; on Pashtuns, 230;
    regional reports on, 220–21; on
    suicide attacks, 106, 115, 184, 199
Musam Ghar, 200–202
My Afghan Library program, 133,
    136–37
Mya Neshin, 223

N
Najib, Pervez, 6, 233
Nasemi, Amon: death of in Zabul
    attack, 7, 138, 139–40; family of, 6,
    136, 145; memorials for, 158–59;
    ramp ceremony for, 142; service
    of, 144
Naseri, Mohammad Ashraf, 19, 44,
    92, 150, 153, 190
naturalization ceremony, 123
Neumann, Ron, 193
Nguyen, Wesley, 93
night raid, simulated, 41
Noorzai, Ehsan, 33
Noorzai, Saleh Mohammad, 23

O
Obama, Barack, 87, 94
observation balloons, 221
Odierno, Raymond, 118
officers, Afghan, 42, 60, 156
Omar, Mohammed: and the cloak of
    the Prophet, 16, 75, 106; Eid-al-
    Fitr message by, 217, 221, 224, 230;
    uncertainty about, 174

O'Neill, Joshua, 109
opium poppy cultivation, 63, 183
Orthodox Easter Service, 163–64
outreach: to Afghan police, 132; as
    an embassy function, 4–6, 233–34;
    cables on, 107, 113; in countering
    violent extremism, 89; in health
    care improvement, 157, 234; to key
    leaders, 234; religious, 112, 114–15;
    schools in, 234
Overman, Steve, 139

P
Pak, Jason, 79
Pakistan: fatwa from, 128; narrative
    of, 117; suicide bombing in, 204;
    and the Taliban, 221; violence
    blamed on, 42
Pakistani diplomats, 63–64, 116–17,
    190
Pakistanis: casualties among, 85;
    dislike of, 55; in Kandahar, 181
Panetta, Leon, 79
Panjwai: air power in, 66; casualties
    in, 11; civilians in, 154; civilians
    killed in, 214; IED explosion
    in, 167; Taliban resisted in, 174;
    treatment of captured Taliban
    in, 129; uprising in, 109–10, 114,
    131–32, 133, 201
Panjwai campaign, 66–67, 88
Panjwai DST, 67, 71
Panjwai PRT, 38–39
partnership dinners, 70
Pashtuns, 223, 230
Patyal, Qadim, 6, 162, 233
peace talks, Doha, 183, 191, 199, 201
Petraeus, David, 59, 60
Pierce, David, 71–73
Poe, Keith, 124
Poet's Night, 177
police, Afghan: and captured Taliban,
    129; in green-on-blue attack, 10;

outreach to, 132; Pakistanis on, 117; soldiers killed by, 22; study on, 194; in Taliban attack, 219; in Zaray, 99
political discourse in the U.S., 94
Popal, Abaidullah, 55
poppy cultivation, 63, 183
power plants, 234–35
Price, Job, 87
provincial courts, 104–5
provincial elections, 113, 117
provincial reconstruction teams (PRTs): civilian leadership of, 157; closure of, 26, 116; described, 16; in Kandahar, 17, 25, 58–59, 96; in Panjwai, 38–39
Purple Heart pinning ceremonies, 3, 25, 47, 167
Pushto proverbs, 23, 76, 82, 125, 222

Q
Qalat, Zabul, 43, 67

R
Rabat Melon Cooperative, 35
Ramadan, 71, 197, 199, 201, 204, 220
ramp ceremonies, 3–4, 22, 130, 142
Razziq, Abdul, 12–13, 102, 120, 195
realities of war, 3–4
regional reporting: as consular function, 234; January, 2013, 86; June, 2013, 178, 181, 184; July, 2013, 198–99, 203–4; August, 2013, 214, 219–21, 223, 230
Registan Desert, 27, 38, 217
reintegration, 17, 31, 72–73, 75–76
religiosity in Kandahar, 102, 108
Return of a King (Dalrymple), 134
Rhea, Trenton, 170
rhetoric, GIRoA/Taliban agreement on, 102
RIAB (radio in a box) program, 213

Robinson, Scott, 171–72
Robles-Santa, Wilbel, 153
rocket attacks, 89, 159, 215, 220, 226
Romanians, 163–64
Rufi, Mohammad Zaman, 104
Ruiz, Clinton, 49, 58
rules of engagement, 66, 182
Russell, Phil, 15, 17–18

S
safety equipment, 10, 186, 236
Sakari Karez, 54
Sangin, Amirzai, 179
Santos, Delphin, 153
Sarhadi, Niaz Mohammed, 11–12, 47, 99
Sariposa Prison, 105
schools: in Arghandab, 76–77; enrollment in, 19; local, 39; madrassahs, 106; in outreach, 234; private, 98; Taliban destroying, 199; Urdu taught in, 214; vocational, 230. See also education
Scialdo, Marc, 132
security: bilateral agreement on, 64, 66–67, 87, 90; in DST closings, 67; handover to Afghans, 67; military responsibility for, 236; new procedures, post-Zabul attack, 149; Pakistani concerns on, 117; senior military staff on, 188; signs of improvement in, 56; in southern Afghanistan, 64; videos on, 9; worldwide, 213; in Zabul, 19
senior civilian representative (SCR), 2, 216
sexual harassment, 198
shadow governors, 135–36
Shah Wali Kot, 55–56
Shannon, Zachary, 132
Sharif, Nawaz, 190
Sheie, Marc, 59
shrine of Mohammad's cloak, 5, 16, 24

shura (Afghan tribal council): on energy issues, 184, 189; July 24, 2013, 206–7; June 2013, 178–80
Sidiqui, James, 126
Sipe, Rob, 155
Smedinghoff, Anne, 6–7, 137–39, 144, 162, 188
Sopko, John, 94
SpeakEasy, 229
Spin Boldak, 1, 28, 124, 154
Stanikzai, Abdul Ghafar, 110, 156, 233
Stevens, Christopher, 20
suicide attacks: by an Afghan girl, 23; in Helmand, 167, 175–76; mullahs on, 106, 115, 184, 199; in Pakistan, 204; Pakistani fatwa justifying, 128; on rescue team, 224–25; suicide vests in, 181, 225
suicides, 55, 58, 60, 87
survivor's guilt, 154, 173, 228, 236
Swindle, Jason, 32

T
Taliban: in the 2013 fighting season, 136; as Afghan citizens, 236; and the Afghan Independent Human Rights Commission, 156; agreement on rhetoric, 102; American civilians targeted by, 183; assassination of Wesa attempted by, 16; attacks by, 22–23, 51, 175, 211, 220; civilians killed by, 185, 214, 217; confidence of, 61; credibility of, 219; deaths of in Shah Wali Kot, 56; detainees, reports on, 217; finances of, 198, 218; in green-on-blue attacks, 58; image of, 108, 201; infighting within, 109, 110; Khalid Ibn al-Walid campaign, 166; killed in Panjwai, 42, 206; in Maiwand, 213; murders by, 111–12, 214; order

to shoot, 128–29; organizational issues of, 218; and Pakistan, 221; peace talks with, 183, 191, 199, 201; post-withdrawal threat of, 65; reintegration of, 17; resiliency of, 19, 87; resistance to, 109–10, 174; schools destroyed by, 199; shadow governors, 135–36; suicide vests used by, 181; summer campaign of, 18; sympathy of Maulvi's for, 115; threats by, 19, 219
Tanweer, Shamsuddin, 104
Tarin Kot, Uruzgan, 20, 31, 44, 180–81
Thanksgiving Day 2012, 64–65
Third Infantry Division, 64, 80–81, 177, 195
To End a War (Holbrooke), 121
Tracy, Lynne, 90
transition planning, 116
translators, 146, 158
tribal elders, 55, 77, 133
Trofimov, Yaroslav, 178, 179
troop levels, 53, 119
"two Malalas" story, 41, 43, 44, 48, 107, 210

U
ulema (learned religious scholars), 72–73, 106, 114–15
Unity of Effort Conference, 46
Ureta, Horacio, 211
Uruzgan: Australian raid on, 16–17; development in, 155–56, 157; impressions of, 181; IPA closed, 154; memorial in, 30; VBIED attack in, 130–31
USAID (United States Agency for International Development): cold storage project by, 35; at Kajaki dam, 128, 129; slogan of, 165; Spin Boldak project ended by, 124. *See also* development programs

V

VBIEDs (vehicle-borne improvised explosive devices): in Aino Mina, 168; unsuccessful attack with, 130–31; in the Zabul attack, 138, 149, 153
village elders, 93–94

W

Ward, Christopher, 153
Warlick, James, 100
wealth in Afghanistan, 201
weir, Canadian funded, 29
Wesa, Toryalai: Abrams on, 47; assassination attempt on, 16–17; on development, 133, 183; on education, 30; first meeting with, 24–25; on Kandahar, 72, 206; on Petraeus, 59; on soccer, 16, 30, 48
Wesh-Chaman border crossing, 27–28
Western cultural influence, 214, 217
Wilder, Andrew, 120
Williams, Wesley, 78
Willis, Chris, 189
Win, Kevin, 103–4
Wolters, Curt, 66
women: beheading of, 10; female engagement teams, 69, 176; human rights abuses against, 104, 110, 156;

iftar dinner on issues of, 209–10; killed by Taliban, 185
wounded warriors of Afghanistan, 181

Y

Yamashita, Ken, 151
Yepa, Charles, 128
Younce, Michael, 151
Yousafzai, Malala, 41, 43, 210. *See also* "two Malalas" story

Z

Zabul: green-on-blue attack at, 22, 28; handover of security in, 67; provincial council, 40–41
Zabul attack (April 6, 2013): events of April 6, 6–7, 136–42, 148; explosives report on, 222; IEDs in, 138, 149; intended victim of, 160; investigation of, 142, 150; memorial for, 153; narratives of, 147; report on, 185–87, 188, 236; security in, 19; VBIED used in, 138, 149, 153; video of, 152
Zabul PRT, 19, 59
Zabul Teacher Training College, 43–44, 124, 127–28, 169, 190
Zaray, 11–12, 99, 154

ABOUT THE AUTHOR

Born and raised in the mountains of northern Pakistan, **Jonathan Addleton** has served as U.S. ambassador to Mongolia, USAID representative to the European Union in Brussels, and USAID mission director in India, Pakistan, Cambodia, Mongolia, and Central Asia. In June 2014 he received the American Foreign Service Association's Christian A. Herter Award for intellectual courage and constructive dissent. A career Foreign Service officer, he has been married for thirty years and has three adult children.